ALSO BY DAVID MARANISS

When Pride Still Mattered: A Life of Vince Lombardi
The Clinton Enigma
First in His Class: A Biography of Bill Clinton
"Tell Newt to Shut Up" *(with Michael Weisskopf)*

The Prince

DAVID MARANISS
and
ELLEN NAKASHIMA

# of Tennessee

THE RISE
OF AL GORE

SIMON & SCHUSTER

NEW YORK   LONDON   TORONTO   SYDNEY   SINGAPORE

SIMON & SCHUSTER
Rockefeller Center
1230 Avenue of the Americas
New York, NY 10020

10   9   8   7   6   5   4   3   2   1

Library of Congress Cataloging-in-Publication Data

Maraniss, David.
   The prince of Tennessee: the rise of Al Gore / David
Maraniss and Ellen Nakashima.
      p. cm.
   Includes index.
   1. Gore, Albert. 1948–   2. Vice-Presidents—United
States—Biography.   3. Legislators—United States—
Biography.   4. United States. Congress. Senate—
Biography.   5. Presidential candidates—United States—
Biography.   I. Nakashima, Ellen.   II. Title.
E840.8.G65 M37 2000
973.929'092—dc21
[B]

                                             00-055610

ISBN 0-7432-0411-5

*Portions of the chapters contained herein were previously
published in* The Washington Post.

*The authors and the publisher gratefully acknowledge
permission to reprint material from the following work:
Excerpt from* "Anecdote of the Jar." From Collected Poems
*by Wallace Stevens. Copyright 1923 and renewed 1951 by
Wallace Stevens. Reprinted by permission of Alfred A.
Knopf, a Division of Random House, Inc.*

To our parents

CONTENTS

16 CONTENTS

THE PRINCE
OF TENNESSEE

THE LONG ROAD

IN THE FOOTHILLS of middle Tennessee there is a little village called Difficult. Whatever hardship that place name was meant to convey, it could not match the resigned lament of the nearby hamlet of Defeated, nor the ache of lonesomeness evoked by a settlement known as Possum Hollow. It was that kind of land, isolated and unforgiving, if hauntingly beautiful, for the farmers and small merchants who settled the region, families of Scots-Irish and Anglo-Irish descent named Hackett and Woodard, Key and Pope, Gibbs and Scurlock, Beasley and Huffines, Silcox and Gore.

For generations one old road, Highway 70, was the main road west and the best way out, weaving through the hills of the Upper Cumberland past the county seats of Carthage and Lebanon and across the barrens of rock and cedar and flat cactus to the capital city of Nashville. Albert Arnold Gore, then a young superintendent of schools in rural Smith County, regularly drove that route in the early 1930s to study at the YMCA night law school, and to loiter at the coffee shop of the nearby Andrew Jackson Hotel, pining for a brilliant young waitress named Pauline LaFon who would forgo her own law career to become his wife and adviser and, some say, his brains.

Now on the morning of December 8, 1998, the whole Gore family was retracing that original journey, traveling west to Nashville through a dreary gray mist. Al Gore Jr. made the trip in a limousine, braced by his mother, his wife, Tipper, and their four children. His father, the former United States senator who gave Al his name and his life's profession, rode ahead as usual this one last time, at the front of the funeral cortege, his body resting within a solid cherry casket inside a black Sayers and Scoville hearse.

Keep up, son! Keep up! The elder Gore used to bark out as he strode briskly down the sidewalks of Carthage or the corridors of the Capitol with young Al, never slowing to a child's pace, determined to teach his boy that the race went to the swift. His race was at long last done. He had died three days earlier at age ninety in a way that any father might wish to go: in his own bed in the big house on the hill above the cold Caney Fork River, his wife of sixty-one years at his side, his only son, vice president of the United States, holding his hand for the final six hours. Senator Gore, as he was commonly known, seemed to linger long enough for the arranging of all that needed to be arranged and the saying of everything that needed to be said. Carthage folks had become accustomed to his occasional bouts of befuddlement in his final years, yet he seemed sentient at the end, and his last words of fatherly advice—"Always do right," he reportedly whispered—might have been uttered with posterity in mind. But what was the meaning of the old man's life? That was the question the son grappled with as he rode west through the mist down the ancestral highway, occasionally reading something aloud as he revised the text of a eulogy he had composed on his laptop computer.

He had been at it for twenty-eight and a half hours straight, since four on the morning before when he bolted out of bed and began rummaging through a drawer in the predawn darkness, gathering up loose scraps of paper that he had been tossing in there for weeks, usually after returning from his father's bedside. On each crumpled page he had scribbled a few words that represented something more, a family folk tale or serious political theme—scraps of paper that, if pieced together, might bring ninety years back to life. He had taken them out once before, but it was too soon after his father's death, and he could think of nothing, not even an outline. The second time, as he sat at the dining room table of his farmhouse retreat across the river from his parents' place, the words began pouring out. *My father was the greatest man I ever knew in my life,* he began, and he kept writing past dawn and through breakfast and lunch until seven that night, when, as he later recalled, he "showered and shaved and grabbed a bite to eat and went down to the funeral home for the wake and stood in line and shook hands with the people."

Two hours later he was back at the table, writing through the night without feeling tired, until 8:30 the next morning when he packed up his computer, showered and dressed again, and got his family ready for the trip to Nashville for the first memorial service. That Al Gore had pulled an all-nighter was characteristic in one sense. Going back to his prep school days at St. Albans in Washington, when he would persuade classmates to cram for midterm exams while devouring hamburgers past midnight at the twenty-four-hour Little Tavern on Connecticut Avenue, he had shown a propensity for avoiding some subjects until finally focusing on them with seemingly inexhaustible energy. But this eulogy represented more than another essay test. Funerals honor the dead but tend to reveal more about the living. In trying to tell the world who his father was and what he meant to him, Al Gore was explaining his sense of self as well; doubling back on his father's life, he unavoidably encountered many of the markings of his own unfinished biography.

ONLY TWO WORDS on a scrap of paper were needed to remind Gore of a story he had to include in the eulogy: *Old Peg*. This was the tale his father told more than any other, embroidering it through the years with ever more vivid and piteous details, and though by the end Old Peg seemed more comic fable than historical account, the moral revealed something about the early motivations of Senator Gore and the ambition that he passed down to his son.

The year is 1920 and Albert Gore has just finished eighth grade, an age when many farm children quit their formal schooling. He lives with his parents, Allen and Margie, along with his siblings and an orphaned cousin on a farm in Possum Hollow about fifteen miles from Carthage at the edge of Smith County. The Gores moved there when Albert was five, coming down from the Upper Cumberland hills near Granville. Albert has been obsessed with fiddle music for years, so much so that his classmates call him *Music* Gore. He has his own $5 fiddle and one night there is a hoedown at his parents' house and musicians venture down from the neighboring hills, among them a one-legged traveling mandolin player named Old Peg, who stays the night.

Albert is mesmerized by Old Peg, and the next morning helps hitch up the harness for his horse and buggy. "Each time he told this story, the buggy grew more dilapidated," Al Gore, in his eulogy, said of his father's version of the tale. "Before long it had no top; the harness was mostly baling wire and binding twine. He counted that scrawny horse's ribs a thousand times for me and my sister, and then counted them many more times for his grandchildren." All leading up to the punch line: As they watch sorry Old Peg and his sad-sack horse and crumbling buggy ramble down the road and out of hearing range, Allen Gore, known for being a dead-serious man, puts his arm around his son and deadpans, "There goes your future, Albert."

The difficult life, if not defeated. In retelling the story at his father's funeral, Al Gore used it not just as a reminder of a road not taken, but of the distance this branch of the Gore family had traveled in one generation to reach the heights of national power. People looking at Al Gore today see a product of the American upper crust: a presidential contender born in Washington, reared in a top-floor suite of a hotel along Embassy Row, his father a senator, his mother trained in law, the high-achieving parents grooming their prince for political success at the finest private schools in the East. It was as though his entire future had been laid out in front of him on the direct route he took to school as an adolescent, 1.9 miles up the hill of Massachusetts Avenue from the Fairfax Hotel to St. Albans, passing on the left along the way the grounds of the Naval Observatory, where he would live as vice president.

All true enough, yet misleading if considered without the prologue in Tennessee. Gore's father could find poetry in the hardship stories of his early days in Possum Hollow, recalling droughts so bad that they had to cut down trees to let cattle suck moisture from the leaves, but most of the romance was in the telling, not the living. He was determined to escape. "There was but one way to go from Possum Hollow—that was up and out," he once said. "You couldn't get out except by going up, and once you got out, you still were pretty far down that pole." What is it that lifts people from provincial obscurity? Luck seemed barely a factor in the case of Albert Gore. His father, a strict disciplinarian, first placed his hopes in the oldest son, Reginald, but he had gone off to fight in World War I and came home incapacitated, one lung destroyed by mustard gas, leaving the family's future to Albert, who was twelve years younger but precociously eager. The "ethyl in my gasoline," as he once described it, was an intense pride in achievement, something that first overtook him at the end of the first week of first grade when his teacher in the one-room schoolhouse in Possum Hollow praised him for mastering the alphabet in five days. He hungered for that sensation again and again, and that is what led him toward education and law and politics—and out of Possum Hollow.

During his late teens he was the only member of his generation from Possum Hollow to go to college, attending the state teachers school in Murfreesboro, while also hauling livestock to market, raising a tobacco crop, and selling radios door-to-door for the furniture man in Carthage. He began teaching, long before he had a degree, over in a one-room schoolhouse amid the hollows of Overton County in a place known informally as Booze, and soon became principal in a community closer to Carthage called Pleasant Shade, living where he could, sometimes in the homes of his students, who took to calling him Professor. He thought of himself first as a teacher from then on, always looking for lessons to pass along, a pedagogical style that his son inherited, for better and worse. Albert loved the sound of his own mellifluous Tennessee mountain voice and seemed enthralled by the art of speechmaking, which he had been practicing since his Possum Hollow childhood. They would be working the fields and his father would turn around and Albert had disappeared and they would find him "on a stump somewhere speaking to an imaginary crowd," recalled Donald Lee Hackett, an old family friend.

THE FIRST POLITICIAN Al Gore mentioned in the eulogy to his father was a former congressman from middle Tennessee who "made all the families in this part of the country proud" by becoming secretary of state under Franklin D. Roosevelt and winning the Nobel Peace Prize. For anyone seeking to understand the origins of Gore's political personality, routinely characterized as stiff and oddly formal, there are clues to be found in the direct line that traces back through the family to their political hero, Cordell Hull. During Hull's teenage years in the Upper Cumberland hills, he often "ran the river" with Allen Gore, floating logs down the Caney Fork and Cumberland toward Nashville and taking a steamboat back. Albert Gore grew up hearing his father's stories about those days and watching Hull's political rise, and wanted nothing more than to be like him. When he was teaching in Pleasant Shade he often drove twelve miles down to Carthage at the end of the day if he heard that the congressman— Judge Hull to his constituents—was back in town. After sifting through his mail while eating a late lunch, Hull would sit under a shade tree on the front lawn of the Smith County Courthouse and talk with the checkers players. Albert Gore, hovering close by, listened intently and came away "greatly impressed."

Many of Hull's basic political convictions—his belief in progressive taxation, internationalism, and free trade—were bequeathed to Albert Gore, and then to son Al, but also notable was the style that was passed along as well. Hull's public manner was invariably formal and correct, as if to insist that he never be taken for a hillbilly from the hollows of middle Tennessee. Gore Senior consciously modeled himself after Hull, adopting the same formal bearing for the same reason, but then slightly exaggerating it: always in dark suit, white shirt, and tie; courtly, but rarely relaxed in public, little small talk or informality, always on, speaking in complete sentences full of Latin-rooted words, as if his thoughts were being recorded for history. In the eulogy, Al Gore took wistful note of this last trait, saying that he "always marveled" at his father's vocabulary and archaic pronunciations—"for example, instead of 'woond,' he always said 'wownd.' " Others viewed it as a symptom of grandiosity, someone trying too hard to impress. "He did try to compensate for perceived inferiority to a degree," said historian Kyle Longley. "He went out of his way oftentimes to use very SAT language—the only time you see those words is on the SAT [exam]." During Albert Gore's later days in the Senate, colleague Robert Kerr of Oklahoma stopped a committee hearing and said, "Wait a minute, Albert, what did you say?" Gore repeated a seldom-uttered word, prompting Kerr to direct an aide to bring him a dictionary so he could look it up on the spot.

The senator from Tennessee was not to be treated like a country bumpkin. His colleague Birch Bayh said that with his shock of premature white hair and stately bearing, Gore "looked like a Roman senator—all he needed was a toga." Bernard Rappoport, a Texas financier who befriended progressive southern Democrats in Congress, called them all by their first names when he visited their offices on Capitol Hill, with one exception. "It was always Senator Gore. He demanded to be treated like a statesman." This formality at times was taken for aloofness. Francis Valeo, who served as secretary of the Senate during Gore Senior's three terms there, described him in an oral history as "a very egotistical man" who "sort of lived in his own world." Jesse Nichols, a librarian on the Senate Finance Committee and the first black appointed to a clerical position in the Senate, recalled that "Senator Gore used to come in and out of the clear blue sky he would say,

'Jesse, bring me a Coca-Cola.' " Other members of the committee, Nichols remembered, would put money in the kitty for him to buy coffee and sparkling water. But "Senator Gore would ask time after time for a Coca-Cola. So one time, Senator Kerr and I were in the room together, and I told him, 'Senator, he asks for a Coca-Cola as if I'm a daggumbed servant—and he hasn't put nothing in the kitty!' "

If there was a bit of the Senator Claghorn archetype in old man Gore, who considered his every utterance profound, he was his own man, not the creation of staff. "The staff could help him get the mail together, but when it came time to voting, he took care of himself," said one longtime aide, Jack Robinson Sr. "If you saw a vote up there 94 to 2, you knew he might be one of the two." Gore never had a press secretary, and for decades made the rounds of the galleries, dropping off press releases himself. He also had the touch of country common sense. When much of America was shaken by the Russian success with the first Sputnik satellite in 1957, Gore was part of a small delegation from the Senate Foreign Relations Committee that toured the Soviet Union. Upon his return, Robinson asked him whether he was impressed by the rival superpower's scientific prowess. "Jack Robinson," said Gore, shaking his head. "They don't build things *plumb* over there!"

And despite his tendency toward public pomposity, there was an occasional exuberance to Albert Gore that came out mostly when he was telling stories in Tennessee, or showing off at the center of a crowd, or playing his fiddle. The tale of Old Peg may have been a cautionary tale to his son, but it also captured the depth of his love for fiddling. When he arrived in Washington and began living the congressional life, he put the instrument down, but only after his wife, the more sophisticated Pauline, beseeched him to, saying that fiddling was beneath a statesman's dignity. But back when he first ran for Congress in 1938, he was seen strolling up and down the streets of his home district like a pied piper, trying to persuade local musicians to come along and join his campaign. Donald Lee Hackett, a singer and guitar player with the Roving Trio, heard the pitch and went on the trail with Gore, sometimes bringing his band. "I pulled a right mean bow at that time," Gore once recalled. Perhaps too mean, by Hackett's account. Gore, he said, was such an energetic fiddler that he could not find the beat. "He couldn't keep time at all when he started out. I told him to listen to the rhythm and not get thrown off too much. He really liked to put on a show, and he'd get all out of time, rolling up the bow and jumping around."

For the most part, even, or especially, when he was dealing with his son, Senator Gore maintained a serious reserve. Al's childhood friends in both Carthage and Washington were struck by what Bart Day, who attended St. Albans and Harvard with him, called "the formality of their relationship." The father, Day remembered, "spoke in a very sonorous tone, and it seemed to be the same way with Al." Donna Armistead, Al's Carthage girlfriend in his teenage years, noticed that his demeanor would harden abruptly and a stoical look would wash over his face when he was around the old man. "His father would want him to listen and he would want to impress Al and it was kind of a battle back and forth," Armistead said. "Like, 'Hey, Dad, have you heard this?' And the father was, 'Why, yes, son, let's discuss that.' The stoicness would come through then." James Fleming, a Nashville doctor who was a college friend of Al's older sister, Nancy, described it as "the worst thing in the world" to get trapped in a conversation with Gore father and son. "One day I had to sit on the back porch up in Carthage with Albert and Al, and you know they don't talk baseball and they don't talk about sex or girls, they talk about issues and politics and things that ordinary people have no interest in whatsoever, so it was very difficult to be included in that," Fleming said, using a touch of hyperbole to make his point. "Every now and then they'd ask, 'So what do you think of the Federal Reserve?' I wasn't up for the Federal Reserve. It was awful!"

That is not to say that the son became a duplicate of his father's personality. Few have accused the younger Gore of loving the sound of his own voice. Nor, on the other hand, did he develop his father's maverick flair. Gore Senior's aura of independence, which allowed him to break away from his more conservative southern Democratic colleagues on issues of race and oil tax breaks and the Vietnam War, was stimulated, he once said, by his isolated childhood in Possum Hollow, "where every boy was pretty well on his own out in the woods and on the lonesome hills." There was no comparable experience in young Al's formative days, especially not at St. Albans, where the emphasis was not on independence but on a sense of team. But the son did carry his father's formality into public life, a character trait accentuated by something detected by Charles Bartlett, the veteran political reporter from Chattanooga who observed Tennessee politicians for more than six decades. From Gore Senior to Gore Junior, there was one telltale physical sign of the culture of the Upper Cumberland, coming down through the genes, Bartlett believed: "It's the eyes. The one way he is most like his father is that he does have that distant look in his eye. It's a mountain thing. It's the look of people who don't quite trust anybody. I see that distant look in Al and it reminds me of his father."

BARTLETT found a touch of pathos in Albert Gore's hard eyes: They seemed to predetermine his fate. "It was kind of sad in a way with Senior," Bartlett said. "His ambition exceeded his personality. And he paid a price for that ambition." The price-paying Bartlett alluded to came first in 1956, when Adlai Stevenson, the Democratic presidential nominee, opened the vice presidential nomination to the floor of national delegates and Senator Gore eagerly volunteered himself, challenging his home-state colleague, Estes Kefauver, who had been a presidential candidate and was favored for the vice presidential nomination. In his eulogy, Al Gore used his father's vice presidential aspirations as a joke line. After reading a quote in which Gore Senior reflected that he never truly lusted for the presidency, but "there were times when the vice presidency seemed extremely attractive," the son added dryly, "Now that's humility."

Al was eight years old during the 1956 convention. He watched it at the farmhouse of Gordon (Goat) Thompson, a childhood friend whose parents oversaw the Gore farm just off old Highway 70 on the southern rim of Carthage. Young Al sat transfixed in the Thompsons' living room near the coal fireplace, staring at the black and white set while his father, behind the scenes in Chicago, worked himself into a frenzy the likes of which no one had seen before from the stately senator. "He went wild," remembered Bartlett. In trying to plead his case to Texans Lyndon Johnson and Sam Rayburn, he was almost unrecognizable, according to an LBJ Library oral interview with George Reedy, a former Johnson aide. "A man came running up to us, his face absolutely distorted. . . . His eyes were glimmering. He was mumbling something that sounded like 'Where is Lyndon? Where is Lyndon? Adlai's thrown this open, and I think I've got a chance for it if I can only get Texas. Where is Lyndon?' And we suddenly realized we were talking to Senator Albert Gore of Tennessee," Reedy recalled. "I have never seen before or since such a complete, total example of a man so completely and absolutely wild with ambition, it had literally changed his features."

Senator Gore was overwhelmed by the prospect of national renown, but his inflated notion did not last long. It was punctured by a man who was normally his ally, Silliman Evans Jr., publisher of the Nashville *Tennessean*. Newspapers in Tennessee were lined up across an ideological divide in that era. On the conservative side stood the Nashville *Banner*, Knoxville *Journal*, and Memphis *Commercial-Appeal*. On the liberal side were the Knoxville *News-Sentinel*, Memphis *Press-Scimitar*, and above all the *Tennessean*, a potent force in state politics, having helped defeat the political machine headed by Edward H. Crump, the conservative Memphis insurance man who controlled Tennessee politics for two decades. The *Tennessean* staunchly supported progressive Democrats, and had a personal link to Gore, whose sister-in-law was the publisher's secretary. But the political ties were even closer to Kefauver, who reached the Senate in 1948, four years ahead of Gore. Not only had Kefauver arrived first, but many liberals believed that the coonskin-capped, shambling intellectual had shown more courage in confronting the state's reactionaries. For Gore to challenge him now was seen by some as an act of family treachery, made worse by the fact that his firmest support seemed to come from his erstwhile enemies, the Dixiecrats. Between the second and third ballots, Evans found Gore near the convention floor, grabbed him by the lapels, and thundered: "You son of a bitch, my father helped make you and I can help break you! If you don't get out of this race, you'll never get the *Tennessean*'s support for anything again, not even dog catcher." Gore backed down.

The man who prevailed instead, Estes Kefauver, is in his own way as central to the Gore political story as Cordell Hull. Hull was the prototype, Kefauver the antitype, not in ideology, where they were similar, both southern liberals, but in political personality, where they were near opposites. In examining the image problems of Al Gore Jr., there is a generational parallel to consider: Kefauver was to the father what Bill Clinton is to the son.

Kefauver's eyes were as soft as Gore's were hard. That those eyes might have been softened by excessive alcohol (Albert, in contrast, did not drink) was less important on a superficial level than the fact that they seemed inviting and friendly, not distancing. If Kefauver became perhaps too close to some of his female constituents, as historians later documented, his ability to connect on a personal basis with the average voter was striking, and in direct contrast with Albert Gore. "Everybody always tried to befriend Estes and to look after him, particularly women, because he was always bumbling around," recalled Jim Sasser, the former senator who as a young man worked in the campaigns of both Kefauver and Albert Gore. Sasser would long remember the day when he drove Kefauver through the little Tennessee town of Gallatin. "There were three garbage workers on the side of the road, all black, collecting garbage. Nobody in the car except myself and Estes. 'Stop the car!' he says. So he got out of the car and walked back to all three of those garbage workers and chatted with them and he came back and I said, 'Senator, just out of curiosity, why did you want to talk to those fellows?' He said, 'Well, those fellows don't have much to look forward to and talking to a senator, that probably would make their month.' "

Kefauver understood, as Bill Clinton later did, the powerful effect that a soft personal touch could have on voters. Whenever he traveled in Tennessee, Kefauver made sure that an aide was walking directly behind him, whispering into his ear the names and histories of people coming toward him, whom the senator then greeted as long-lost friends. Another member of his Senate staff did nothing but read local papers from back home and clip notices of funerals, births, weddings, beauty pageants, 4-H contests—all of which would elicit a personal note from the senator, addressed informally on a first-name basis and invariably signed with the warm scrawl of "Estes." Ted Brown, an Atlanta lawyer who once worked for Albert Gore and spent a year at the University of Tennessee cataloguing Kefauver's political papers, was struck by the different approaches of the two men. "Gore was a lot more formal. He rarely sent those types of letters out, and if he did they would always be addressed to Miss So-and-So and signed 'Albert Gore,' " Brown noted. "I asked him one time if he had ever thought about doing something similar to what Senator Kefauver had done, and he said, 'No, I don't know those people.' Kefauver's perspective was, 'I don't know them but I need to know them.' " Another story captured the contrast between the two men, according to Wayne Whitt, a veteran political reporter at the *Tennessean*. "It was said that if you asked Gore Senior how he felt about an issue like admitting Red China to the U.N., he would still be answering thirty minutes later, whereas Kefauver would simply say, 'What do you think?' "

Perhaps it was more style than substance, more image than reality, but with the father and Kefauver as with his son and Clinton, the contrast in personalities tended to work against the Gores, accentuating the aura of distance conveyed by their eyes.

THEY SAY opposites attract, Al Gore wrote in the eulogy to his father, explaining the marriage of his parents. Pauline LaFon, a descendant of Huguenots, or French Protestants, shared some characteristics with Albert Gore. Like him, she came out of relative poverty in the provincial south and believed from an early age that circumstances could not deter her. But she was more sophisticated and politically savvy than her husband. "Pauline was the brains and Albert was the pretty blond," is how one former Tennessee journalist put it, stretching the reality to make the point. No one familiar with the family disputes the idea that Albert would not have gone nearly as far in life without her. Once, according to family lore, Pauline became so exasperated with her husband that she said, "I think I'll leave."

"Why, that's a good idea," Albert responded. "I believe I'll go with you."

Tennessee is so diverse and wide (Mountain City in the northeast is closer to points in Canada than to Memphis) that until recent years it was regarded internally as three separate jurisdictions, known as Grand Divisions: east Tennessee, middle Tennessee, and west Tennessee. Each division had its own geography, history, economics, politics, and culture. Pauline LaFon came out of the west. She was born in the small town of Palmersville and moved in early adolescence to Jackson when her father Walter L. LaFon, disabled by an arm infection, gave up his country store and took a job with the highway department dispensing gasoline tickets to road crews and highway patrolmen. Her mother, Maude, tended a vegetable garden and rented rooms to boarders. Maude was an orphan from Paragould, Arkansas, who had been only sixteen when she married Walter, then working in Arkansas on a railroad crew. Word of their teenage union spread through town like this: *What kind of man did Maude get? She didn't get a man at all, she got a slick-faced kid!*

They produced six children, and the three girls, who came first, Verlie Mae, Thelma, and Pauline, were encouraged by their father to compete in the male-oriented society. The early feminist streak in Pauline's father was said to arise from an inheritance battle that traced back another generation, to when his mother was denied land she felt was rightly hers but was given instead to her brothers "because they were supposedly strong and could grow things on the land and women couldn't." Though not a lawyer, Pauline's father tried to help his mother in a long court battle, and he spoke of the injustice frequently at the LaFon dinner table—"fuming," as Pauline later recalled, "about women not being allowed to do some things men could do." All three of his daughters eventually went to college, including Thelma, who was legally blind and wrote on a special Braille typewriter.

Pauline attended Union College in Jackson, but felt uncomfortably restricted by cultural expectations. "There were so few things that were interesting to me that were open to women," she said later. "I didn't want to be a nurse. I didn't want to be a teacher. I didn't want to be a secretary." While working in a restaurant in Jackson to pay for her tuition, she had an epiphany. Most of the customers she served were lawyers, and all of them were men. She listened to their conversations, found them interesting, and concluded that she certainly could do anything they could do. So she borrowed $100 from the Rotary Club of Jackson and rode the bus to Nashville to attend Vanderbilt law school, where she became the tenth female graduate. She paid back the loan by again waiting on tables, at night at the Andrew Jackson coffee shop. One of her regular customers was Albert Gore, the evening law student who was stoking up on caffeine before making the drive back to Carthage on old Highway 70. Albert could not get enough of Pauline, with her handsome cheekbones and piercing blue eyes and strong but comforting bearing. "He'd stay over sometimes and see that I got home all right, which was just a couple of blocks away," she recalled. "That went on almost the whole three years we were in law school."

They took the bar exam together and then Pauline endured one unsatisfying year practicing law in Texarkana, a half-state away from Albert, who was launching his political career as state commissioner of labor, an influential post for progressive action in those New Deal days. On May 15, 1937, they slipped away to Tompkinsville, Kentucky, and got married. There was a certain mystery to the ceremony. Their families were not there, and a handwritten notation on the certificate directed that news of the marriage not be published. Perhaps the secrecy was prompted by another fact revealed on the certificate—that Pauline had been married once before and divorced, a part of her early life that she never again wanted to discuss. Once they were married, Albert and Pauline Gore seemed to meld perfectly. "They weren't two people, they were one," said Louise Gore, a second cousin whose father, Grady Gore, had grown up with Albert in Possum Hollow. "They were as close as two people could be." In his eulogy, Al Gore said that "of all the lessons" he learned from his father, "perhaps the most powerful was the way he loved my mother. He respected her as an equal, if not more."

Here was another contrast with Bill Clinton, who sat among the mourners at Albert Gore's memorial service in Nashville. Clinton grew up with an alcoholic stepfather who abused his mother; he reacted by trying to become a peacemaker, constantly seeking to soothe or conceal the rough edges, and to go out into the world to achieve and redeem the family. Gore, on the other hand, said that his parents' strong marriage allowed him to grow up "secure and confident" that his needs would be met. While his parents expected much of him and instilled in him fierce competitive instincts, he never seemed driven, as Clinton so clearly was, to win the approval of strangers. He had a high enough opinion of himself.

Soon after joining forces with Albert, who announced for Congress within a year of their marriage, Pauline decided to put aside her own law career and channel her considerable talents into the rise of the Gore family. "I was interested in everything he was doing and we were very ambitious—for both of us," she explained. She traveled with her husband, polished his speeches, spoke as his stand-in without hesitation, and talked policy with him at the dinner table, usually pushing him to be more liberal (her politics were modeled after Eleanor Roosevelt's, for whom she worked answering letters during the 1930s). While Albert had the instinctive ambition, that wild-eyed look that LBJ's boys noticed, Pauline always knew what to do with it. "Albert had a real good woman that was driving him," said Whit LaFon, Pauline's brother, who became a judge in west Tennessee. "She stayed on his duster." After her husband had spent sixteen years in the House, Pauline encouraged him to reach higher and run for the Senate against the Democratic incumbent, Kenneth D. McKellar, the ancient and powerful chairman of the Senate Appropriations Committee.

As they traveled around the state that summer of 1952, the Gores noticed placards tacked to trees, utility poles, and vacant storefronts declaring *Thinking Feller Vote for McKellar.* "I found it repeated every time I turned a curve, and by word of mouth," Gore later recalled. "I saw we had to get an answer to that. So Mrs. Gore and I came home one Saturday night after a hard day of campaigning and she cleaned off the kitchen table and made a pot of coffee and said, 'Albert, sit down here. Here's the pencil. Here's the paper. I'll get a pencil and paper. We've got to answer that placard.' So we wrote doggerels and rhymes and riddles and finally came to one we thought would work. So we got our country printer up early the next morning and ran a bunch of placards answering that of the opposition. And on Monday morning my friends started fanning out over the state. Wherever they found one of those *Thinking Feller Vote for McKellar* signs they tacked one just beneath it which read *Think Some More and Vote for Gore.*"

Where Albert tended to go his own way, Pauline mixed more easily with people, reflecting the cultural differences between the lonesome hills of middle Tennessee and the southern flatlands of the west, where social graces were more valued. "She was always trying to calm Albert down," remembered Charles Bartlett. As she once put it, "I tried to persuade Albert not to butt at a stone wall just for the sheer joy of butting." Although her politics were liberal, she did not have a maverick personality, "and she transferred that [caution] to Al," said historian Longley. Along with her softer edges, she possessed a keener sense of the political world. She was constantly "looking out from behind for the guys with the knives," according to David Halberstam, who covered the Gores for the *Tennessean* early in his journalism career. "She was smarter, tougher, more calculating." If Al Gore took his formality, his distant eyes, and his pedagogical style from his father, his political instincts came more from his mother. "You have to understand Pauline to know Al Junior," said Bartlett. "She was the leavening influence."

THE OLD MAN was always teaching, his son said in the eulogy. "And I thank God he taught me to love justice. Not everyone was eager to learn. One unreconstructed constituent once said, in reference to African-Americans—though that was not the term he used—'I don't want to eat with them, I don't want to live with them, and I don't want my kids to go to school with them.' To which my father replied gently, 'Do you want to go to heaven with them?' After a brief pause came the flustered response: 'No, I want to go to hell with you and Estes Kefauver.' "

In the political narrative of the family Gore, stories of race appear regularly, often in the form of little morality plays. Gore Senior entered politics at a time when Jim Crow segregation was still a bitter fact of life in the south, and though he was considered a moderate, his positions on race were complicated by the political realities of that time and place. He voted against the imposition of a poll tax in 1942, but there were relatively few blacks in his congressional district in middle Tennessee then, especially in contrast to the Memphis region to the west, which was controlled by Boss Crump's Democratic machine. As venal as Crump's operation was, it included blacks in the power base, spreading money to handpicked black leaders to control the vote. So when Albert Gore and other reformers took on the Crump machine, they also ran the danger of alienating powerful black leaders in Memphis.

The Gores personally felt the evils of segregation during the long car trips they began making in 1939 between Carthage and Washington after Albert was elected to Congress. They took along a black nanny, Ocie Bell Hunt, to look after their young daughter, Nancy. On the first drive, according to historian Tony Badger, they could find no rest rooms for Hunt to use and had an exhausting time searching for a motel that would lodge an interracial traveling party. Finally they came upon a little motel in east Tennessee that would allow the Gores and Hunt to stay overnight, provided they arrived after dark and left before the other guests in the morning. The trips continued in this humiliating fashion year after year, until well after Al Gore Jr. came along. He later said that he thought he had some early memory of those incidents, but realized that perhaps he merely remembered being told the same stories so many times. "That was a key lesson in injustice that was being driven home," he said. "And it was reinforced by frequent commentary from my parents."

Racial injustice was a common theme in the conversations of Pauline Gore. Friends say she was the one who fed the family's convictions, her west Tennessee roots giving her more of a deep personal witness to racism. When Nancy was old enough, Pauline urged her and a friend to read Harper Lee's *To Kill a Mockingbird*, and then had them read it again until the theme was etched in their memories. The ideal of a southern lawyer committed to principles of truth and justice that transcended race and prejudice was one that Mrs. Gore thought "really hit at the heart of the whole matter," recalled Nancy Fleming, the daughter's friend. Pauline's sensibility was unusual among her peers: She often recounted the time during the 1940s when she addressed a black acquaintance by the title "Mrs." instead of a condescending first name, and was struck by the look of horror that simple act brought to the face of another Tennessee congressman's wife.

Of all the decisions made by Senator Gore during his long career in Washington, one dramatic act of rejection established his reputation as a supporter of civil rights. It came on the floor of the U.S. Senate in 1956, when colleague Strom Thurmond of South Carolina approached his desk with a copy of a segregationist document opposing the federal effort to desegregate southern schools and said, "Albert, we'd like you to sign the Southern Manifesto with the rest of us." The entire southern press corps had been alerted ahead of time and looked down on the scene from the balcony. Senator Gore, his voice rising so loud that he was certain he could be heard in the press gallery, grandly declared "Hell no!" and brushed Thurmond and the document away. He later called the Southern Manifesto "spurious, inane, insulting" and "the most unvarnished piece of demagoguery" he had ever encountered. It does not lessen the importance of his denunciation of the manifesto to point out that Gore was joined in opposition by his colleague from Tennessee, Kefauver, and that the senator's most powerful friends back home, including the editors at the Nashville *Tennessean*, also opposed the racist proposition and would have criticized him had he done anything else.

With every gesture Gore made in support of civil rights came a mailbag of angry letters from segregationists. One year after denouncing the manifesto, he voted for the 1957 Civil Rights Act and further enraged some constituents by nominating two young black students from Memphis for appointment to the Air Force Academy. "I was literally astounded to read that you had appointed two Negroes" to the academy, wrote one voter who called himself the senator's friend. "It appears that some of your staff must have slipped up very badly to make such a mistake as this." While politely thanking the letter writer for "calling this matter to my attention," Gore noted that Selective Service boards did not take race into consideration when calling young men for the draft and so "it had not occurred to me that I should do so" in the case of the Air Force Academy.

AFTER THE MEMORIAL SERVICE in Nashville, the funeral cortege turned back toward Carthage, traveling east through the mist not on old Highway 70 but along Interstate 40, the other main road in the life of the Gore family. Al Gore had planned the return route—

what he called his father's "last trip home"—as another metaphor for his life's path. As a senator in 1955 and 1956, Albert Gore had helped write and pass legislation creating I-40 and the rest of the Interstate highway system, the largest public works project in American history. That is where the son's interest in politics and government began, when Senator Gore brought him along to hearings of the Senate Public Works Committee in Room 412 of the marbled Russell Senate Office Building and the eight-year-old boy became captivated by the debate over where the superhighways would go and how wide the lanes would be and what color was best for the road signs, blue or green. The issues seemed understandable, and the results amazingly clear; there could be no better lesson in turning an idea into reality. The Gores traveled by car between Washington and Tennessee as many as six times a year, and as I-40 was being completed the trip got shorter year by year, until what had been an arduous two-day journey, with an overnight stop in Roanoke or Bristol, could now be finished in one day.

"Making the connection between those people sitting in that room, discussing and debating, voting and enacting a law on one hand, and the bulldozers pushing the earth, and the pavement laid down, and my family being able to get home faster—that connection was very powerful," Gore said decades later. The Interstate project made a lasting impression on him; it served, in a sense, as the generational precursor of his own later work in Congress promoting the Internet's information superhighway. The father passed down to his son something else, it seems: an overeagerness to take credit. Although Albert Gore was an important figure in the Interstate highway bill, there were many other key participants in Congress and the Eisenhower administration, but he never shied away from calling the system his own. It was not unlike Al Gore's later boast that he had paved the way for the widespread use of the Internet—stretching an indisputably important role into a seminal one.

The funeral procession rolled toward Gordonsville, slowing briefly as it approached Possum Hollow, in silent honor of where it all began with the childhood oratory on the tree stumps in the back field. Then the line of black limousines snaked north toward Carthage, approaching the big house on the hill where the old man had died, with its big magnolia tree shading the circle driveway; its spacious living room dense with oriental antiques and political artifacts and portraits of Al and Tipper and the children; and its kitchen walls lined with black and white photographs chronicling a family's rise: Senior with his fiddle, Senior with John F. Kennedy (who entered the Senate with him in 1952), father and son picking strawberries and standing by the water pump, the family bouncing along in a jeep. And beyond the house, the Gore farm, 250 acres bending down to the Caney Fork.

Here were the fields that the son had eulogized hours earlier. It was sometimes reported that his father went back to this farm at the end of his political career, but that was misleading, because in fact "throughout his entire life in public service he never left his farm," the son had said. "He loved to raise Angus cattle. In the audience today are quite a few Angus breeders from around the country who were among his closest friends. It was his recreation. He always said, 'I'd rather find a new black calf in the weeds than a golf ball in the grass.' Our farm was also an important school where he taught me every day. He must have told me a hundred times the importance of learning how to work. He taught me how to plow a steep hillside with a team of mules. He taught me how to clear three acres of heavily wooded forest with a double-bladed axe. He taught me how to take up hay all day in the sun and take up the neighbor's hay after dinner by moonlight before the rains came."

The stiff preppy Geeing and Hawing mules behind a hillside plow? The very notion has prompted doubts and some ridicule. And though it certainly was not an everyday occurrence, it *did* happen, in the summer of his fifteenth year. Gore's Carthage friends are puzzled by the skepticism. Steve Armistead, Edd Blair, Goat Thompson, and Terry Pope all worked alongside Al for several summers. They fooled around when they could—filling the cattle trough with cold water and diving in, driving jalopies wildly down the farm hill, hypnotizing chickens—but not when the old man was watching. He paid his son and the other boys 30 cents an hour for a half-day's work when they were teenagers, sometimes rousting them out of bed before dawn to bale the hay and move the electronic cattle fences. "Senior always wanted Al to do this and do that," said Steve Armistead. "His dad really wanted him to work." Perhaps there was a long-range political purpose to Albert's insistence that his son learn the ways of rural life, but the intent did not seem to be that Al could later use the farm as a convenient counterpoint to his Ivy League schooling. Gore Senior believed that farmwork was invaluable in and of itself. Pauline later recalled one afternoon when she and Albert were inside the big house, looking out the picture window toward the Caney Fork, and there was Al down below, behind the mules, and the father said contentedly, "I think a boy, to achieve anything he wants to achieve, which would include being president of the United States, oughta be able to run a hillside plow."

The Gore farm was more than a quaint getaway for the father or training ground for the son; it was also a business enterprise. Albert Gore was never a financial wizard, but he had an entrepreneurial streak that hovered between compulsive and comical. Carthage folks would shake their heads when discussing his multifarious business schemes over the decades—chicken coops, feed stores, flea markets, virtually anything he could get his hands on. He was known to buy seemingly useless plots of hardscrabble land—"holes in the ground," as one friend politely described them—and then persuade gravel and construction companies to come by with detritus to fill the holes so that he could try to sell his property as prime acreage. The elder Gore's predilection for landowning was passed along to his son, who bought his first piece of property, a twenty-acre field on the edge of Carthage, when he was home from Harvard during the spring break of his senior year in 1969, borrowing the money from a rural credit union.

There were two principal enterprises on the Gore farm, cattle and tobacco. In raising Black Angus, Albert Gore pursued an avocation enjoyed by many of his social acquaintances, including cousin Grady Gore and Senator Kerr and Occidental Petroleum chairman Armand Hammer, the international whirlwind: cutthroat businessman, world-class philanthropist, art collector, and, in his early days, secret agent for the Soviet Union. Hammer first met Gore at a cattle auction in 1952 around the time of the Tennessean's election to the Senate. They became political allies as free trade internationalists, and also developed a mutually beneficial business relationship, with Gore occasionally easing the way for Hammer's dealings with the federal bureaucracy and Hammer in return offering the senator entrée into his moneyed world, first introducing him to the social scene of wealthy cattle owners, then, decades later, hiring him to run an Occidental subsidiary in Kentucky, Island Creek Coal. Gore and Hammer shared a cattle manager, Leo Cropsey, and eventually became partners in the raising of several bulls, including Ankonian Dyno Gore, a Black Angus stud of some renown. To Hammer, who kept a cattle ranch near Red Bank, New Jersey, the senator was but one of countless associates with whom he might deal, but Hammer loomed larger from the other side. He was a part of the Gore family saga, a special guest at weddings and inaugurals, the middleman in land acquisitions, a mysterious figure who might help provide the fuel for the father's dynastic ambitions.

At its peak, Senator Gore's Black Angus herd totaled two hundred head and was regarded as one of the top herds in the land. Twice a year, cattle breeders from across the country, some of them encouraged by Hammer, found their way to Carthage for a big sale in which a third of the herd might be auctioned off, grossing $100,000 or more. There was often a celebrity or two in the crowd: one year the sale was graced by a visit from Joe DiMaggio. Tom Burke, a noted sales manager from Smithvale, Missouri, came down to run the auction with Cropsey, who stayed as a guest at the Gore house. The senator relished these occasions. He would not miss the auctions for anything, once even turning down a competing birthday invitation to dine on Hammer's yacht. As much as he took to his work in the Senate, he seemed obsessed by his herd of Black Angus. "He'd be sitting up there in a hearing while somebody else was busy with the committee work and he'd be reading this catalogue on these cattle," recalled Senate Finance Committee aide Jesse Nichols. He regarded the cattlemen with at least as much respect as his fellow politicians at the Capitol, referring to them as "my fellow breeders." According to Cropsey, the senator showed off his farm wearing his finest suits—"Oh, yeah, you betcha, he never dressed down for those catalogue sales." Pauline Gore dressed up, too, as the hostess of a festive barbecue for out-of-town guests on the sale's eve. At some point during the barbecue, on cue, a neighbor would turn to Albert and call out a tune, and *Music* Gore would haul out his fiddle in honor of Old Peg.

Al and his summer friends washed and scrubbed the cattle and put in the bean hay, but none of them could keep pace with the old man. "He could outwork three or four field hands . . . and he had real strong hands," remembered Edd Blair, a neighbor boy a few years older than Al. "The cattle feed used to come in paper bags that were five or six layers thick. Most of us were strong but we couldn't take a fifty-pound bag and pick it up and tear it, but he could just tear it in two and put it in a feed trough. Mr. Albert could do it all day."

As proud as he was of his cattle, Senator Gore seemed equally enamored of his favorite crop of tobacco. Cropsey, the cattleman who became a Gore family friend, noticed that whenever a new person visited the farm, "the first thing Albert did was take them to see the tobacco acreage. Beautiful tobacco plants—he was always so proud of that." Tobacco had been part of the culture of the Upper Cumberland region for generations: virtually every farm family, including the Gores, had their federally regulated allotment and followed the seasonal rhythms of planting and spiking and stripping and hauling to the warehouse on Main Street for auction. Tobacco was not mentioned in the son's eulogy to his father. Only a decade earlier, while campaigning in a presidential primary in North Carolina, he had delivered an ode to tobacco ("I put it in the plant beds and transferred it. I've hoed it. I've chopped it. I've shredded it. Spiked it. Put it in the barn and stripped it and sold it."). But now he wanted nothing to do with it. And that, in a sense, is where he started. Along with all of his friends, Al detested working the tobacco field as a teenager. It was "hot and dirty" work, according to his pal Goat Thompson, whose hand still bears a V-shaped scar caused by the slip of a tobacco knife. "You get wringing wet with sweat. Your pants and all just sop. Looks like you've been floating in a river. . . . If you've ever been in a tobacco patch, you'd be hunting a way out."

DOWN PAST THE FARM, at the edge of Snow Creek, the funeral procession stopped at New Salem Missionary Baptist Church for a second memorial service, this one smaller, for old Carthage friends and neighbors. This was the Gores' country church, though old-timers said the only regular Gore worshiper was Margie Gore, Al's grandmother, who often brought along her grandson when he was home for the summer. There was some concern among the locals when they first got word that an Episcopal bishop would lead the funeral service, and a woman no less. But Al Gore asked that honor go to Jane Holmes Dixon, the suffragan bishop of the Episcopal diocese of Washington, who had been one of Nancy Gore's best friends at Vanderbilt. The vice president's wishes on this day were not challenged. As Bishop Dixon opened her soft sermon on the theme of resurrection, she was startled by a sound that she had never heard in her own high church.

Her every sentence elicited a hearty round of amens from over on the left side, where old men in dark suits sat in what they called Amen Corner. The response left Dixon "beside herself" with appreciation for this blending of faiths and traditions. When she finished, two verses of "Amazing Grace" were sung in powerful solo voice by Jerry Futrell, who had run the Reed Bros. Pharmacy in town where General Patton, wearing two ivory-handled pistols, once came in on break from military maneuvers and ordered two milk shakes. The congregation joined Futrell for the final verse.

Then the black hearse led the way back through town, past Fisher Avenue, where the Gores had lived in the summers of Al's early childhood, Albert and Pauline and Al and sister Nancy in one house, grandparents Allen and Margie next door, where Allen had taught his grandson how to spell his first word—G-R-E-E-N. Up at the end of the street stood the Greek Revivalist Cullem Mansion, where Albert had once taken his son, then seven, for another lesson: What could Senator Gore's refusal to sign the Southern Manifesto mean to a youngster? Here was what it meant. Through the elegant front parlor and down the back staircase to the dank basement, way in the back, *Look up, son! Look up!*—slave rings hanging from the ceiling, remnants of shackles that once locked on the wrists and ankles of slaves who built the mansion. The sight was an utter shock to young Al, the first startling lesson on life's contradictions—the "stark contrast," as he said later, "between the undeniable and palpable presence of evil having existed in my hometown, my neighborhood, on the one hand, and the gentleness of Carthage as I knew it."

It was dark by the time the funeral cortege reached the cemetery, and a winter drizzle dampened the grass along the fifty-yard walk from the driveway to the burial site. Local men had dug the hole by shovel, and would fill it again after everyone left. The funeral home brought in a generator and set up construction lights to illuminate the scene. Al Gore had been awake for thirty-eight hours straight dealing with the meaning of his father. He sat with his arm around his mother as they watched Albert Arnold Gore Sr., dressed formally, as always, in a blue business suit, resting inside his solid cherry coffin, descend into Grave 3 in Lot 18, Section C of the Smith County graveyard. He was buried next to his daughter, the ebullient Nancy, who had died of lung cancer fourteen years earlier at the premature age of forty-six. The ceremony done, son and mother moved slowly through the evening darkness to the waiting car, past rows of grave markers memorializing the people of the Upper Cumberland hills of middle Tennessee, ancestors named Cowan and Burton, Hood and Butler, Ligon and Dixon, Bowman and Lankford, Massey and Gore.

CHAPTER TWO

PRINCE
OF THE FAIRFAX

D URING HIS EARLY YEARS as a senator's son in Washington, Al Gore was often the smallest one in the crowd, a pint-size boy with dark hair and freckles who lived with his prominent parents in Suite 809 atop the Fairfax Hotel along Embassy Row. If this experience made him different from you and me, to borrow F. Scott Fitzgerald's phrase, it was not from being rich, but rather from being apart. He grew up in a singularly odd world of old people and bellhops, separated from the child-filled neighborhoods of his classmates at St. Albans and further still from his summertime pals at the family farm in Tennessee.

The Fairfax still advertised itself as "Washington's Family Hotel," but most of the families were gone by the mid-1950s. Directly below the Gores in Suite 709 resided grumpy old Senator John McClellan, who complained every time Al bounced his basketball. Down one dark hall lived the exotic widow, Madame Brambilla, who spent half the year at the Excelsior in Rome and maintained a second suite for her considerable wardrobe. The hotel was owned by Grady Gore, the senator's cousin, who had grown up with Albert in Possum Hollow, but now had transformed himself into a society figure, answering to the title Colonel, voting Republican, living in his capacious Marwood estate overlooking the Potomac, and arriving at the Fairfax each morning in the back of a black Cadillac.

There was not much for a young boy to do at the hotel once the thrill of riding an elevator was gone. The best playground, it seems, was the hotel's flat roof, which Al reached by ascending a metal staircase.

He and his friends now and then played Frisbee up there, an entertainment often cut short by a gust of wind. They also tied plastic toy figures to spools of thread and dangled them down to the front entrance, hoping to discombobulate a hotel guest by bopping him gently on the noggin as he left the building. And they dropped water balloons on limousines parked in back or on the hoods of cars waiting for the light to change at the corner of 21st and Massachusetts. But for the most part, these occasional caprices aside, Al adapted to a staid environment by behaving as a perfect little gentleman. Sam Williams, a school friend who lived in the suburb of Bethesda, was struck during visits to the Fairfax by his classmate's unusual life: He came to think of Al as "almost political aristocracy" existing "all alone in the big old apartment building." Al was invariably courteous to his elders and seemed uncommonly earnest, sometimes too much so and prone to tattling.

His only sibling, Nancy, was a decade older and in some ways his opposite, radiant, easygoing, and full of mischief. Nancy attended Holton Arms, a private girls school then located on S Street near Dupont Circle. On weekends, she often stayed home to look after her little brother while their parents were on the political circuit. Barbara Howar, a friend from school, sometimes joined her and they had the run of Suite 809. Although Nancy by all accounts adored her brother, at times like this she wanted nothing to do with him. He was the sort of pest who would seek attention by popping out of nowhere, reciting in singsong voice the latest television commercial he had memorized ("Got a little ant . . . Got a little fly . . . Real-Kill! Real-Kill! . . . Watch them die!"). The two teenage girls would hole up in a room, fiendishly puffing on nonfilter Pall Malls while furtively dialing and redialing a Hollywood telephone number they had dug up for Marlon Brando, on whom they both had crushes. Their efforts to evade the watchful eye of Little Al met with no apparent success. "Every time we tried to do something, Al would catch us and say, 'I'm telling! I'm telling! I'm telling Dad!' " Howar said. "He was an egregious little tattletale."

His compulsion to adhere to the expected order extended beyond the common practice of snitching on an older sibling. One day in May 1958, Al's lower-school class at St. Albans went on a field trip to Andrews Air Force Base in Maryland. Their bus broke down outside the base entrance, and the boys and teachers walked the rest of the way in. When the tour was over, they waited in the sweltering afternoon heat for the arrival of a replacement bus, and many of the boys took advantage of this idle time by scampering around an open field. A young science teacher named Alexander Haslam was surveying his boisterous brood when young Al approached and politely inquired: "Sir, is this the time to be rowdy?"

Perhaps no human being, not even a candidate for the American presidency, should be judged decades later by the way they were before they reached adulthood, but it is true nonetheless that in seeking to understand why people think and act as they do, the early days often provide the richest veins in the biographical mine. Al Gore underwent a series of life-changing experiences after his school years—serving in Vietnam, marrying and rearing a family, losing his sister, nearly losing his son, following his father into politics, losing a premature bid for the presidency, serving two terms as vice president—yet in many ways the child remains the father of the man. Many of the behavioral patterns of the figure who would run for president in 2000 are best explained by the boy he once was.

Young Gore learned to adapt within the confines of a disciplined life, a structure imposed on him by his parents and teachers, and against which he rarely rebelled. He presented himself to the world as serious and earnest, always striving to do right, but at times revealed flashes of a more complicated struggle within, his stoic front masking a hidden artistry, sarcasm, and loneliness. He made himself the son that his parents wanted and the very model of a St. Albans student, but if he was good, he was never the best. He was a smart boy who was tested twice for IQ and scored 133 and 134 ("absolutely superb, that means tremendous ability," said a high school counselor of those numbers), but his grades rose and fell depending on his interest, while athletic success came to him only with considerable effort.

HERE IS A MORNING TABLEAU at Suite 809 drawn from remembrances of the family and hotel workers: Al's mother, hoping to make the hotel seem more like home, bakes her own bread and prepares Al's morning meal. He eats hurriedly, gathers his books, and leaves for school at precisely the same time each morning, scooting past the green chinoiserie desk with the silver goblet, past the big red sofa with the tufted back, and out the green door and down the hallway to the elevator, descending to the lobby and sprinting to the Fairfax's front door "like a rocket," as the elevator man later recalled, crossing Massachusetts Avenue to wait for the N-2 or N-4 bus that will take him up the hill to St. Albans. As their son stands there waiting for his ride, Albert and Pauline gaze down on him from the eighth-floor window, fairly bursting with pride, and one turns to the other and declares, "Isn't it fine?"

It had been that way since his birth, which came at Columbia Hospital in Washington on March 31, 1948, nearly ten years after Nancy's and just when the Gores, according to Pauline, "had almost despaired of having another child, much less a son." They regarded their nine-pound, two-ounce boy as "kind of a miracle" and wanted the world to know that he was special. Albert had gone so far as to instruct the Nashville *Tennessean*'s Washington bureau while Pauline was pregnant that "if I have a baby boy, I don't want the news buried on an inside page [as the birth of a daughter of his competitive ally, Estes Kefauver, had been]. I want it on Page 1 where it belongs." And so it was. "Well Mr. Gore, Here He Is, On Page 1," read the headline.

Did this reflect how demanding his parents would be from then on in their expectations? "Not really," Gore said once when asked to look back on his childhood. "But," he added, "I suppose I got the message" that their expectations were high. Their ambitions for him were not always subtle. Albert imparted lessons to his young son much as a strict mentor would to a pupil, using daily encounters as the course work for an ongoing political philosophy class. Pauline later used the dinner table in Suite 809 for the same purpose. "Al always listened to what his father was doing and how his father was doing it," she said. "If we had important people . . . I liked for Al to be able to be there. I selected guests for us; if it so happened there was a great guest who was a good conversationalist and the issue was proper for me and my son, then I would see if I could wedge Al in." Once, when serving a meal to young Al and his cousins Mark and Jamie, she asked, "Which one of you is going to be president?" It was a rhetorical question, Mark recalled, but all three knew she was talking to her son. Albert, perhaps putting his aspirations into the boy's mouth, told acquaintances about the time he and Al were crossing the street and his son looked up at him and announced, "One day, I'm going to be somebody."

When Al was six, his parents called a reporter at the Knoxville *News-Sentinel* to relate a story about how he had talked his father into buying him a 98 cent bow and arrow rather than the 49 cent set they had originally agreed upon—a tale that in its recounting seemed like nothing more than a promotion of the boy's political future. "There may be another Gore on the way toward the political pinnacle," the story began. "He's just 6 years old now. But with his experiences to date, who knows what may happen." The climax of the piece came when Al was alone with his mother and boasted of his dealings with his father: "Why Mama, I out-talked a senator." And that, the article concluded, under a photo of the boy drawing a suction-tipped arrow across a bow with the help of his father, "is why Al Gore is a young man to be watched from here on in."

Pauline never spanked her boy. She believed in "using your wits instead of your switch" to steer him in the right direction. She and Albert were not smothering stage parents; they were too busy with the senator's political rise to oversee their son's every step, but they did have a definite path they wanted him to follow. Pauline canvassed the prep schools of Washington before deciding on St. Albans as the proper place, with its liberal yet disciplined atmosphere. At first she was told there was no space, but she persisted, visiting the campus week after week until the headmaster relented and let young Al enroll.

OFFICIAL WASHINGTON was as much of a small town in its way as any backwater spot in Tennessee, with its own rituals and mores and circle of families. Diane Kefauver was in Tricia Nixon's class and her little sister was in Julie Nixon's class, and their fathers ran against each other for vice president and their houses were just around the corner, and the family dogs, both cocker spaniels, "got married and had puppies together," as Diane Kefauver later put it. Private schools were the coalescing institutions for the sons and daughters of the political class. The girls were sent to National Cathedral School and Holton Arms and Madeira; the boys to St. Albans. From fourth grade to seventh, these children of the elite were brought together on Friday nights at Mrs. Shippen's Dancing, a pre-debutante training ground located at the corner of Wisconsin and Fessenden run by the white-haired, whistle-toting dowager Florence Hawley Brush Shippen, a director of the Robert E. Lee Memorial Association and the Society of Colonial Dames. Mrs. Shippen and her staff instructed their young charges in the rudiments of social grace along with the fox trot and the waltz. St. Albans was not as snobbish as the top New England boarding schools, but when Gore arrived in Form C, or fourth grade, he was thrown in with boys whose fathers were much like his—prominent men in politics, diplomacy, the law, and journalism. In the apt phrase of Brooks

Johnson, a St. Albans coach and teacher, the school featured "one of the highest distillations of second generation power in the country."

There were Alsops and Restons, Grahams and Stewarts. One boy arrived from the Maryland suburbs every morning in a beige Lincoln Continental with beige upholstery driven by a beige chauffeur in a beige uniform. Young Al's first school pal was Mead P. Miller, whose father was a Texas lobbyist and whose mother was a protégé of the legendary hostess, Perle Mesta. Mead's father kept a suite at the Mayflower Hotel, where he drank shooters and told tall tales on soft summer nights with friendly newspaper correspondents and the southern power brokers in Congress, Speaker Sam Rayburn and Wilbur Mills and Lyndon Johnson, who decades earlier had received his first job from Mead's grandfather, Roy Miller, a dairy lobbyist ("butter-n-egg man") whose dress shirts were monogrammed eight inches down the left sleeve. With the election of John F. Kennedy in 1960 a new set of Democrats held sway in the political village. Young Al attended school with their children and caught glimpses of their fathers at night at the Jockey Club, the trendy new restaurant that Jimmy Gore, Grady's son, opened on the first floor of the Fairfax as the Washington version of New York's 21. Pierre Salinger spread the word, making it the *in* place for the Kennedy administration. Jimmy Gore secured a table in back where Robert Kennedy, the new attorney general, could plot in private with a group of Cuban exiles. Peter Lawford and some members of the Rat Pack set up shop at a banquette when they were in town, their table cluttered with hard liquor that they ordered by the bottle, not the glass. It was quite a change from the 1950s, when the Fairfax's restaurant did not serve alcohol and its most reliable customer was Senator Alexander Wiley of Wisconsin, a teetotaler.

St. Albans still clung to an older time. It had opened in 1909 intended as a school for choirboys at the National Cathedral, whose Gothic towers now loom above the school, and over the decades it had remained a terminally Anglophile place. The Glastonbury thorn tree in the circle fronting the school was said to bloom whenever English royalty arrived on American soil. Grades were called forms and student leaders were known as prefects. A St. Albans boy was instructed to keep a stiff upper lip, British public school style. There was no such thing as a snow day. During one blizzard, a student arrived at one in the afternoon and was not reprimanded for being late but honored for showing the proper fortitude. There was a structure to everything. Coat and tie were mandatory; Al knew how to tie a Windsor knot by age nine. At precisely 8:20 every morning the boys lined up in front of the school and pledged allegiance to the flag, then walked in two orderly rows up the drive to chapel, and on to class. At lunch in the refectory, they rotated from one faculty member's table to another every four to six weeks. Every boy had to engage in some form of athletics, from varsity football, the favored sport, to an after-school program for the less athletic students dubbed Troop 19. The regimen could end as late as six. It was "all about structure," said George (Buddy) Hillow, one of Al's classmates. "Not about personal freedom. Not about personal discovery and exploration."

The school was defined as much by the figures who ran it as by the old stone chapel and school building—men who helped develop Al Gore's mind and shape his values during his nine years there. Foremost among them was Canon Charles Martin, "a Mr. Chips character, a great leader," as Gore later remembered him, who drove around in a clunky Ford Woody, accompanied by his bulldog, symbol of the old man's determined spirit. Martin, wearing a clerical collar under his dark jacket, preached a muscular Christianity intended to prepare his charges to choose "the hard right" over the easy wrong and to make a contribution to society, serving the community in God's name. He was fond of saying that he was preparing his boys "for the kingdom of heaven, not the kingdom of Harvard." He believed in developing the whole boy: mind, spirit, and body. The barrel-chested headmaster thought nothing of dropping to the floor of the faculty lounge to pump out a few one-handed push-ups. In this respect he was much like the senior Gore, who at home often challenged his son to do fifty or more push-ups a day. Martin had a viselike grip and used it often, clamping down on a boy's shoulder. "My gosh," he would say, his hard G turning into a hard C in his New England accent. "Good to see you, my boy!" He shared another trait with Al's father, frugality. The headmaster could not tolerate food going to waste. When melon was served in the refectory, he would roam from table to table inspecting the boys at lunch, instructing them to eat it "Down to the rind!"

Canon Martin's right-hand man was Ferdinand Ruge, a tough-talking, Camel-inhaling assistant headmaster and English teacher whose approach was described by one admiring former student as "late-nineteenth-century German." His favorite poem was Shelley's "Ozymandias," a lesson in the fleeting nature of fame and power, and he would stand in front of his class repeating it over and over in a booming voice . . .

> *Nothing beside remains. Round the decay*
> *Of that colossal wreck, boundless and bare*
> *The lone and level sands stretch far away.*

Al Gore was rarely one to disappoint Canon Martin or Ferdinand Ruge or any of his teachers, at least in behavior. There he was, standing straight, chest out, speaking clearly. He was balanced and steady and "didn't go swinging off one way or another," according to Stanley D. Willis, an English teacher and director of admissions. In that sense, Willis believed, Gore "sort of did in a way exemplify the St. Albans boy." While some boys were "restless under discipline," recalled the Reverend Craig Eder, the school's chaplain, Gore used discipline "for its main purpose, which is to get things done." Year after year, his report cards from the lower school included comments about the all-around good lad. "Al is a careful and precise worker," was one assessment. Then: "An enjoyable boy with a fine sense of humor." At the end of one year, he was lightly admonished for schoolwork lapses. "Al was careless in his arithmetic examination—thereby lowering his grade. In essay type questions he fails to develop his answers as fully as he should." The comment Eder remembers writing most often on Al's report card was "Good Boy, Doing Well."

If there was uneasiness among the St. Albans faculty about the senator's son, it was that he seemed constrained by circumstances. They were all too familiar with the demands placed upon children of the political world, and though they believed Al generally handled the pressure well, they were also struck by his inordinate caution. John C. Davis, a sacred studies teacher, regarded Al as "a dutiful son" who seemed well trained to watch what he said. "It was almost unnatural for a boy to be that well behaved," he said. Davis was impressed by Pauline Gore, finding her a "very smooth, very charming" woman who "made every effort to be interested in the school." He also sensed that she was silently plotting Al's rise, and though she never said it aloud, to him or anyone else, "she wanted to have her son exactly where he is now, and perhaps president." To Eder, young Al seemed "sort of grown up early." Some of his early exchanges with teachers, such as his query to Haslam about the appropriate time for rowdiness, made him sound like a junior faculty member. His C-Form homeroom teacher, Lawrence Smith, a proud Vermonter, would never forget when young Al approached him in the hallway on the morning after the state had elected its first Democrat to Congress in generations.

"Vermont elected a Democrat! Hah! Hah!" Gore chuckled, assuming that his teacher was a Republican.

"I know, Al, I voted for him," Smith responded.

"You did?" Al asked incredulously.

The pleasure Smith derived from the exchange came both in surprising his student and in realizing that a boy of ten had paid such close attention to an obscure congressional race in tiny Vermont.

HE THOUGHT OF HIMSELF first as a southerner. During winter afternoons at the lower school at St. Albans, the boys would play a make-believe game they called North and South, and Al joined with his pal Mead Miller and others in the smaller gang from the South. In the real world, he considered himself a son of Carthage, not of Washington, and could not wait for school to let out so that he could get back to Tennessee. In his early years, his parents owned a house on Fisher Avenue just off Main Street in Carthage, within walking distance of Reed's Pharmacy and the Ben Franklin five-and-dime and Clyde White's Western Auto store. (Gore then and always repeated his father's exaggerated pronunciation of this last establishment, with a hard T and two separate and equally accented syllables—"awe toe.") His sister kept her horse Dagger out back, and he had a Lionel train set in the basement. He loved to sleep next door at his grandmother's, swallowed up in the big feather bed in the sitting room underneath a painting of Daniel in the den looking up at the sky, encircled by a pride of becalmed lions. The painting became one of the lasting images of the boy's life, a declaration of faith that made such an impression on him that he asked for it when his grandmother died and later hung it in his office in the West Wing of the White House.

In the summer of 1959, Pauline brought in Shorty Hunt and one of the Silcox brothers to oversee the construction of a big house made of Tennessee stone, marble, and cypress on their farm to the south of town near the community of Elmwood, where Al would hang out with Goat Thompson, Edd Blair, Steve Armistead, and some other local boys. They camped out in pup tents and played cowboys and Indians (Al was always a cowboy) and walked along the Caney Fork River and showed cows at the county fair and went to 4-H camp together over at the old World War II German POW camp up in the mountains near Crossville. They joshingly called themselves the Snow Creek Gang or the Tootsie Roll Gang. The latter nickname came to them after a truck hauling Tootsie Rolls overturned on nearby Highway 70 and spilled a bounteous supply of the candy on the roadway. The boys stuffed their pockets with as much as they could and stored it in a hideaway in the hillside woods, peeling away the brown and white paper and chomping on their stash until they could stomach no more. "I've never wanted a Tootsie Roll since that wreck," Armistead said decades later. "About OD'd on Tootsie Rolls!"

The next summer Al underwent a sudden physical transformation from a smallish boy to a husky young man. His growth spurt might have been the inevitable result of genetics, puberty, and hard labor, but Goat Thompson attributed it to the miracle growth pills his mother, Alota, regularly gave Al. Everyone in town seemed to notice the change. One day Donna Armistead, Steve's red-haired older sister, was sitting in her car with a girlfriend, waiting for her mother to get off work. The fifteen-year-old girls were talking about how they were not going to date that summer when Donna caught sight of a strapping young man approaching. It was Al Gore, then only thirteen, yet almost "as big as he is now," she recalled later. He asked her to go out that night. They went to the movies, driven by Donna's older brother, Roy, and the next day Al introduced her to his mother, stole his first kiss, and asked her to go steady. Donna would remain his Tennessee girlfriend until he went off to college. Whenever he "came home" from Washington, she said later, he would be "walking like a city boy" and it took "about two weeks" to straighten him out. They played basketball one-on-one (her hook shot was deadly), swam off the big rock in the Caney Fork River, and walked in the woods along Snow Creek near the cold spring where local kids were baptized by Preacher Gibbs.

The Tennessee life took much of the stiffness out of Gore. As soon as he arrived in town, he and Steve Armistead would have a contest to see who could sneak up on the other first and shout "Punk!" He would impress Donna by unscrewing the receiver on a telephone in his basement room so they could listen secretly to his father's conversations with important people in Washington. After taking in several lectures on sex from his mother and her grandmother, they once teased their concerned elders by jumping on a bed until the springs squeaked loudly. Donna's mother came hurtling into the room only to find the young couple "dying laughing, holding hands, jumping." He also wrestled with Steve Armistead, and during one scuffle in the big house broke one of his mother's antique lamps. Instead of fessing up, Al and Steve found a look-alike replacement in the basement storage room, which was full of antiques (Pauline Gore loved few things more in life than antiquing). They threw the broken lamp off the Cordell Hull Bridge at dawn.

Al had obtained his learner's permit when he was fourteen, and quickly established a reputation for reckless driving, a counterpoint to his innate caution. "He was constantly running us into hog feeders and running us off the road," Steve Armistead recalled. One morning, as Gore was returning from a summer school class at Castle Heights Military Academy in Lebanon (there was always another lesson to be learned, his father insisted), he tried to speed past a truck on a narrow road near the big house, but the truck weaved to the left and sent him upside down into a ditch overgrown with honeysuckle and weeds. He told his pal Steve Armistead that he was so disoriented he did not know whether he was up or down. "I rolled that window up seventeen times before I thought of just crawling out." He escaped unhurt, but his father's 1962 Chevy Impala was totaled. His daredevil streak was evident in other ways: Water-skiing on early summer evenings at Cove Hollow on Center Hill Lake, where his father kept a speedboat, he loved to stand on his head on the outboard motor.

There were, in the end, limits to Gore's antic behavior, his Carthage friends noticed. If they were playing sports, he did not want to joke around, he wanted to win. His intense competitive streak was always there, whether in Ping-Pong, checkers, basketball, or cards (rook was the local game) — even discus, an event Al picked up at St. Albans. Steve Armistead, who described himself as "happy-go-lucky, running my mouth, carrying a bunch of BS," said Gore eventually would become irritated by such behavior. "I could provoke him to the point where he'd almost want to fight, to that point of 'I'm better than you!' " Armistead said. "He always had that aggressive part of him. No play. That nature carries over in the way he does his day-to-day business. I could see that going back to when he was a child — being aggressive and wanting to be perfect. He always wants to be perfect."

• • •

BART DAY would forever remember the day he first met Al Gore, who would be his classmate through high school and college. It was an autumn afternoon and Day was the new student at St. Albans, an aspiring quarterback tossing a football on the school's lower field. Along came Al, fresh from the shower, his hair still wet, neatly dressed, spinning a basketball nonchalantly on his index finger. There was something about the juxtaposition of what Gore was doing and how he looked that struck Day as "a funny sort of contrast." Day held that image in his mind as a symbol of the tension between appearance and reality that would define his friend throughout his later political life.

By the time Gore reached the upper grades at St. Albans, he was an unavoidable presence. Everyone knew him. He was not only a senator's son, but now bigger than most of his peers, with many talents, involved in virtually every aspect of school life. He started as a center on the varsity football team in his sophomore year and also threw the discus on the track-and-field team and played basketball. At the same time he was active in art and in Government Club, where he eventually assumed leadership of the Liberal Party. Yet as a sometime boarder (when his parents were traveling) and more frequent day student, he was not part of any clique, and did not appear to have a best friend. "He wasn't somebody you got to know real well," said classmate Gordon Beall. "He had his own world." Another classmate, Bayard "Stocky" Clark, considered Gore "very close-to-the-chest" and thought he was consciously or subconsciously trying "to live up to the often-unspoken ideals as they are reflected by the great father." Diane Kefauver was a frequent date of St. Albans boys, and knew as well as Al the strains of being the offspring of a famous man. Yet she sensed that he, more than any of them, carried the burden of the future. "He drank beer and he danced and he seemed like he was one of you, but you always just felt he had this other thing going on that was more serious," Kefauver said later. "He just dabbled in being one of us."

Many of the fifty-one boys in the class of 1965 came to adopt a cool and cynical affect, modeling themselves after J. D. Salinger's ironic Holden Caulfield, refusing to buy into Canon Martin's muscular Christianity. Gore was more aligned with the gung ho jocks, but smarter than most, though by no means the class brain. Peter Van Wagenen, who became class valedictorian, was struck by Gore's "athletic prowess and leadership, [but] in terms of academics, not as much." Charles Saltzman, who taught English, Gore's favorite class, described him in words that he would hear often enough throughout his life—"a very competent young man" but "not scintillating." The transcript of Gore's St. Albans years shows that even in English he received only C's and B's, his highest mark a B+ during one reporting period of his junior year (known at St. Albans as Form V). He pulled C's and C+'s through three years of French, and C's and B's in various history and social studies courses. His strongest grades came in chemistry, physics, and sacred studies, where he received mostly B's and a few A's. His class rank reached its zenith during his junior year—the crucial year for college admissions—when his grades placed him seventeenth out of fifty-one boys. By his senior year he had dropped to twenty-fifth, settling precisely in the middle of the pack.

What set Gore apart was his air of supreme confidence, something that was not considered universally endearing. "Al didn't wonder if he could cut it in life. I don't think that was ever a worry for him," said classmate Geoffrey Kuhn. "A lot of his investment was in competitiveness. He wasn't anybody to mess around with. . . . Nobody would mistake him for a victim." Buddy Hillow was one of those who felt estranged from Gore. His father ran a restaurant, not the government, and he had come to St. Albans in his freshman year from the public schools. Gore, to him, seemed like the very model of a self-possessed preppy, and the fact that he seemed to excel at everything became tiresome to Hillow. "I remember in the locker room, in the field house, Al would sing . . . 'The Lion Sleeps Tonight' . . . a-win-a-weh-a-win-a-weh . . . the air filled with steam, I remember Al singing a lot; I also remember hating him a lot because he had a beautiful voice." The friction between the two boys led to a fight in Earl R. "Doc" Arnds's math class. Hillow sat in front of Gore and had a habit of rocking back in his chair until it reached the precarious balancing point. Once, as he was rocking, Gore extended a finger and lightly touched the chair, upsetting the balance. Hillow turned and hissed, "If you do that again, I'm coming!" Gore did it again, Hillow leapt at him, and the two boys engaged in a fierce wrestling match, tumbling around the room, bowling over desks. "I only wish I could say that I ended up on top, but I didn't," Hillow recalled decades later. "All I remember is Doc Arnds standing over us, yelling 'Stop it! Stop it!' But it sounded like cheers."

Gore possessed a sarcastic side that some classmates found offputting. Though seemingly not a cruel or vindictive person, he let it be known to classmate Bruce Rathbun once that he thought Bruce was a veritable loser. The class had a paper due and Rathbun had skipped school for a number of days to finish it. He returned without completing the assignment, and Gore scoffed. "The paraphrase," Rathbun said, "was something like: 'You're a jerk if you took all this time off and still didn't do this paper. Taking time off is ridiculous to begin with.' " In his disdain Gore seemed to be conveying the mores of his school. At St. Albans, as the disciplinarian Ferdinand Ruge instructed his young charges, the ultimate sin was not doing something wrong, but something stupid. Skipping school and still not finishing a paper fell into the latter category.

Depending on the situation, Gore could seem selfless or self-serving. In basketball, point guard James T. Hudson considered him an incorrigible if deadly gunner from the left corner. "What I remember mostly was his goal seemed to be to score as many points as possible in order to get his name in the paper." Yet Dan Woodruff, another teammate, recalled once getting ejected and nearly coming to blows with a referee at a tournament, until Gore intervened. Gore "saved me from what would have been an embarrassing moment for me and the school," Woodruff said later. After the game, which St. Albans lost, Gore sat with his teammate to make sure that he was okay. "It was one of those moments," he said, "that I've never forgotten." And the hint of bullydom that Rathbun felt was nowhere evident in Gore's dealings with Andrew Stevovich, an artistic soul in the class behind theirs who felt that he was "the odd boy out," being neither wealthy nor Anglo-Saxon Protestant. Two students were taunting him one day, mocking his Slavic name, and when Gore suddenly appeared on the scene Stevovich's first thought was that he was "sort of the same" as the taunters. "But he told them to get off my back," Stevovich recalled. "They let off." Bruce La Pierre, who came in as a new kid for the final two years, said the clubbiness of St. Albans was almost too much for him, but he found Gore "outgoing and gracious even to a newcomer."

Gore did not always choose the hard right over the easy wrong, but he seemed as steeped in Canon Martin's doctrine as any of the St. Albans boys. Once, in math class, he and Jorge Tristani realized that Doc Arnds was passing out an old exam that they had used to prepare for the test, so they inadvertently knew the answers. "We just looked at each other and it was sort of an automatic reaction on both of our parts," Tristani recalled. "We just turned ourselves in."

• • •

IN PAULINE GORE'S initial calculation of what school her son should attend, one factor in her choice was that St. Albans had begun admitting black students and was more liberal on issues of race than most Washington prep schools. "I wanted him to know that blacks have the same right to go to school that whites have," she explained later. That is not to say that St. Albans was in the vanguard of racial diversity. There was a lone black student in Gore's class, James Gray, who was so distraught by his singular situation that he frequently broke out in hives during his first year on campus. The first black faculty member, Brooks Johnson, was hired during Gore's years there, first to help coach track and football, then to teach history. Johnson sensed that Gore, unlike many of the other students, seemed "very comfortable around strong black people." This was certainly Pauline Gore's intention; for years she had undertaken a modest amount of social engineering to ensure that her son was exposed to blacks. When he was a young boy and the family was back in Carthage for the summer, she hired a black youth from the neighborhood, Abe Gainer, the son of a laundry woman, to be Al's companion. His older sister, Faith, had played with Al's sister, Nancy. Gainer was several years older than Gore, and served as both playmate and baby-sitter for him during the early 1950s. "We got to the point where we sort of became inseparable," Gainer said later. "I remember that I could not leave in the evening until Al would go to sleep."

There had been an altruistic component to Pauline's actions, though she did not step far outside the racial norms of that time. For a semester in 1953, she had brought Abe to Washington with the family and enrolled him at Francis Junior High, which while all-black offered an academic program superior to the segregated little schoolhouse he attended in Carthage. During his semester in Washington, Gainer lived not with the Gores but with the family of a black hotel worker. After school, he came over to the Gore suite and washed dishes, cleaned rooms, and occasionally donned a white jacket to serve dinner guests at the senator's table. Gore eventually befriended another black teenager, Jerome Powell, who worked as the hotel's doorman and was lead singer in his own band. In one of Gore's rare explorations of the soul of the city, he persuaded Powell to take him to the Howard Theater to see James Brown. As they drove to the theater at Seventh and T in Powell's little blue Ford, Gore seemed "happy as a lark," Powell re-

called. The senator's son was one of only a handful of whites in the audience and stood out as much for his restraint as the color of his skin.
His rhythm, apparently, was no better than his father's offbeat fiddling,
and less demonstrative. "He would applaud . . . that's about the best Al
would do," Powell said. "He wasn't a jump-and-scream guy."

Senator Gore's reputation as a dauntless progressive on matters of
race grew so much in later years that it is difficult to think of him as he
was back in the early 1960s, at times the most conservative member of
his own family. His wife often privately nudged him on racial matters.
His daughter was close friends with David Halberstam, Fred Graham,
and other journalists who had covered the early civil rights movement
for the Nashville *Tennessean*, and she brought the commitment and
passion of their world into the family orbit. The senator considered
himself an economic populist more than anything else. He believed in
a gradual approach to desegregation, arguing that it could only happen
over time as job and educational opportunities improved. He never
claimed to be "a white knight for civil rights," noted historian Tony
Badger, but rather "a moderate who believed in the Constitution . . .
and who had compassion for oppressed fellow Americans."

His cautious approach faced its stiffest test during the Senate de-
liberations over the landmark 1964 Civil Rights Act. He feared the act
sought to accomplish too much too quickly. While distancing himself
from the segregationists who bitterly opposed the measure, he spoke
out against it in his own way, arguing that it would place excessive
power in the hands of federal bureaucrats who might arbitrarily with-
hold funding from hospitals and schools perceived to be violating the
law. Among the places the senator had to defend his position was within
the confines of the family suite atop the Fairfax, where son Al, then sixteen and a junior at St. Albans, sparred with him in dinner table debates
as intense as the ones on the Senate floor. "I, as always, respected what
he had to say," Gore said later of his father. "But I disagreed with him."

Civil rights leaders in Tennessee disagreed with Albert Gore also,
and briefly turned away from him. The Tennessee Voters Council, an
influential statewide black organization, withheld its endorsement in
the 1964 Democratic primary, recalled Russell Sugarmon, a founding
member of the organization who went on to become a Memphis
judge. "It was a way of slapping his wrist. We wanted to make a point,
but not so hard that it defeated him in November." Indeed by November Gore was back on the slate. The senator never acknowledged to his

son or anyone else that there might have been a political motive to his vote, that he might have been more fearful of losing white voters than black support that year. "Not openly. Never. Never. It was not in his nature" to confess to political considerations, Al said later of his father. But survival undoubtedly was part of the calculation. A conservative mood was spreading across the state and Gore seemed increasingly vulnerable.

If his vote was in part a realistic assessment of what he had to do to survive, it worked. He won reelection and returned to Washington, and from then on acted like an unflinching southern progressive attuned to the needs of his black constituents, eventually apologizing for his 1964 vote, calling it the biggest mistake of his career. As his son watched this transformation, he began thinking that perhaps the dinner table debates with his father had had a delayed effect. "I sometimes think that the ferocity, the renewed ferocity that he brought to the civil rights debate . . . came out of what might have been his own sense that he made the wrong call on that 1964 vote," Al Gore said later. "My analysis is vulnerable to solipsism, but I've actually at times thought that the renewed ferocity that I referred to may have been at least in a tiny part for me."

DURING THAT FALL OF 1964, when his father was campaigning for reelection to the Senate, Al began his final year at St. Albans. Because his parents were in Tennessee campaigning much of the time, he moved over to the school again, as he had periodically through the years, this time sharing a third-story room with Geoffrey Kuhn one floor above the chaotic barracks where underclassmen stayed. They had one of the larger rooms, with space for two beds, bureaus, and desks and a view overlooking the circle in front of the Lane-Johnston Building. Kuhn, unlike Gore, was not consumed by competitiveness. Once, after dinner, to test his roommate's resolve, he jokingly said, "Okay, Al, give me fifty!"—and Gore responded immediately, right there in the common room, cranking out fifty push-ups without breaking much of a sweat, then turning to Kuhn with a nonchalant "What else?" Kuhn considered himself "tragically hip," one of the Caulfield types who would sooner throw up than do fifty push-ups. At midnight, he and some other cool senior boarders would sneak into the bathroom to smoke. "Night fog," they called it. Al was usually asleep by then.

As he had for several years, Gore dutifully called Donna every Saturday night at seven and wrote her two letters a day, using a pen and U.S. Senate stationery, his "sloppy" cursive hand detailing his athletics and grades and daily routine, counting the days until his next trip to Tennessee. Donna was working as a car hop at "a little burger place" down the hill from the Gore farm. "I think he was lonely at times, but he never dwelled on it," she said. "A passing thing, like, 'I was expecting Dad at the ball game Saturday.' Or 'Dad didn't get to make it.' Or 'I was hoping to go see Mom, but Mom had a meeting.' Stuff like that." (Gore's father, in fact, never attended one of his football games.) The letters had been going back and forth since tenth grade, and some of the boys knew about Al's country girl, though they never saw her.

The letters from Donna had meant so much to Gore that he once punched an old friend, Mead Miller, over them. Miller had grown long hair during his final years at St. Albans, and one night Gore and a few other boys tiptoed into his cubicle when he was asleep and "snipped off a few hunks" before he woke up. "I was pretty pissed," Miller recalled. "I was as mad as I could be." So he entered Al's cubicle and stole a batch of "puppy dog" letters from Donna and hid them. When Gore discovered what Miller had done, he tracked him down, confronted him in the cloisters area on the side of the school, and smacked him in the nose.

The year was a mix of accomplishments and frustrations for the senator's son. He was chosen to be a prefect, an elite group of students who meted out discipline to classmates who had committed minor infractions. To work off one demerit, a boy would spend fifteen minutes cleaning the fields or washing windows. Gore tended to be a rules-follower himself, but was more likely to cajole his classmates than write them up for punishment. In a close election for the top job, or senior prefect, he finished second to Dan Woodruff, a star athlete. This would become a repetitive theme in his life, to be overshadowed by someone just a bit more talented or charismatic. He was relegated to being the prefect in charge of announcements at lunch. But he scored 1355 out of a possible high score of 1600 on his SAT (625 Verbal, 730 Math) and was recommended for admission to Harvard by the school's college adviser, assistant headmaster John Davis. The recommendation was tantamount to acceptance in those days, when St. Albans had a direct pipeline to the Ivy League. Gore's middling class rank and decent but not overwhelming transcript of mostly B's and C's meant less

to Harvard than the school he attended and his status as a senator's son
and an athlete.

"In Al's case, he was what Harvard most wanted at that time,"
Davis said later. "What they wanted was competent academic performance plus future potential. And they were very impressed by the
fact that he was a political son. Colleges like Harvard, Princeton, and
Yale were just as excited to get important sons as top academic schol-
ars. They wanted our boys as much as our boys wanted them. And . . .
any nice big boy was welcome if he played football."

Gore not only played football, he was elected captain of the team.
That accomplishment might have helped him get into Harvard, but it
also left him greatly frustrated, as he found himself leading a squad that
was undersized and hobbled by injuries and indifference. Bart Day
had a strong arm, Woodruff was a swift and powerful wide receiver, and
Gore was a steady presence at center and middle linebacker, but there
was not much else for Coach Glenn Wild to work with that year. Captain Gore tried to rouse the troops, enthusiastically leading them in
jumping jacks in pregame calisthenics, shouting "Good job!" after
every sharp tackle or block, or chiding his teammates when they
sloughed off—"C'mon, guys! That wasn't very smart. Let's pick it up!"
He had been known for his spirit since his sophomore year, when he
first started at center, a big unpolished kid, and faced off against a
schoolboy legend, Cadwell Tyler, the ferocious middle guard for rival
Episcopal, who was good enough to demand three nicknames, Ty Ty,
Igor, and the Monster. Tyler, a first-team All-Metropolitan behemoth,
was known for winding up his right hand behind his back like a baseball bat and whacking the opposing center on the helmet at the snap of
the ball. He tried this on Gore, but could not stop the feisty St. Albans
underclassman from blocking him, until finally the mighty Ty Ty grew
so frustrated that he kicked and punched Gore during a pileup. All the
referee saw, unfortunately for Gore, was his retaliatory punch, which
got him kicked out of the game.

It was that very spirit of standing up to Tyler that led his teammates to elect Gore captain two years later. And now, in his final season, he felt responsible for his team's performance, on and off the field.
St. Albans was not a football factory, but football mattered. There was a
metaphorical quality to it. Through football one proved oneself and
the spirit of team play. And you proved yourself to Canon Martin, who
came to every game and paced the sidelines while his bulldog, Marc

Antony, slobbered near the bench (and once threw up on a player's cleats). With their opening game loss to Mount St. Joseph's, the St. Albans Blues were on their way to a miserable season. Their second defeat, against Georgetown Prep, was particularly frustrating, a game that they should have won. The student body seemed unconcerned by the losing, and many of the boys were bewildered by the headmaster's enthusiasm for the game, which included praying out loud for the team at chapel. *Would the football double-reverse get you into heaven?* asked Peter Van Wagenen sarcastically in his valedictory address. Even many of the players seemed unperturbed by the team's losing ways that fall; losing in football, they thought, showed their cool detachment. "We thought it was perfect for our senior year that our football team would go in the tank," recalled classmate David Everett.

Gore had to win. He had to please Canon Martin. What could he do? On Saturday morning he walked over to Coach Glenn Wild's brick duplex on 38th Street and knocked on the door. Wild was taken aback. Never before, in all his coaching days, had a player paid him a surprise visit at home.

"Al," Wild said. "What are you doing here?"

The captain said he was troubled by the team's slide and thought he knew the problem. Too many of his teammates were breaking training rules, he confided. Though Al did not get more specific, Wild understood that he meant drinking and smoking. No names were mentioned, but he wanted the coach to know about the problem and take remedial action. Wild thanked him, and during the team meeting on Monday, he lit into the lackadaisical boys. But there was to be no dramatic turnaround. Gore joined the list of wounded, banging up his knee, and the team finished the year with a 1-7 record.

Wild could vividly remember Gore's visit even thirty-five years after the event. It was a rare boy, he thought, who had such a strong sense of responsibility to do the hard right. It showed the stunned coach how determined—and competitive—young Gore was. Gore's perception of his action changed over the years. He came to feel guilty later, he said, when he thought back on how Wild "kind of cracked down" on the team after his conversation, leading him to the conclusion that he would not do it the same way again. At the time, he said, plummeting morale and the prospect of a losing season overwhelmed him. "I didn't know what to do," he said. "I had the responsibility."

There was a bit more spirit to be found in Government Club,

which met for debates on Thursday evenings at 7:30 in the somber wood-paneled library around a horseshoe-shaped table under the tutelage of history teacher Francis (Froggy) McGrath. As leader of the Liberal Party, Gore was not a fiery orator ("He read his script. . . . He sounded much like he does today," recalled classmate John Siscoe. "Earnest. Careful. Slightly dull. He was responsible, but hardly scintillating."). But he tried to make up for it by being prepared, tutoring his fellow liberals on the issues of the day. "He could tell you about the virtues of the TVA when he was fourteen or fifteen," said Siscoe. Classmate Matthew Simchak found Gore's interest in public policy unusual for a teenage boy, and thought "to some extent he may have been coached by his father." Gore was moderate even then, and "not a risk-taker," recalled Bill Yates. When conservative leader Brent Taylor proposed a bill advocating a ban on trade with Communist bloc countries, Gore countered with a proposal for a limited increase in trade, adhering to his father's free trade principles. Taylor was frustrated that he could "never get much of a debate going" on defense issues "because we were both fairly conservative on defense." One of the more memorable debates concerned China, with Gore and his liberals advocating United Nations recognition of Red China, which Taylor and his conservatives opposed. When liberal colleague Tom Carroll questioned his party's position, Gore told him, "It's world reality. We've got to let China into the United Nations. . . . With their size and population we've got to deal with them."

Where could Gore escape the weight of responsibility? Perhaps only in Dean Stambaugh's art class down in the basement, a hideaway of stunning color and originality amid the muted private school atmosphere: ferns and bamboo, birds chirping in cages (including a bullfinch named Bud and a back-flipping Chinese nightingale), Brahms and Beethoven, Mingus and Bird playing in the background, boys sitting at rows of large drawing tables, dropping their poses, picking up the tempera or watercolors, and becoming painters. Stambaugh would stroll through the room, hands clasped behind his back, his gait rising and falling on tiptoes as he gazed over shoulders, advising on shades of darkness and light, trying to bring out the spiritual side of his students.

Gore took art for nine years, including four times as an elective, and through his art showed a side of himself that stunned his classmates, hinting that perhaps there was more to him than they saw during the rest of the day. With his tie tucked between the second and third buttons of his shirt, he worked intensely with tempera on letter-size pieces of paper. "His painting was bold, abstract, vibrant, and his personality was not," said Buddy Hillow. "He wasn't concerned with painting reality, with making a realistic statement. . . . He used his painting as a sword. I think there's something about the way a person paints or gardens that is a much more powerful expression of personality than words." Gore might have "played the St. Albans game beautifully, he was the quintessential St. Albans student," Hillow thought—"but in the art room, he was someone else."

But there was one thing about Gore's art that seemed eerily familiar, even in his most abstract portraits. It was in the eyes. When friend Bart Day saw those painted eyes, it reminded him of Al's father. In those eyes, Day said, "there was always a steady kind of sharp appraisal going on all the time." Day thought of it as a "uniform gaze" that symbolized "the self-consciousness of this weight of having to be always on."

AS GRADUATION APPROACHED, his classmates had some satirical fun with Al Gore. Under his photo in the yearbook they ran a quote from Anatole France—"People who have no weaknesses are terrible"—and went on to say: "Al is frighteningly good at many things. . . . He would seem the epitome of the All-American Young Man. It probably won't be long before Al reaches the top." Just as telling was a drawing in the yearbook that showed Gore replacing George Washington in one of the National Cathedral's statues. He is dressed in a business suit, standing on a pedestal, carrying a football under one arm, a basketball under the other, a piece of paper in one hand, a discus in the other, with a tourist looking up and snapping a picture of him. To classmate John Lillard, the cartoon got it right. "Al was not the brightest guy in the class, but he seemed to know how to meet expectations," Lillard reflected. "You conserve your energy and give people what they want without spinning your wheels. It's a lesson for everyone, to give people what they expect. It's a lesson I learned late in life. Al knew it back then." When John Davis, who taught Gore sacred studies and wrote his recommendation for college, looked at the cartoon, he, too, thought the yearbook editors captured him perfectly. "He was the wooden Apollo."

But wooden Al got the last laugh. He had always been attractive to the girls. Schuyler Gott, who watched Hawaiian surfing movies with Al in the cozy darkness of Bill Yates's basement, remembered him as "quite a good kisser." At senior prom night it seemed at first that James S. Wright Jr., son of a noted federal judge in Washington, would be the envy of his graduating classmates. He came with a knockout date—Mary Elizabeth (Tipper) Aitcheson, a fun-loving junior from St. Agnes who drove a VW Beetle and knew how to downshift a five-speed and played the drums and had gone out with many of the St. Albans boys, including Mead Miller and David Baker and Gordon Beall. At a party after the prom, Gore caught sight of her, turned to his roommate Geoff Kuhn, and asked, "Who's that?" Kuhn introduced them, and her field of boyfriends began to narrow.

"I thought, 'Oh, boy! He's good-looking,' " Tipper later recalled of her first impression of the senator's son. "We had a good conversation. We connected." The next day Gore got her phone number and asked her out for the following weekend, and their relationship began. That summer he worked in Arlington as a radio dispatcher for the Heritage Cavaliers tour guide company, and every day for his lunch break he rode his motorcycle over to the Aitcheson house on 26th Street in Arlington, not far from National Airport, where Tipper invariably gave him a bologna and cheese sandwich and a Coke.

"Can't you make anything else?" he eventually asked.

"No," said his future wife.

CHAPTER THREE

LOST AND FOUND
AT HARVARD

H E WAS ASSIGNED a room in Harvard Yard, on the bottom floor of Mower B, assuming his place among the elite of his generation when he arrived in Cambridge that fall of 1965. He seemed to have all the proper credentials: graduate of St. Albans, son of a U.S. senator, a three-sport letterman with decent grades and relatively high SAT scores, so confident of his standing that he had applied only to Harvard, the thought of a safety school not even crossing his mind. His freshman class of 1,211 was larger than usual, its ranks swollen by the desirability of student deferments after a doubling of the military draft call over the summer. The incoming class of 1969 also reflected the Ivy League institution's goal of recruiting more exceptional public school graduates from middle America, and many of these best and brightest teenagers tried to conceal inner doubts about whether they belonged at Harvard.

Peter Goldberg of suburban Milwaukee arrived frightened and convinced that he was "the mistake." Roberts Bennett, the smartest kid in his Jacksonville high school, felt "awed and overwhelmed." Richard Hyland from Grossmont High in California immediately hated the place, finding it "enormously pretentious without reason to be." David Friedman from Los Angeles quickly became "disoriented" amid the posturing of his peers. Even a prep school product like John Bandeian Jr. from St. Paul's in New Hampshire worried about "competing against all these other smart young men." Did Al Gore, still six months shy of his eighteenth birthday, share those anxieties?

Some of his peers and teachers certainly thought so. One student who sat near him that first year in a discussion section of Economics 1 vividly remembered Gore's demeanor this way: "He looked scared, and overmatched. It seemed that he didn't open his mouth in class the whole year." His instructor grew so concerned about Gore that he asked a senior economics major to tutor him, saying that the politician's son was struggling in the course, could not keep his mind on his work, and seemed in need of counseling. But if Gore was struggling, he would not acknowledge it. Asked decades later whether he had any self-doubt during his early days at Harvard, he quickly responded, "No. I didn't. . . . Should I have?"

The undergraduate journey Gore and his classmates began on that New England autumn thirty-five years ago turned out to be far different from anything they might have imagined. The Harvard experience was perilous and intimidating in its own way, but less for the academic demands than for the difficult personal and political choices they confronted during four tumultuous years. Gore, like many of his peers, struggled with the alternatives that his past and present offered, vacillating between idealism and cynicism, responsibility and freedom, diligence and laziness, conformity and rebellion, ambition and withdrawal.

Here he was the class president debating the quality of meat loaf served in the Freshman Union. There he was the Dunster Funster playing pool, watching Johnny Carson on television, downing chocolate frappés, smoking dope, and crashing on a couch in the basement lounge of Dunster House. Here he was busting with pride that his father, Senator Albert Gore of Tennessee, had spoken out against the war in Vietnam. There he was confiding to friends that he had missed having a normal childhood and that his old man thought his hair was too long. Here he was enthralled by literature, a young writer evoking the quaint and lovable characters of rural Tennessee. There he was back in the world of politics, role-playing for a government class, pretending that he was President Kennedy in the Oval Office dealing with the Cuban Missile Crisis. It was during his Harvard years that Gore first showed the ambivalent relationship with politics that he repeated later in life, arriving with great political ambition, then turning away from his father's profession, then returning after concluding that public service was the one endeavor, as he put it, where he felt "the wind in my sails." It was also during his college years that Gore first showed the competing characteristics of farsightedness and caution, selflessness and self-aggrandizement that have defined him, for better and worse, during his political career.

Harvard was on the cusp of a cultural transformation during his freshman year. There were still coat-and-tie dress codes at dinner, parietal hours, Friday night mixers, even panty raids. Radcliffe girls under twenty-one were warned that spending a night in a man's room could lead to prosecution under the Massachusetts fornication law. The paternal nature of the place was captured by the first-day sight of a nattily dressed Nathan Pusey, the Harvard president, strolling down the sidewalk, offering to help Carl Vigeland carry his popcorn popper into his new dorm room. In his welcoming remarks to the students, Pusey had noted that the university, like the papacy, was "one of the last surviving medieval institutions." The spring riot was not an antiwar protest but a prank of mock rebellion, hundreds of guys blocking traffic on Memorial Drive, searching on hands and knees for a fictitious contact lens.

Yet change was next door, literally and figuratively. On his second night on campus, Terrence McNally, another freshman in Gore's little Mower dorm, wearing Weejuns, madras shirt, and flattop haircut, ventured next door to the Phillips Brooks House and "walked straight into a different world, the 1960s"—a crowd of long-haired students nodding to an ode to LSD from Timothy Leary, a former Harvard faculty member. While Richard Nixon, the former vice president, could discreetly hole up in a Cambridge hotel suite to interview Harvard law students for his New York firm, campus visits by Lady Bird Johnson and a few LBJ aides elicited protests from SDS, Students for a Democratic Society, which started passing out leaflets and staging antiwar rallies. In the *Harvard Crimson*, the student newspaper, lengthy articles described an emerging radical student movement on campus "that dwarfs every other political movement in the past quarter century."

Gore's first political move at Harvard seemed anything but radical. During a get-acquainted meeting of freshmen in Mower B, the young men sat around sipping beer and telling each other what they wanted to do in life. Gore said that he intended to be president of the United States. "That pretty much brought the house down," recalled classmate David Wylie. "Right, Al!" Wylie remembered Gore at that moment as seeming "very directed." Gore was already running for one presidency, of the Freshman Council, campaigning door-to-door in the North Yard. John Tyson, who became his suitemate in later years, recalled their first encounter—when "this guy came in the room with a big smile and a handshake" asking for votes. After the senator's son left that day, Tyson's freshman roommate, Glenn Price, who was running for the same office, threw up his hands and moaned, in a lament that in retrospect might prove all things are relative, "Look what I'm up against! He's a professional already!"

Soon enough, Gore the young pol was chairing Freshman Council meetings. Decades later, Roberts Bennett, another council member, found a yellowed document in his files titled "Freshman Council Minutes/Nov. 4, 1965 Meeting" that evokes the lingering innocence of that transitional semester and the mundane yet vital concerns of Harvard dorm life:

"The meeting was called to order by Chairman Al Gore at 7:05. . . . Council members were urged to sign up and also show up for work at the Princeton mixer. . . . Henry Bernson complained about football tickets. . . . Ed Tabor suggested that the University Police take care of the drunks in the Yard over the weekend. . . . Al Gore will write a letter of complaint. . . . Protests were made about room cleaning, and also about the food randomly put together. Specific mention was made about the turkey salad and meat loaf. . . . A movement to adjourn was made at 8:00, but Al continued with announcements. . . ."

Gore's involvement in Freshman Council provoked mild ridicule from his new pals in Mower B, who were more interested in Radcliffe and Wellesley girls, trips across the Charles River into Boston, jazz clubs, classical music, sports, poetry, art, and theater. One of his suitemates, Ballinger Kemp, was a hip black student from California (Gore had made a specific request to live with a black student) who wore oversized sunglasses and bellbottoms and was cool in a way that most of his new classmates had never seen before. Another suitemate, Roger Mennell from Cleveland, was a brilliant scholar who reminded the others of a hyperconscious character out of a Dostoyevsky novel. Student government was "high school," in the cutting phrase of another Mower dormmate, the sardonic football-playing actor Tommy Lee Jones of Texas (more commonly known then as Tom Jones). "Tommy Lee would rib him about it. He would rib anybody about anything. He was very challenging and competitive and would brook no bullshit. Class president—that's kind of bullshit. High school," said another classmate in their group, Michael Kapetan, a talented sculptor from Michigan. Another member of Gore's circle, Bob Somerby, a philosophy student from San Francisco, thought college was not the time to run for office but to "sit around in black turtlenecks and read poetry and be depressed."

Gore got the message. After that freshman presidency, he never again showed the slightest interest in student government, and receded from leadership roles for the remainder of his undergraduate years. "We had some good parties, dances, and it was almost meaningless. And I'm searching to justify the word 'almost,'" he recalled of his council presidency decades later. The peer pressure he felt to withdraw from student government, Gore added, brought to mind "what Mark Twain said in his autobiography about Silver City, Nevada. He said, 'There was gambling, drinking, cursing, gunshots. It was no place for a Presbyterian and I did not long remain one.'"

HE WAS ALWAYS fiercely competitive, and at Harvard this trait found new means of expression. He did not go out for football, but when he heard his friend John Tyson, a talented running back, boast about being the school's beer-chugging champ, Gore immediately challenged him to a drinking duel. Tyson was all technique, wide openings punched on both sides, huge gulps—he could down a can in three seconds. Gore studied Tyson's method and duplicated it. "He said, 'Let's go,'" Tyson recalled. "We were outside in the North Yard, standing there with sixteen-ounce cans. One, two, three, chug. We had an even start and we came down with the can at pretty much the same time and we argued for the next hour who won and settled on a tie. He was the only one who even came close to me. Throughout our undergraduate years, that was our relationship. Handball, Frisbee—there was always some sort of competition."

If Gore claimed later not to be intimidated by the talent that surrounded him at Harvard, it was nonetheless an uneven time for him, when he seemed to either underachieve or bump up against the bounds of his own abilities. Economics 1 was not the only course in which he struggled. He scored a C in Social Sciences 8 and a C+ in Humanities 2, his two other graded courses his freshman year, ending up in the fifth rank of his classmates, the lowest group without flunking out. His only B was in physical education, but even in that realm his skills now seemed unexceptional. At prep school he had made himself a star basketball player through sheer perseverance, staying after practice in the St. Albans gym—catch, turn, jump, release, catch, turn, jump, release—refining his shot from the corner hour after hour. At Harvard he made the freshman basketball team, but found himself sitting near the end of the bench with the other scrubs, getting playing time only when a game was out of reach.

Barth Royer, one of his Mower suitemates and a starting forward on the team, thought Gore "suffered from white man's disease; he was a little slow and didn't jump real well. But he was nothing if not tenacious"—a competitive instinct that, during those few minutes when he was on the court, invariably landed him in foul trouble. During his long stretches on the bench, Gore sat next to Robert Shetterly Jr. of Cincinnati, who had the same build and plodding playing style. "We would talk about the game, what it was like to have this different sense of ourselves as players, seeing our limitations," Shetterly recalled. "We both had been fairly big fish in small ponds."

There was a parallel experience for Gore that year in the classroom. He made the cut and was accepted into an exclusive freshman seminar, then found himself in a subordinate role, surrounded by classmates who seemed quicker and who were making intellectual or ideological leaps while he tried to keep both feet on the ground. The seminar, titled "Problems of Advanced Industrial Society," was taught by a first-year instructor named Martin Peretz, who later would become publisher of the *New Republic* and serve as an unofficial adviser to Gore, often urging him to take more hawkish positions on foreign policy issues. Peretz seemed like a very different fellow back in the fall of 1965, when he strolled Harvard Yard with what his students remembered as a "satyrlike" appearance. He had long hair and a bushy red beard, set off his button-down Oxford shirts with bright paisley ties, and viewed the world through his thick glasses with a fearsome stare. Sporting an immense vocabulary, a proclivity for political and social theory, and a provocative pedagogical style, he was a particular favorite of left-leaning students drawn to his unorthodox appearance and eclectic tastes. "He was not exactly the bad boy, but not the staid professor," explained Dave Forman. "He was pushing the edges at Harvard a little bit." Another student thought of him as "the school's pet radical."

In later years, Peretz would think of himself as "the great disenchanter" of radical students, but his rightward movement in response to what he saw as the excesses of the counterculture was not immediately apparent that first year. His ambivalence was noticed by one of his faculty advisers, conservative Soviet scholar Adam Ulam, who said to him, "Marty, you are in a political trap. You are located in one place. It can be described either of two ways: You are the extreme right of the left or the extreme left of the right."

More than one hundred freshmen applied for the seminar, and Peretz interviewed each one in his book-cluttered warren at Kirkland House, handpicking the dozen or so he wanted. He quizzed young Gore about the Vietnam War, his political philosophy, and what he knew about social theory, which though limited was apparently satisfactory. Others in the class thought it was not mere happenstance that the seminar included both Gore and Don Gilligan, whose father was a rising Democratic congressman from Ohio. Others in the seminar, including Alan Moonves, Barth Schwartz, and Dave Forman, had progressive to radical credentials, and the only conservative was James Truesdale Kilbreth III, latest in a long line of Harvard-going Kilbreths. This same Jamie Kilbreth later became the most radical of the bunch, an SDS leader who turned with a passion against the establishment from which he came.

The seminar began with readings in Marx and his theory of alienation, then went on to C. Wright Mills and the power elite and finally to Freud, with what Gilligan called "a lot of impenetrable stuff in between"—all of it in different ways challenging the establishment and the status quo. Peretz believed that the seminar would not work "unless the people get agitated; you have to be a little bit egregious, and then sometimes you confess to the egregiousness." Part of his egregiousness was the equation with which he ended one lecture: "Marx plus Freud equals Truth." This was said "not as a devotee," Gilligan recalled, "but as someone who was trying to challenge a bunch of kids."

Gore was by no means the star of the class. Schwartz and Forman were what Peretz called "the dazzlers," with incandescent minds and an eagerness to debate any theory their instructor threw at them. Peretz suspected that his dazzlers had always been told when they were younger that they were the smartest of their peers, whereas of Gore he said: "I would guess that Al was never told that. Al was told other things—the responsibility to do important work in his life." What struck Peretz first about Gore was his politeness. Since he was only a half-dozen years older than his students, Peretz asked them to call him "Marty," and all obliged except Gore, who persisted for months in greeting him as "Mr. Peretz." Later in the year, when the boys were invited to the Peretz house for dinner, Marty's young wife walked into the room and Gore rose and addressed her as "ma'am," causing her to turn to see if someone was behind her.

In "a curious way," Peretz said later, he also thought of Gore as "far less political" than his seminar colleagues. The others would try to goad him into taking ideological positions, but he seemed to have what Peretz called "an allergy to unprovable assertions. He would never let a dazzling phrase end a conversation. He wanted to know what it meant." Gilligan was often Gore's lone ally in the room, the two isolated by the others because their fathers were politicians. "I have this memory of lots of discussions in which one or the other of us would be saying, 'Yeah, but that isn't really the way the world works,'" Gilligan recalled. "I would try or Al would try to bring it back into a framework that we considered reality, but that we were more comfortable with because we understood. There were sometimes hoots of derision because we were trying to make things more pedestrian as far as those other guys were concerned."

The Peretz seminar had varying degrees of influence on the freshmen. "I don't think it's unfair to say that Marty radicalized some of his students and then didn't know what to do with them," said Jamie Kilbreth. "I was politely going about my way, playing lacrosse, having a social life, doing all the things that a traditional Andover guy whose family had gone to Harvard for generations did. On the other hand, I was trying to deal with all these ideas, many of which said all this other stuff didn't make much sense." Even as they struggled to hold the middle ground, Gilligan and Gore were changed by the seminar, from then on more conscious of the hidden structures of the society around them. "That seminar pretty thoroughly blew away my whole worldview," said Gilligan. He entered the class interested in traditional politics and came out fascinated by the interplay of economics and culture, eventually concentrating on the origins of the Puritan revolution in England. Gore, who remembered the seminar as "a time of great growth and learning," said it might have had the opposite effect on him. He had been turning away from his father's profession anyway that year, but the memories of the debates about Freud and Marx and Mills stayed with him, keeping a pilot light of political interest burning quietly inside him until the fire returned.

AL GORE AND TOMMY LEE JONES were never literally roommates at Harvard, as many accounts through the years have implied, but they were at the center of a group of friends who coalesced as freshmen at Mower and later moved on together to Dunster House. The young men in this group were not aesthetes or intellectuals or clubby types, but mostly took their cues from Jones and Gore—jocks with a creative side. Jones, not Gore, was the dominant character. "When I first met him I was shocked. He was like a man and we were all these little kids," said Bob Somerby. "He was a year older, but beyond that was his attitude, a whole different way of presenting himself." One of the lingering memories of many classmates is of the charismatic Jones, who played guard on the football team, pacing along a path near the Charles, wearing a blue velvet jacket and holding a rose, reciting lines from *Coriolanus* in his hard, crackling Texas voice. Gore's first encounter with Jones seemed straight out of a Beckett play. On the first day of school, he enters the Mower suite, the lights are out, he assumes the place is empty, then he flips a switch and sees a figure sitting silent and motionless in a straight-backed chair in the middle of the room. "Hi," says Gore. "Hi," says Tommy Lee Jones. Nothing more. "Then I thought to myself," Gore recalled later, " 'This is going to be interesting.' "

Gore in his early college days thought of himself as an artist much like Jones. He told Tipper Aitcheson that he intended to be an author, and his letters to her often included lines of poetry. For a freshman writing tutorial, he spent countless hours at his desk, gazing into the somber shroud of a Cambridge winter, typing out installments of what he hoped would be a Faulknerian novel about Carthage, the colorful hometown of his Tennessee summers (an untitled and unfinished tome that appears lost to history). Unlike many of his peers, who seemed eager to reinvent themselves into hipper 1960s figures once they reached Cambridge, Gore chose to retreat into his past and recreate it, using the idiosyncratic characters of the small town in the Upper Cumberland to populate his fiction.

(The one Carthage character likely missing from his fiction was Donna Armistead, his old country girlfriend. He had written her a few times from Mower B, using Harvard stationery, but that had been the end of it. Donna got married that year, and one night she turned to her young husband and said, "We've got to go down to the little branch, I need to do something." She went to her dresser and fished out the batch of letters from Al, bundled in pink ribbons, and had her husband drive her down the dirt road to a point where Snow Creek was so low it could be forded by car. This was the place where she and Al used to go to talk and neck. It was a cold night and her husband stood back by the car, the motor running, while Donna walked down to the creek with the pack of letters. She struck a match and held it to a letter and threw it to the ground, then tore more letters apart, feeding dozens into the fire. "This was several years going up in flames," she said. "I thought I would have more emotion, but I didn't.")

Gore's friendship with the Texan Jones, who insisted on calling him Albert, encouraged him to accentuate his southernness. "There was this funny little dynamic going, as if Tommy Lee was the occasion for Al to assert his roots," recalled Bart Day, who had come up to Harvard from St. Albans with Gore and lived with him in college. At one point Gore took to wearing bib overalls as an expression of Dixie hip. But if Jones, who kept his radio tuned to the only country music station in Boston, was the superior actor, he also tended to take himself even more seriously than Al. "He was always acting. He was always on, always on stage," said John Tyson. "So what we would do—Al would instigate this—he would say, 'Let's ignore Tommy Lee!' So Tommy Lee would walk in and no one would lift a head up. Then he would start acting and we would ignore him and say, 'Anybody seen Tommy Lee?' After a while he would start screaming. He just couldn't take it. Then we would burst out laughing."

Gore competed with Jones in the telling of down-home tales, and was regarded by most of their friends as the funnier of the two. Among the publications flowing into the suite, along with *Sports Illustrated, Time,* and *Playboy,* was the *Carthage Courier,* the little Tennessee weekly whose masthead shouted an irrefutable boast: "The Only Newspaper in the World That Gives a Whoop for Smith County." Gore also gave a whoop, combing the *Courier* in search of material for his novel and odd stories to read to his pals. "The *Carthage Courier* was always a treat," said Mike Kapetan. "Al would read it in Tennessee dialect." Gore loved his Tennessee characters, Kapetan thought, but he also loved to tell stories about his other, far different world, the high culture of St. Albans. One of those tales was about the Washington society family that decided to learn Spanish "the intense way, by not speaking English. So they all sat down to dinner and no one spoke a word."

They were both small towns, in different ways, Carthage and Washington, and with all their eccentricities and insularity they might have seemed comforting to Gore as he became more aware of the darker forces of history and human nature. David G. Nichols, a former classmate from St. Albans, visited Harvard for a few days, sleeping in the lower bunk usually occupied by Bart Day, who was out of town. Nichols was struck by the gloomy nature of a long conversation he had with Gore one night in the darkness of the dorm room. Gore could not take his mind off weapons of mass destruction. He told Nichols "in almost biblical" terms about how his father the senator had visited a weapons storage facility out in the Plains states where "as far as the eye could see there were canisters and tanks holding nerve gas and substances so deadly that an amount equal to an egg in the water supply could kill the whole world."

After rooming their first year on the Yard, Harvard men were distributed among the school's traditional houses, which served as combination dormitories, fraternities, and tutorial colleges. Gore and eight friends requested to be assigned to Adams House, which had a literary reputation, but were sent as a group instead to Dunster, named for Harvard's first president, the Reverend Henry Dunster, and regarded as one of the lesser houses, stocked with science grinds and assorted characters who affected a Wild Bunch image, riding motorcycles and staging all-night high-stakes poker games. Dunster was an aging Georgian structure with a red-topped clock tower, no elevators, no air-conditioning, and unreliable hot water heaters, but it had certain advantages, among them its own kitchen and wood-paneled dining room, squash courts and a grill in the basement, an elegant library facing the river, fireplaces in many suites, and the privacy that came with being all the way down by the Charles River, the furthest of the houses from the campus, an eight-minute walk from 935 Memorial Drive up to the Yard. While overseen by a master from the old school, the aptly named Alwin Max Pappenheimer, Dunster also harbored an interesting collection of young tutors, including a classics instructor named Erich Segal who was conceiving a novel on college life that would become *Love Story*.

Gore and Bart Day lived during their sophomore year in what they called the "bird's nest" apartment on the fifth floor, directly above a large suite that housed the others in their gang. Their room was the most popular hangout, largely because Gore had the best stereo system. The friends called themselves the "motley crew," and included in their set a few girlfriends, including Tipper. Al and Tipper's relationship had grown increasingly serious since the Christmas break of his freshman year, when he had invited her down to the farm in Carthage to meet his parents. She was still in high school then, and when she graduated he asked her to "please look at schools up here," and she had obliged, enrolling first at Garland, a two-year women's college, before transferring to Boston University.

While he and his friends were becoming increasingly preoccupied with the Vietnam War and the military draft, Gore's interest in politics reached a nadir during his sophomore year. He left it to others to run for house president or representative to the Harvard Policy Committee. When a former Kennedy aide spoke at Dunster and asked, "Who in this room is actually going to go into politics?" Gore kept his hand down. His one notable public act was organizing a protest against the nightly servings of fried chicken and gravy in the dining room; after ballooning to 210 pounds, he successfully lobbied for less-fattening fare.

Interviews with several dozen Dunster men from his graduating class revealed a range of impressions about Gore during his college days. Some agreed with one classmate's characterization of him as a "stoic and machinelike" figure, a princeling who had to have "everything in his life orchestrated for him." Even his participation in Dunster's all-night poker games, according to this view, was carefully "arranged for him so that he could experience what it was like to play poker." The poker regulars let Gore into the game five or six times with the understanding that they would teach him how to play while relieving him of his money, a few hundred dollars at a time. The word was that the old man, Senator Gore, was his silent, if reluctant, backer, replenishing his wallet after every loss. A few classmates considered Gore a dullard and were stunned by his later rise to national power. "There were a few geniuses in the mix and you remember them," said one. "Gore was not that kind of person. He didn't have a magnetic personality. I liked the guy, but president? What a kick!"

Most regarded Gore as neither princeling nor stiff. Dennis Horger remembered him as "a good listener, and with all the egos in a place like that, it was not a quality many people had." Horger's view of Gore had been shaped by his experience in freshman basketball, when he competed with Gore for a guard spot and was cut from the team during tryouts, then allowed back on after Gore and a few other players went to the coach and argued that he had made a mistake and that

Horger deserved a spot on the squad. Robbie Gass considered Gore "a straight guy in the best sense of the word. Not a straight arrow, but a good guy. He talked straight. You knew where you stood. He was not a game player." Peter Goldberg thought back on Gore in the dining hall at breakfast leading a "funny and interesting" discussion of what was in that morning's *New York Times*.

But the most common memory of Gore retained by his Dunster classmates placed him down in the basement lounge. It seemed as if he and his pals were there almost every night, playing pool, chomping on hamburgers, watching the news and *Star Trek* and Johnny Carson. Gore became hooked on television as purveyor of pop culture. "He used to tell me that I didn't watch enough television," recalled Warren Steel, who was ushered into the motley crew although he was a year younger than the others. "He studied it, you could tell that even from his watching, the comments he would make watching regular television shows. He made astute comments about *Star Trek* or *Lost in Space*." By the spring of 1967, the second semester of their sophomore year, beer-chugging contests were a thing of the past and marijuana, as Dunster classmate Jonathan Ritvo recalled, "had almost completely replaced alcohol as the substance of choice." Dunster House had its own in-house grass supplier, and though Gore and his motley crew were not considered potheads, they were known to smoke, and also to consume "magic brownies" laced with marijuana. When the issue of past drug use by presidential candidates first arose during the 1988 campaign, Gore readily acknowledged that he had smoked dope in his college days. Said housemate David Friedman, "A number of us had a joke: It's a good thing Al Gore 'fessed up that he inhaled, because a number of us saw him passed out on the Dunster House couches."

GORE'S ACADEMIC INTEREST was English during his first two years at Harvard, but that field grew increasingly difficult for him. He became frustrated by what he called the "headwind" he faced in his literature courses. "The apocryphal story that I tell, which doesn't tell the whole truth, is that Chaucer was okay, but when I began to get into the antecedents of Chaucer, I began to think, 'Is this really for me?' " Gore recalled. "I liked part of it, but I didn't like the rest of it." In fact, he said, if he had "more of a gift for writing," he might have "stayed that course." After discarding his unfinished novel about Carthage, a place that he loved and romanticized, Gore began looking at his past in a more clinical way, spurred on by a popular course he took from Erik Erikson, the legendary psychologist who had written *Childhood and Society* and coined the phrase "identity crisis." Erikson was a proponent of psychobiography, seeking to understand the evolution of human personality and ego through the psychological struggles one faces at each stage of life. He believed that identity was not immutable but could change over a lifetime, depending upon how successfully a person dealt with the tests of each stage.

Gore considered Erikson "a man of tremendous insight" who had "a big influence" on his thinking at what he once called "an awkward stage" in his life. For a course paper, he traveled to Washington and interviewed his father to write a psychobiography of him. Senator Gore told his son about how his older brother, Reginald, in whom the family had invested most of its hopes, was disabled by a gas attack while fighting in France during World War I, and how that setback had motivated Albert to succeed for the family. The themes Gore studied in Erikson's course found their way into conversations he had with his close friend Mike Kapetan, one of six children of working-class parents from Wayne, Michigan. "Trying to establish his own identity is what Al was about," Kapetan concluded from their discussions.

"Al took Erikson and the development of the human being and fulfillment of the psyche, he took that very much to heart," Kapetan said. "And I can see why he would. In many ways he was deprived of childhood. The problem of being a famous man's son—he would talk about that. Around our dinner table there were six hungry mouths, around his there were senators and congressmen and ambassadors. Unfortunately, that is where he learned his behavior to be still and sober and circumspect." Kapetan came to understand that Gore envied "the way I talked about my dad and the kind of relationship we had. From the earliest days I could remember I would accompany my dad on Saturday chores. 'Daddy, what is this?' 'Daddy, what is that?' There was always something else to talk about between Al and his dad."

Kapetan and Bart Day both had a sense that their friend was struggling with his past to prepare for his future, that even as he was telling them that he did not intend to follow his father into politics, at some level he knew that it was inevitable. "I guess you might argue that he almost kept it from himself in a way," Day said. And if they were the motley crew, Al was indeed Prince Hal. "There was this pull to something, almost like he was born to it."

The pull became much stronger in his junior year, when Gore took his first class from Richard E. Neustadt, professor of government and director of Harvard's Institute of Politics. Neustadt was a leading presidential scholar whose book *Presidential Power* was already a classic, with the special blessing of the late President John F. Kennedy, Harvard's favorite son. His course on the American presidency attracted hundreds of students, even though by 1967, as Neustadt now says with a certain bemusement, "I was regarded as a sort of semi-reactionary. I had worked for Kennedy and was a consultant to Johnson. I don't think I was in very good odor with the radicals." His lectures in Emerson Hall were not a dry recitation of presidential history or theory, nor an attack on establishment politics, but a method of political empathy, in a sense, showing the students how it would feel to sit in the Oval Office and have to deal with an endless array of dilemmas and complex decisions. He used specific stories, some real, others imagined, to illustrate specific points. He treated the Vietnam War as "a series of close decisions called wrong, made under uncertainty by beset people."

Twice a week the students gathered in small sections to role-play many of the dilemmas Neustadt brought up in the lectures. Gore's section man, as teaching assistants were called, was Graham Allison, who was completing a book on the Cuban Missile Crisis. Allison was fascinated by the way Kennedy reached his decision not to bomb the missile sites but rather impose a blockade against Soviet ships, and how he then sold those decisions to his advisers. In the students' role-playing, Gore was the one who "naturally gravitated to the role of president," Allison recalled. "That was the role he either chose or was chosen for." Gore played JFK, Allison said, "with intensity and seriousness—you could see the political possibilities coming alive. He was very much engaged with the notion of presidential power as the power to persuade." The experience was "an eye-opener," Gore said later, reawakening in him "the same sense of excitement" that Peretz's seminar had stirred in his freshman year. He realized that when he talked about solving problems in government, he suddenly felt more at ease, a sensation overtook him that this was where he belonged, as opposed to when he tried to resolve the same societal problems through writing, when he felt that he was straining.

When he mentioned his fascination with Neustadt's class to his parents, they apparently did not tell him directly how they felt—they tried not to overtly guide his life—but they were privately overjoyed. They had been concerned that he was struggling at Harvard, groping for motivation, showing signs of alienation, turning away from them and the values of public service that Albert and Pauline Gore had so thoroughly inculcated in him. Now, they told friends, with his renewed interest in government, the spark relit by Neustadt, he had been saved—saved from Chaucer, saved from some outer darkness. At least for the moment.

CHAPTER FOUR

THE TUMULTUOUS
SUMMER

THERE SAT AL GORE inside the International Amphitheater in Chicago, listening intently as Hubert Humphrey delivered his acceptance speech at the Democratic National Convention. At age twenty, Gore was somewhat of an anomaly by his very presence in the convention hall that eventful summer night of August 29, 1968. Thousands of his college-age contemporaries were demonstrating in the streets outside, chanting and jeering and clashing with Mayor Richard Daley's head-bashing police in protest of the Vietnam War and the party's nomination of Lyndon Johnson's loyal vice president over peace candidate Eugene McCarthy.

Gore also opposed the war and had supported McCarthy that summer back home in Tennessee, a futile effort in a state whose military tradition was evoked by its "Volunteer" nickname. Yet while many of his peers were turning away from establishment politics and had little or no interest in Humphrey's convention address, Gore found it utterly absorbing. He parsed the message line by line in search of signs that the presidential nominee had listened to the younger generation and was changing with the times. In his own mind at least, Gore that night was not only a witness to history, but also a minor figure in the shaping of it.

The way young Gore later often told the story, he had been interviewed the day before by Charles Bartlett, the veteran *Chicago Sun-Times* columnist from Chattanooga, a family friend who had known Albert Gore Sr., the senior senator from Tennessee, since his early days in the House. Bartlett "had passed the apogee of his career" by 1968 but was "still a very eloquent writer," Gore said, and was one of those helping Humphrey with his speech at the convention. "And he came and spent an hour with me, asking what people my age thought about the war." As Gore sat in the convention hall and looked up at Humphrey in the spotlight, he thought that he heard his own words coming back to him. He was convinced that the vice president's speechwriters had incorporated his suggestions into the acceptance speech—evoking "the end of an era," the promise of a "prompt end to the war," the assertion that no one wanted "a police state," the call for "young Americans . . . to continue as vocal, creative, and even critical participants in the politics of our time." Hearing those phrases, Gore said later, led him to the conclusion that "there was no doubt Mr. Bartlett had faithfully conveyed some of the feelings that I had tried to describe."

But was Gore only imagining his role as interpreter for his generation? According to Bartlett's description of those long-ago events, that might be the case. "I had nothing to do with Humphrey," Bartlett said in a later interview. "I had no contact with Humphrey at all. If I talked to Al, it was perhaps for a story. I had absolutely no link at all with Hubert Humphrey in 1968."

When presented with Bartlett's response, Gore quickly retreated from his earlier recollection. "Faulty memory. Faulty memory," he said of himself and his oft-told story. But whoever wrote Humphrey's speech, he quickly added, "did a good job of figuring out what millions of us were thinking and saying, because he gave me the impression that he was speaking directly to my feelings about it."

There is in Al Gore an occasional propensity to enhance his role in events. The 1968 convention episode might fall into that category of solipsism. But the uncontested facts in that scene—that he was in the convention hall to hear the speech and was impressed by what he heard—accurately reflect his political disposition that summer and all through what was to follow during his tumultuous senior year at Harvard. After turning away from his father's profession during his first few years in college, Gore now seemed back on the political track. His earnest behavior during the Democratic convention was of a piece with the caution and respect for authority that he exhibited from then until his graduation one year later. His final semester at Harvard climaxed with a student takeover of University Hall, the main administration building, and a bloody encounter with police that repeated on a smaller scale the generational confrontation in Chicago—and this time, as before, Gore stayed close to his elders and observed the event from a safe distance. Some radical classmates considered his behavior apolitical, but he was in fact thinking politically on a longer arc, taking into account not just his feelings at the moment, but also how his actions might affect the political futures of himself and his father.

All during this period, even as he was making another turn back toward politics, Gore struggled not to succumb to the occasional waves of despair that had been washing over him throughout the 1960s. First the assassination of President Kennedy in 1963, then the vitriol directed at his father for his opposition to the war starting in 1966, then the assassinations of Martin Luther King Jr. and Robert F. Kennedy earlier in the year—his inherent instinct to believe in the system, he said, was constantly being challenged by "a cumulative process of disillusionment."

IN THE SUMMER OF 1968, Gore was working his way through the thicket of late 1960s politics. A few months before the Chicago convention, he had come out in support of McCarthy after several discussions with his friend and Harvard tutor Martin Peretz, a leader of the McCarthy movement in New England. How active he was in that campaign is unclear. In a front-page article in the July 18, 1968, *Carthage Courier*, Gore was described as the new state chairman of a Youth for McCarthy organization. He said that his father was aware of his role, adding: "But my activities are completely separate from his. He has not endorsed either candidate yet"—meaning Humphrey or McCarthy (though Gore Senior eventually cast his delegate vote for a third candidate, his Senate colleague George McGovern).

Steve Cobb, the Tennessee coordinator for McCarthy, said later that "there wasn't a Youth for McCarthy organization in the state, although the whole campaign was laughingly called that." Cobb was a twenty-three-year-old graduate student. He remembered Gore paying a single visit to the campaign at its dusty old warehouse state headquarters on Eighth Avenue in Nashville and agreeing to write a letter to delegates to the state Democratic convention. "I remember Al one time coming into headquarters. We talked. We had both gone to Harvard," Cobb said. "We were delighted to have his support. The more important thing for him I think were his own personal plans—what he was going to be doing and his father's reelection coming up in a couple of years."

One of Gore's other interests that summer explained why he was not in Nashville more often—and also offered a hint of his political ambitions. He attended summer school at Memphis State, taking a course in Tennessee history taught by Charles Crawford, a leading young historian. "He just showed up one day," recalled Crawford, who remembered Gore as being "preppy casual." The class met from mid-July to mid-August at seven each morning for two hours, going over Tennessee's geology, archaeology, Native Americans, early white settlements, black history, developing political structures, and religious, social, and economic institutions. Taking that course was classic Al Gore, incessantly industrious and focused on the future. "With Al, knowledge was power," said Bart Day. "It was something you could acquire and grab hold of and assimilate. He was very good at it." Some of what Gore grabbed hold of and assimilated from Crawford's class would prove beneficial to him years later when he would present himself to state voters as a native son who understood the local culture, rather than as an interloper from Washington.

On the final weekend of August, Gore drove to Chicago from the family farm in Carthage with his older sister, who by then was living in Mississippi and married to lawyer Frank Hunger. Nancy Gore Hunger was a vibrant activist closely aligned with Mississippi's integrated Loyalist delegation, which was seated by the national Democrats that year in place of old-line segregationists and included liberal newspapermen Hodding Carter and Curtis Wilkie. In those years of protest, Nancy attended two peaceful antiwar demonstrations, large acts in the small conservative town of Greenville, where she lived. She had her mother's sharp instincts and was perhaps the most politically savvy member of a thoroughly political family, and as such felt especially protective of her younger brother, in whom she saw a great political future.

Hodding Carter later remembered Nancy saying that she had brought Al in from Grant Park and had him sleep in her hotel bathtub to make sure that he steered clear of the trouble in Chicago. It was an apparently apocryphal tale (Gore insists that he stayed in his parents' hotel all week) that nonetheless captured the tensions and crosscurrents of the times. While none of Gore's closest friends were in the streets, he was acquainted with many of the young demonstrators. Several of his Dunster housemates were there, including Robbie Gass and Jonathan Ritvo, who had driven out from Cambridge in Gass's VW bus and stopped in Chicago on their way to Wyoming. Just when the situation turned ugly and police started bashing heads, they slipped away and took an El out to the calm of Evanston. Former St. Albans classmate Bruce Rathbun was there as a member of a street theater troupe presenting skits on race and peace.

Many Democratic politicians worried about what their sons or daughters might get into that week. Jack Gilligan, an antiwar Senate candidate from Ohio who had just earned the Democratic nomination and was struggling to hold the support of organized labor, took the precaution of making sure that his sons, including Gore's Harvard classmate Don Gilligan, were nowhere near Chicago. "My brother and I were planning to go, and then a few days before the convention my father appeared with an untypical offer," Don Gilligan recalled. "He said, 'Here's a couple hundred dollars and a car. Why don't you guys go up to Michigan for a week? Sure this is enough money?' He was afraid that we'd get arrested in the park and didn't want to antagonize the unions with two goofy college kids."

Although the senior Gore also seemed politically vulnerable, he showed no similar paternal alarm. He encouraged his son to attend the convention and used him as an adviser, welcoming his suggestions for an antiwar speech the senator delivered that Wednesday, the very day that Humphrey's nomination was overshadowed by a harsh confrontation between police and protesters. Al did not witness the most violent clash. But decades later he could call back one incident etched in his memory: He stepped outside the hotel, the sidewalks and curbs brimming with angry demonstrators, and watched as an Army jeep moved slowly down the street "with a couple of film cameras . . . taking pictures of the faces of everybody. . . . I remember that camera focusing on me, because it had a feeling of intimidation about it, and it was inconsistent with what I felt this country must be all about."

The passion that eerie encounter stirred in young Gore stayed with him as he helped his father craft his speech, he said. John Seigenthaler, then editor of the Nashville *Tennessean*, chatted with Senator Gore in the press section before it was delivered. "He gave me a copy of the speech and said, 'Look this over and tell me what you think about it,'" Seigenthaler recalled. "So I looked it over—an antiwar speech. I said, 'There's some powerful stuff in here.' And he said, 'Young Al helped me with the speech.' And I said, 'Helped you to what extent?' And he said, 'Well, I went over it with him at great length.' "

This was by no means the elder Gore's first antiwar statement. He had once been a cold warrior, a strong supporter of President Truman's policy during the Korean War, but slowly came to doubt the alliances the United States was making in Asia, which he said seemed "about as reliable as a label on a piece of canned goods." He had been troubled by the administration's Vietnam policy since the first big American troop buildup in 1965. "It's going to be one of the worst mistakes the United States is going to get into—I tried to talk the president out of it," he confided to his Carthage doctor, Gordon Petty, shortly after calling President Johnson to question that early decision. And he had become increasingly outspoken since the spring of 1966, when the Senate Foreign Relations Committee, of which he was a member, held televised hearings on the issue. Al was a freshman at Harvard then, and from that point on he and his father had bonded in their opposition to the war, each feeding proudly off the other's opinion. In a letter to girlfriend Tipper Aitcheson after the committee hearings, Al wrote of his father: "He was so pleased when I told him I missed two or three days of classes to watch him on television. He tried not to show it and said I shouldn't have missed class, but he was awful pleased." By 1968, Senator Gore was a popular speaker in antiwar circles, known for his questioning of the morality of American foreign policy.

The convention speech that Al helped draft for his father in Chicago was short (361 words) and biting in its contention that Johnson—and by extension Humphrey—had betrayed the promises they had made in the 1964 election. "Mr. Chairman, fellow delegates, four years ago our party and the nominee of our party promised the people that American boys would not be sent to fight in a land war in Asia," Gore Senior began. "The people made an overwhelming commitment to peace. They voted for our distinguished leader, President Lyndon B. Johnson, but they got the policies of Senator Goldwater."

Antiwar delegates roared their approval, and young Al watched as his silver-haired father raised both hands and then lowered them in a signal to hush. "He felt so strongly about getting all of it into the record of the proceedings, delivering every word, that he insisted that nobody applaud because they were taking up his time," Al Gore recalled. "He kept pushing his hands down—keep on going!" The senator continued. "Almost immediately combat troops were sent to fight in a steadily widening Asian war. Twenty-five thousand American men have died. What harvest do we reap from our gallant sacrifice? An erosion of the moral and spiritual base of American leadership, entanglement with the corrupt political clique in Saigon, disillusionment, despair here at home and a disastrous postponement of imperative programs to improve our social ills." The American people, he said, "think we made a mistake, and yet . . . read the proposed platform. We are called upon not only to approve this disastrous policy, but even to applaud it. I wonder how many of the American people are applauding it. They don't want to applaud it."

It was one of Albert Gore's finest moments, thought his son. "I felt passionately about the war policy," he said later. "I was intensely proud of what my father was saying." But his pride in his father was mixed with bewilderment over what he saw as the increasing polarization in American politics. He was upset, he told friends, by the growing tendency among his antiwar peers to dismiss what they called "the system." To make matters worse, he said, people working for change within the system, such as his father, were in danger of losing their jobs.

From his Chicago hotel room, Gore placed a call to Mike Kapetan, his Harvard suitemate and a working-class artist and philosopher who had thought about coming to the convention but could not afford to leave his summer job, which helped pay his tuition. There was an ironic resonance to his work. At a factory in Plymouth, Michigan, he was earning $3.15 an hour building boxcars for the Southern Pacific Railroad—cars fitted with special absorbers to carry munitions to be used in the war. He was against the war but shared Gore's concern that things were falling apart. "We talked about how sorry the situation had become, and how the regular Democratic Party did not seem able to contain the radical forces, and the kids who wanted to be radical weren't doing anything constructive," Kapetan said. "It was hard to see anything good that was going to come from that. Al and I thought along similar lines."

On election night a few months later, Gore and Kapetan and a few friends stayed up until three in the morning in Gore's room at Harvard watching the returns that carried Richard Nixon into the White House instead of Humphrey. Another Democratic casualty that night was Don Gilligan's father, Jack, who lost the Senate race in Ohio. Not long afterward, Gore was cutting through Harvard Yard, past University Hall, when he caught sight of young Gilligan, who had just returned from the election battle. The two felt a special kinship, sons of politicians, and now as they stopped and talked it was apparent that their bond included a shared sense of loss. After expressing his sorrow at Don's father's defeat, Gore said matter-of-factly, "I'm going to be in the same position in two years. My dad's going to get beat and there's nothing we can do about it."

GORE'S POLITICAL EDUCATION continued apace even as he worried about the fate of his father and the cynicism of his peers. Once each week during his senior year, he left his Dunster suite and walked over to a seminar room in the little yellow house at 78 Mount Auburn that was home to Harvard's Institute of Politics. There, for two hours, he sat with the institute's director, Richard Neustadt, occasionally joined by one of Neustadt's instructors, Graham Allison, and they discussed the issues of power and the presidency. The private tutorial was entirely Gore's idea. Neustadt was preoccupied that year with establishing the young institute and writing books and papers and at first told Gore that he had no time. But Gore pleaded with him, said he would take the tutorial for no credit, that he had much to learn and only wanted to learn it from Neustadt. "I have a soft spot for good students who seem to be really turned on and really want to carry on with me and do something serious," Neustadt recalled. And there was Gore—"this big, hulking, serious guy who is so interested. How can you resist?"

For the first few months their discussions ranged across a lengthy reading list that Neustadt had compiled in preparation for Gore's senior thesis in the Department of Government. "He wasn't a bit shy. He was respectful, earnest, and serious—and sometimes funny. He was capable of being quite funny," Neustadt recalled. "But what was challenging about Al was his interest had been stirred, and when it was stirred he was relentlessly pursuing the subject." As the year progressed, their talks deepened and focused in greater detail on the chapter drafts of the thesis. The topic seems as relevant to Gore the presidential candidate three decades later as to the college senior in the late 1960s. The eighty-four-page paper's title was "The Impact of Television on the Conduct of the Presidency, 1947–1969." The essence of Gore's thesis—less obvious at the time than it appears today—was that television had replaced newspapers as the central means of communication and in so doing had forever transformed the presidency. Television had an inherent bias toward individuals over institutions, he wrote, and inevitably would bring more attention to the president and less to the other branches of government. This would appear to give the president more power, and "given time the change in perception could possibly work towards a change in reality." This in turn would make the effectiveness of future leaders increasingly dependent on their television skills. "Because of this," Gore concluded, "it is possible to speculate that a 'role requirement' of the President in the future might become 'visual communication.'"

Using his father's connections as well as Neustadt's contacts with former White House officials, Gore was ushered into offices in New York and Washington that normally might be closed to a college senior doing research. "He was well prepared, asked good questions, listened carefully, took lots of notes—the model of a good student," recalled Bill Moyers, a former Johnson press secretary who years earlier had worked with Gore's sister, Nancy, at the Peace Corps. He thought he saw in Gore "the makings of a journalist," and urged him in that direction, "but even then, unless memory is playing tricks on me, [I] could sense a pull in other directions." George M. Elsey, who had worked with Neustadt in the Truman White House, met Gore in his office overlooking Lafayette Square, and there they discussed the 1948 election. Elsey remembered less about the interview itself than about a call he had received from Neustadt beforehand. "Dick, as I recall, said, 'This guy's got a real future. I don't know what it is, but I can guarantee he's got a real future.'"

Would it be as a politician—or writer? It was not immediately apparent that Gore had the "visual communication" skills required of a future president, but to Neustadt, as to Moyers, he seemed to have the aptitude of a first-class reporter. "What is interesting about that thesis was not that the content was so specially analytical or revelatory, but that the interviewing on which it was based was so damn good," Neustadt said later.

Here it was again, in his last year at Harvard, the tension between what he was good at and what he was expected to be, the choice of a life's path, his past tugging against his future.

CHAPTER FIVE

THE WAR AT HOME

THE WAR HAD ALWAYS been there, since their freshman year, waiting for them outside Cambridge. How they would deal with it was a decision that seemed a long way off for most of the young men, though reality occasionally intruded into their sheltered lives. They had been at Harvard less than a year when Denmark Groover III dropped out in April 1966 and joined the Army and went off to Vietnam. Some of Denny's classmates called him "a fool," Al Gore wrote in a letter to Tipper. "They're running him down all the time. They just can't understand." Gore was against the war, but he also considered himself a southerner, like the Georgian Groover, and he thought he understood. "I admire him a great deal," he confided. "I admire his courage and rashness. I'm not sure at all that he didn't do the right thing."

The next year at Dunster House there were more acts of rashness and courage, and the stakes seemed higher. Carl Thorne-Thomsen from Illinois withdrew from school in April 1967 and enlisted in the Army. Five months later he was in Vietnam, pulling duty as a radioman. He wrote back to his brother in Lake Forest that he thought the war was unjustified, that what kept him going was not patriotism but the camaraderie of his fellow soldiers. One morning that October, while the Harvard boys ate breakfast in their wood-paneled dining hall, the news swept through the room like a shock wave: Carl was dead, killed in an ambush near the Cambodian border.

That same autumn, Robert Shetterly Jr., who had sat next to Gore as a benchwarmer on Harvard's freshman basketball team, became

Dunster House's first resister. He was wearing a beard and sandals when he went down to a rally at Yale, dropped his draft card into a box, and had it sent back to his draft board in Cincinnati. He was immediately reclassified 1-A delinquent and called to a preinduction center in Boston, where he refused to sign a loyalty oath and was grilled by Army intelligence officers who told him that he was acting out of shallow romantic ideals and hurting his country and his parents. Two FBI agents later appeared at H Entry on Dunster's third floor and interviewed Shetterly. "They seemed to think I was a dupe of some larger conspiracy and kept asking me who put me up to it," he recalled. "I kept trying to say it was a personal decision." His act of civil disobedience, he said, grew from his belief that the war "was a terrible mistake, and if I was being asked to die and kill for this cause that I thought was morally wrong, I had to do something comparable to stop it."

Year by year the war closed in on them, and now in their final senior semester, it sometimes seemed as if it was the only thing. The counterculture was in full bloom in the spring of 1969, dope abundant, long hair and beards, exclusive clubs on the decline, the New Left teeming with factions and contentiousness, women sleeping in men's houses, officials halfheartedly struggling to maintain some measure of decorum, students wearing flannel shirts and jeans to dinner, or ties and undershorts, or ties made of toilet paper, anything to challenge authority. But most of it, in the end, came back to the war and the decision that awaited them, the beginning and end of many conversations.

"This is what we were talking about. This is what everyone was talking about," Tipper Gore recalled decades later of that time when she was studying at Boston University and her boyfriend was about to graduate from Harvard and they and their friends were consumed by passion and fear. "It was on everyone's mind. I try to explain it to my children, but it is hard to understand now because the times were so different. The feelings, the climate, the intensity, the consequences, what was happening, what our country was standing for or not standing for. How you felt about that. Bumper stickers: America Love It or Leave It. Neighbors not talking to neighbors. It was a very intense, very hate-filled and idealistic time."

Few places were more intense than Dunster House, where Gore lived that final year in the A Entry wing with his pals Mike Kapetan and J. G. Landau, a jocular baseball player from Long Island, down the hall from their friends Tommy Lee Jones and Bart Day and Bob Somerby. Only a few years earlier, Dunster was known for its poker games and motorcycles. Now it housed many of Harvard's leading young radicals, and debates over the war, the draft, and the university's relationship with the military and "the system" raged from the breakfast table in the morning to the basement lounge at night. Left against left, left against center, center against right, the arguments were incessant, said John Tyson, Gore's roommate from the year before, who by now had an Afro and a beard and a bum-knee limp, the former star defensive back having denounced football as a gladiator sport for rich white alumni. It was not uncommon at Dunster to hear Shetterly, the hoopster-turned-draft-resister, getting into a fierce argument about antiwar protest tactics with Jamie Kilbreth, old-boy conservative-turned-radical-firebrand, leader of the Maoist faction of Students for a Democratic Society. Or to hear another leftist, Richard Hyland, preposterously comparing Dunster history tutor Doris Kearns to a war criminal, turned off by the fact that she had once worked for LBJ, dismissive of her outspoken opposition to the war as being "too respectable." The New Left was by no means a majority at Dunster, but its adherents dominated the debate, overpowering some classmates, challenging them all. "In the system or not—what are you going to do? That was the first question," Tyson recalled.

"It was complicated for everybody. We were all idealists," Mike Kapetan said later, speaking in the plural of Gore and his friends, the self-described motley crew. "I did not like SDS. I would go to meetings and I didn't like the rhetoric." Gore stayed away from those meetings but had a few heated discussions in the dining hall with Kilbreth, a classmate he had been debating from both sides of the ideological spectrum since they sat together in Marty Peretz's freshman seminar, when Kilbreth was the token conservative. "I'm just frustrated talking to this guy!" Gore lamented one afternoon after hearing his now-radical classmate ridicule the system as a fraud and belittle the university and Congress as puppets of the capitalist elite. The democratic system still worked, Gore insisted, it had just been contorted by the war. He also got into breakfast debates with Shetterly, who found Gore "trying to make himself open to and aware of other people . . . out there talking about issues. And just for my tastes he wasn't going far enough. What I attributed that to was, he was already a politician and seeing well beyond the moment." As his government tutor Richard Neustadt described him, with a measure of sarcasm, young Gore was then the essence of the "wimpy moderate."

Some of Gore's friends believed that the radicals tried to engage him in hopes that recruiting a senator's son would enhance their cause. Kilbreth said that notion never crossed his mind. "Recruiting anybody was useful, but I don't think any of us at the time thought Gore was that interesting. We were much more interested in the people who were activists and intellectuals. Gore was none of those."

THE WAR STORY played out on two levels at Harvard that spring. One was deeply personal: what each man would do when the time came to face the military draft. Among the motley crew, Kapetan figured he would flunk the physical for being too tall. He was nearly six foot ten. Day and Somerby had no idea what they were going to do. Day was thinking about the Peace Corps, Somerby about teaching in the inner city. Tommy Lee Jones, John Tyson, and J. G. Landau had sports injuries that might get them out. None of them seemed worried about how their decision would be viewed by strangers, or how it would be regarded sometime in the future. Only Al Gore was burdened with those concerns. And he was the only one who talked about enlisting.

The other question was how they should express themselves until the moment of decision arrived. Some buried their anxiety in books, sex, drugs. For other students, much of their frustration and anger was being directed at the closest target, the Harvard administration, and especially at its most obvious connection to the military, the Reserve Officers' Training Corps. The hostility toward the ROTC had already forced its instructors to move their weekly drills, held every Monday afternoon at four sharp, from an outdoor field to a large room inside its headquarters on Francis Avenue several blocks north of Harvard Yard. But in February and March, the mood on campus grew more hostile and demands more strident. When the faculty voted to diminish the ROTC by removing its academic credit, even that decision was decried as too little too late, a token gesture that did little to absolve the university's complicity in the war.

During spring break it became an open secret along the student grapevine that some SDS leaders were pushing for bold action against the school, comparable to what their Ivy League counterparts at Columbia had done a year earlier when they had seized an administration building. After the break, something would happen. Professor Neustadt heard it from his son, who was also in the senior class and worked at the campus radio station. Richard Hyland and a few other Dunster radicals issued a warning to Marty Peretz. Do you realize, they said, that this university is about to blow? Peretz stood in the middle, or what he described as "no-man's-land." He had once served as a mentor to many of these angry young men, a behind-the-scenes sponsor of the early SDS. But they had moved the other way while he was turning rightward, a process that began for him with the Six-Day War in 1967, when he had been disturbed by the level of anti-Israeli sentiment on the left. After the McCarthy campaign in 1968, he had continued in the antiwar movement through the fall of 1968, helping to organize the October moratorium rally in Boston. But that was his last. The next big antiwar rally in November, known as the Mobilization, or Mobe, had a more confrontational edge and was too much for him. "I've done my bit," he said to himself, according to his later recollection. "Let someone else end the war."

Now, in the spring of 1969, Peretz was alarmed to see his students turning on the very institution that he thought had lit the political and intellectual spark in so many of them. "I felt how strange it was that universities had become the anointed enemies," he said. Where once he had loved nothing more than to spend hours engaging radical students in debate, enthralled by their facile young minds, he now found their rhetoric tiresome. They, in turn, rejected him as all talk and no action, a dilettante more interested in maintaining his stature at the university than in changing the world. He now felt more comfortable dealing with moderate students like Al Gore. While Gore had not been one of his closest disciples, their friendship deepened that spring, and Gore's suitemates noticed the bearded teacher coming around more often, looking for the senator's son, who shared his discomfort with "this highly fraught radical culture."

At the lunch hour of April 9, Gore came down the hallway toward his suite and announced to his roommates Kapetan and Landau that the inevitable had happened. Some of the SDSers had seized University Hall and were now surrounded by police, who had closed off the Yard. "Our first reaction was, 'Oh, let's go there.' So we did," Kapetan recalled. "We all walked down, Al and J.G. and I. There was electricity in the air. Dunster was about ten blocks away, so walking up there, every person had a different rumor to report. There was a break in the fence where you could sneak in the Yard that someone told us about on the way, along the side that faces the Fogg Museum. And we found that hole and got into the Yard."

The takeover had been carried out by the most confrontational wing of SDS, a group of about fifty students at first, including Kilbreth and several Dunster radicals, who marched in, searched the building room by room for administrators, and kicked them out. "It was totally amateur hour," Kilbreth recalled decades later. "A bunch of kids in there who didn't know where anything was, wandering around saying, 'Get out of here now! We're taking over the building!' " A few deans resisted, and there was some unfortunate pushing and jostling down the stairs as they were forcibly removed. Over the next hour, more students joined the protest, so that by the time Gore and his friends arrived, hundreds were inside and even more were out on the Yard, milling around, talking, arguing, wondering what would happen next.

John Tyson was there, engaged in a heated discussion with black student leaders who expressed dismay that SDS was grabbing the attention. "The white folks stole our thunder!" one lamented.

Peretz came by "to gawk." As he later recalled the moment to the writer Roger Rosenblatt, he stood there thinking that "this was a bad thing" and that "it would be very hard for any teacher, ever again, to get automatic and reflexive respect."

Rosenblatt, then a young English instructor and resident dean at Dunster, was also among the onlookers, having just emerged from a classroom where he had dissected a poem by Wallace Stevens called "Anecdote of the Jar." He was lost in thought about the meaning of the opening stanza:

> I placed a jar in Tennessee,
> And round it was, upon a hill.
> It made the slovenly wilderness
> Surround that hill.

Then he was jolted into the present tense by the chaos in front of him: the hubbub of the crowd, the stern faces of the cops, shouts of "Pig! Pig!," the red and black SDS banners, the Beatles song "Revolution" "wafting out" of a freshman dorm room.

As Gore and his pals observed the scene, Kapetan realized that he knew one of the police officers outside, an old Irish cop he had met four years earlier when he worked on a freshman dorm cleaning crew. Now the officer looked saddened by this "unthinkable" turn of events, Kapetan thought. "He obviously had deep feelings about the place." Would he end up struggling with some of the students he had once known? The concern was not really with these campus police, who were familiar to the students, but there were rumblings that a larger squadron of state police was on the way.

Gore agreed with Peretz that the protesters had picked the wrong target. The university was a "convenient" scapegoat, he said, but not the source of the problem. He had sympathy for the cause, "but not the tactics." He soon grew tired of the scene, told his roommates that he had an appointment, and headed back to Dunster House before night-fall. Kapetan and Landau decided to stay with a group of sympathizers who would spend the night on the steps of each entrance to University Hall, hoping to serve as a protective buffer between police and the oc-cupying students. They called themselves the "hostage liberals," not all that keen about the SDS takeover but hoping that the administra-tion would not react too harshly. The mood outside alternated be-tween tension and giddiness. At one point Robert Edgar, a suitemate of Jamie Kilbreth at Dunster, but more theatrical than political, stopped by with members of his finals club. They were carrying a case of cham-pagne, which they wanted to deliver inside.

Dunster men were everywhere inside University Hall. Kilbreth had been there from the beginning. Robert Shetterly joined in, believ-ing "it was important to take this kind of step because the university was refusing to take any positions." But he was a peaceful resister and did not participate in the ouster of the deans. Terrence McNally came along later and met up with a group of the house's underclassmen. Richard Hyland entered the building at midday and was asked to chair a strategy session because he was not aligned with any of the three con-tending factions inside. He took off his shoes, climbed on a table, and began an endless discussion about how to collect trash, get food, keep the perimeter secure, and deal with the press. "People began asking me questions as though I had run a building occupation before," Hyland said later. It was something new for all of them.

Busloads of police reinforcements arrived in the middle of the night, a large contingent of Cambridge cops and state troopers. "I re-member those powder blue shirts and white crash helmets and dark pants, and they were in formation, waiting, waiting, waiting, and it almost seemed to validate what we planned to do," said Kapetan, who had spent the night on the steps. Student runners were sent off to the houses to pull fire alarms and spread the word: The cops were ready to move in. There was to be no negotiating. President Pusey, acting on the advice of his counsel, Archibald Cox, had chosen that the surest course of action was to quell the uprising immediately with absolute force. At a silent signal, the police marched forward to clear the building, their boots clicking in the darkness as they strode directly toward the students on the steps, who were singing "We shall not be moved." As Kapetan confessed later, "never was a more inappropriate song ever sung—because we moved. We broke before them like water before the plow of an icebreaker. We scattered from those steps and that was that."

Many of the people inside had been asleep. Organizers moved through the drowsy crowd: *Get up, the cops are coming!* The two main doors were chained shut. There was a debate over what to do: flee or resist, and if resist, how? "We decided to stay nonviolent, more or less," Kilbreth recalled. They gathered in two main halls on the first floor, which was up the stairs and about twelve feet above the ground. It was "eerie to the point of being surreal. And frightening," said Shetterly. "Just at dawn. A kind of steely blue color in the air. Everybody packed against each other in a solid block, all linked arms, ready for the charge."

Student photographers were inside the building, and one took a picture of a row of students, arm-in-arm, the instant before the confrontation. Terrence McNally looked at that picture decades later and saw himself "dead center in the photo with long hair tied back and scared shitless." The police "came with battering rams to the door on my side, but they couldn't get the chains to break, so they went to the other door," McNally recalled. "I will never forget turning and looking at them as they came in. I expected it to be 'Okay, that's it, kids, march out.' They didn't say anything. They opened the doors and started swinging. Billy clubs on heads. You could hear it." McNally escaped by jumping out a window. Kilbreth and Hyland were clubbed and arrested, among 250 students hauled off in paddy wagons.

The riot spilled into the Yard, where hundreds more students had gathered to watch the debacle. When a policeman moved toward Jonathan Ritvo, he scooted into Thayer South, which had been his freshman dorm four years earlier. "Cops came running into the entry swinging batons and people ran upstairs where freshmen were letting people into their rooms, closing the doors and locking them," Ritvo recalled. Looking out a window of Thayer, Ritvo could see his classmates being taken away in handcuffs and a student marching in front of a stiff line of officers, taunting them with his goosestep. Mike Kapetan saw a policeman clubbing a young woman on the sidewalk and responded instinctively. "I grabbed the gentleman and threw him to the ground," Gore's lanky roommate said. "The next thing I remember is being clubbed like a watermelon on both sides of my head. I remember falling, not hitting the ground. A couple of guys I knew were carrying me by the arms, dragging me out of the way. I was dazed and smiling. And a young woman emerged from the darkness and slapped me across the face and said this is not funny. She thought I was not taking things in the proper spirit. The guys who were helping me explained and she apologized profusely. J. G. Landau found me—we had been split up—and he had some experience with being knocked woozy in athletics, so he asked me, 'How many fingers? What day of the week is it?' "

THAT CHAOTIC MORNING of April 10, known thereafter as the "bust," for all practical purposes ended the Harvard school days of Al Gore and the seniors in the class of 1969. If the tactics of the SDS turned off many students, the response of the university and the brute force of the Cambridge police disturbed them more. "I had been living in a wonderful fool's paradise," said Robert Edgar of Dunster House, reflecting a commonly held view. "It was suddenly shattered by Mr. Pusey's decision to invade," he added. "It was very disheartening."

The cause became at once more urgent and diffuse. The students did what came naturally to them during that era, they called a strike. There were meetings day and night, teach-ins, alternative classes. The campus was flooded with banners, broadsides, posters, buttons, armbands. The two houses with the most radical students, Adams and Dunster, became round-the-clock organizing centers for an array of ad hoc steering committees. At the student production of *Mother Courage,* members of the cast wore different-colored armbands representing various new nonnegotiable demands. The *Harvard Crimson* put out a strike paper with articles on strike literature, strike music, strike rhetoric, strike graphics, even strike games (a column written by future *New York Times*man Frank Rich detailed three types of games: political, escapist, and liberation).

Joe McGrath sat in the balcony at Memorial Hall that afternoon and listened to speaker after speaker rail against the military and the ROTC. McGrath was an ROTC student, wearing his green uniform, and after an hour of denunciations he rose and asked to speak, but his request was muffled in a chorus of boos and hisses. He got up to leave, and looked over at the government professor, Richard Neustadt, sitting nearby. Neustadt shook his head, McGrath recalled, and said, "This is a sad day for the university." McGrath was not the only one drummed into silence. Marty Peretz, rising to address a gathering of protesters at Memorial Church, got no further than a collegial "Brothers and sisters . . ." when he was hooted down by students who no longer considered him a brother.

The exhilaration of a common purpose began to fade after a few days, but not before one last mass meeting, a campus-wide plebiscite at the stadium that filled the seats from the end zone out to the thirty-yard line with undergrads, law students, medical students in their white jackets, and some faculty members. Al Gore and Tommy Lee Jones and Mike Kapetan and the whole motley crew walked over to the stadium together. Jones was the most conservative of the friends, but even he was distraught by the university's police action. Gore also thought both sides had acted foolishly. He said it was another episode that deepened his disillusionment with the political process. The mass gathering at the stadium seemed more encouraging to them than anything that preceded it. Kapetan was struck by a "kind of reasonableness about it—ten thousand people sitting in one place conducting business." Neustadt, who observed the gathering from a perch high atop the stadium, noticed that rather than strident radical voices, "the wimpy moderates had pretty firm control by then. The general tone was: How could the president have so traduced our wonderful university?" From the distance of decades, as passions fade, odd things linger in memory. What Gore's Dunster House classmate Peter Keiser remembers most about the mass meeting that sunny April day was the sight of two dogs scampering across the stadium grass and the male dog jumping on the female and "the whole place starting to cheer as the dogs go at it."

The bust and the strike became part of the lore of Harvard. At the school archive, there is more material documenting the events of that year than any other year in Harvard history. There are files of photographs of the takeover of University Hall, films of damage done to the building, audiocassettes of the student discussion on ROTC the night before, five boxes full of clippings about the "Crisis Spring," and more boxes with broadsides, posters, and paraphernalia. One box was given to the university by counsel Archibald Cox. Inside what is known as the Cox box are two pieces of revolutionary debris taken from the occupied building—a North Vietnamese flag and a jockstrap.

It was within that environment that Al Gore struggled with the most difficult questions of his young life. What should he do about his military obligations after graduation? Should he enlist? Should he wait to get drafted? Should he try to avoid service altogether through a medical deferment? Should he apply for an ROTC graduate program or officer candidate school?

One day that spring, as he was walking along a side street between Dunster and Leverett houses, Gore came across Phil Rosenbaum, another senior. Their lives had followed the same academic path since childhood, first St. Albans and then Harvard, though they had never been close friends. Rosenbaum spent his college years seeking new experiences outside the certitudes of his prep school days, and while he felt no hostility toward Gore, he had always thought of him as too preppy and predictable. But now, in this chance encounter, Rosenbaum suddenly felt a deep kinship with Gore, who for once seemed as uncertain about life as he was. Rosenbaum said he had not decided what to do about the draft, and Gore seemed equally unsure. "It was interesting to me that he was at loose ends, too," Rosenbaum recalled. That "was different for Al. He wasn't usually like that. . . . I did feel that kinship which I don't remember any other time. He made it clear that he didn't know what he was going to do. There was a quality of bewilderment."

CHAPTER SIX

THE OBLIGATION

IT WAS A MESS, that final stretch of college days in the spring of 1969, with the building occupation and the police charge and the student strike, and now even the beloved Dunster House dining hall was closed for repairs, forcing the motley crew to cross the river to eat with the grinds at the Harvard Business School cafeteria. But amid all the confusion there was for Al Gore at least one moment of clarity. He was walking back from dinner with his girlfriend, they paused halfway across Weeks Memorial Bridge, and with the Charles flowing below them, a warm breeze gracing the early May evening, he reached into his pocket, pulled out a ring, and made a decidedly old-fashioned proposition. Tipper Aitcheson said yes, she would marry him, the wedding date put off until she graduated from Boston University a year later.

Nothing else about Gore's future seemed so easy, especially not the question of how he should deal with the draft. He and Tipper talked about it nearly every time they were together. His approach was reasoned, methodical, as though he were mulling over a logic problem, all variables and rational constructs. It worried her sometimes that he was taking too much into account, and she saw it as her job to bring the issue back to what was best for the two of them, not what he felt he should do to please his father or his mother or his classmates at Harvard or the boys his age back in Tennessee.

"There was a huge amount of pressure on him, and I was trying to get him to turn to the focus of *you*," Tipper Gore said later. "What do *you* really think and how are *you* going to feel if *you* do this? I tried to turn it to that, while he might have had these other constructs working in his logical mind. It is you and I that are planning on being together and living with the aftermath of that decision. How am I going to feel if you go and get killed? Or go and get maimed? How are you going to feel if you don't do it?"

It was not a predetermined decision, she felt. "There was a lot of agonizing and there definitely was a choice." A small number of his classmates, perhaps a dozen at most, ended up going to Vietnam. But most of his peers at Harvard were looking for a way out, and finding one. Some took refuge in the National Guard or the reserves, options that might save them from Vietnam. A few resisted or became conscientious objectors or left for Canada. One or two became dining hall gluttons in hopes of appearing too obese to qualify, or alternatively starved themselves to be too thin. Students with no desire to be doctors applied for medical school to secure that rare graduate school deferment. Physical and psychological deferments were the norm, available even to those perfectly fit in body and soul. At a cocktail party in Cambridge, Richard Neustadt heard "a bunch of doctors talking about the grounds on which they were handing out" letters for 4-Fs. "I was shocked," Gore's usually imperturbable government mentor recalled.

Many of his college and prep school friends eventually found their way out with athletic injuries. Mead Miller, his childhood pal, would be saved from the draft with Tipper's unwitting help. He had injured his back during his St. Albans days when he and Tipper had gone out for a Sunday ride and he lost control of her car and rolled and flipped it, leaving Tipper with whiplash and Miller with a back brace and a way to flunk the physical in Baltimore. Gore could have pursued a physical deferment himself. "He talked to me about that a little bit," said Don Gilligan. "I remember Al had what at the time were a couple of legitimate physical deferments." Those included a bad knee that he had injured playing football at St. Albans—not debilitating but real enough that he could have found a doctor to say it was. But as he considered every option in its moral and practical dimensions, that one flunked on both counts.

His dilemma was framed by a contradiction. He strongly opposed the war, wanted it over, and did not want to help perpetuate it, yet for several personal and political reasons he felt an obligation to serve. To borrow a phrase made famous by his future colleague in the White

House, Gore brooded about his situation much the way Bill Clinton did when seeking to maintain his "political viability" at an early age. A physical deferment satisfied neither of his conflicting ideological and political impulses. With that eliminated, what else? "It was a real conundrum for me," Gore said later. "Amplified by the feeling I had that the policy was wrong, which was amplified by all of my friends at college who felt the same way. Of course, Cambridge was a hotbed of opposition to the war policy."

Go to Canada? His mother, Pauline, brought up that notion in conversations with friends and relatives. "I heard Aunt Pauline say with my own ears that she told Al that if he wanted to get to Canada she would help him get there," said Gayle Byrne, a cousin who grew up in Lebanon, Tennessee, not far from the Gore farm in Carthage. While acknowledging that his mother talked to others about helping him if he wanted to go to Canada, Gore insisted that it was never an option and that his mother's words have been misinterpreted to imply that he seriously considered leaving the country. "She said it as a way of underscoring her support for whatever I did," Gore said. "What I deny is that there ever was a conversation between me and her in which I said I'm thinking about going to Canada. It was a figure of speech for her. . . . I never considered going to Canada." He had "no disrespect for those who made that decision," Gore said. "I don't know what burdens they carried. I don't know what they went through. But for me, phew! God, no. Even if I had felt driven to such extremes, there were other ways to accomplish that."

Other ways: Apply for conscientious objector status? Warren Steel, one of Gore's close friends at Dunster House, who had graduated a year ahead of him, was now a CO working with the elderly at an Episcopal church in the inner-city Roxbury section of Boston. He and Gore occasionally talked about pacifism and war and obligations, and respected each other's opinions, but it was clear to the musician from Schenectady that he and the government major from Washington were following "very different paths" and that Gore had to deal with considerations that Steel did not. Don Gilligan, whose life more closely paralleled Gore's, was also strongly opposed to the war and considered becoming a CO during that period. He dropped the idea after being forced to confront the ramifications for his father, who was running for governor of Ohio. Jack Gilligan was a decorated Navy veteran of World War II, but having a conscientious objector son would cost him votes—or so thought one of his top campaign aides, who threatened to quit if that happened. "So my big thing was not to file a CO," Don Gilligan said. "It could have been an issue in Dad's campaign."

Gore faced the same situation. His father was running for reelection to the U.S. Senate in 1970, and Al realized that whatever choice he made would emerge as a subtheme in that contest, which promised to be the most difficult of Albert Gore's career in any case. Since winning a third term in 1964, the senator had become increasingly outspoken: firmly backing civil rights and voting rights bills, opposing the nomination of conservative southern judges G. Harrold Carswell and Clement F. Haynsworth to the Supreme Court, and above all emerging as a leading opponent of U.S. involvement in Vietnam—all unpopular positions in Tennessee, especially that last one in the pro-military Volunteer State.

Nothing seemed more complicated than sorting out the father-son issues. How could the son decide what was best for himself without thinking about what most helped his dad? His roommates considered that question at the core of Gore's dilemma. Even while his mother might say that she would follow him to Canada, they sensed, through their conversations with Gore, that her unspoken message was the opposite. "His mother might say something like, 'Everyone needs to support the father,' " remembered John Tyson. "It was a way of telling him without telling him." Tipper remembered Al constantly asking, "How is this going to affect my dad? How is this going to affect the race?" For nearly two years, he had told friends that he was pessimistic about his father's political future, believing that the senator "almost certainly was going to get beat anyway"—no matter what he did. If he chose to avoid military service, it undoubtedly would further diminish his father's chances, he thought, but even if he decided to enlist in the Army it might not help. There were brief discussions inside the family as far back as Christmas 1968 about the senator stepping down and not seeking reelection, bowing to the realization that his positions had alienated many Tennessee voters, but quitting went against Albert's instincts as much as Al running to Canada did, and the idea was summarily dismissed.

Whenever he considered the consequences for his father, it seemed apparent to Gore that the only option with any benefit was for him to enlist. His logic was taking him to what he later called "a reasoned conclusion" that "the choice that had the most integrity for me personally was to go. And if I was going to look at my decision through the lens of politics and the morality of the war policy, then ironically, because my father was a leading opponent of the war, my decision to go had integrity even within the context of my personal opposition to the war. The most effective thing I could do—and nothing I did would be very meaningful or effective; I didn't have an overblown illusion of it— but insofar as the choice mattered, the most effective way to express my opposition to the war was to go, and help my father."

His father's fate was not the only factor to be considered in that political context. There was his own future to think of as well. Gore then vacillated dramatically on the subject, sometimes expressing deep interest in politics and arguing in defense of the American system, other times uttering declarations of disillusionment and promising never to follow in his old man's footsteps. Most of his friends ignored his disavowals, assuming that he was destined for politics. That assessment was shared by his government adviser, Richard Neustadt, another person to whom he now turned for advice.

Gore met with Neustadt several times that spring, at the little yellow Institute of Politics house on Mount Auburn Street, at the professor's home on Traill Street, and at his cottage on Cape Cod, and in each meeting the professor helped him "think through" the meaning of the choices and "sort out the peer pressure one felt in Cambridge not to go from the political overlay that was unavoidably a part of it." While Gore said that Neustadt "didn't push me," Neustadt's recollection is that he gave young Gore the same advice that he offered his own son, who was also graduating from Harvard that year.

"If you want to be part of the country twenty-five years from now, if you want any future in politics, you've got to serve," is how Neustadt remembered presenting the argument. "That certainly was my view. It was a World War II perspective that didn't prove to be exactly right. But I felt that you've got to be part of the hard experiences of your generation, and mustn't duck this one."

Gore heard the same advice from his uncle Whit LaFon, a lawyer back in west Tennessee and former state commander of the American Legion. LaFon told him that "there wasn't any question . . . if they called you up to do it, you did it." That was the family tradition passed along to young Al, not just from Gore Senior, who took a temporary leave from Congress to serve in World War II. "See, he had three uncles," LaFon recalled. "My oldest brother, he was in the Seabees, five years in the Pacific. My younger brother was in the Army, he was in Europe. His father's brother . . . was a victim of World War I. He was gassed at Argonne. See, this is the kind of thing that would mark you even thinking about it."

IN A SMALL TOWN like Carthage, the cost of war is painfully easy to comprehend. It is etched into a large granite stone memorial that stands in front of the Smith County Courthouse, listing the county's fallen: 138 from the Civil War, one from the Spanish-American War, twenty-four from World War I, fifty-four from World War II, and eight from Vietnam: Joe Taylor, James H. Stilz, Glenn Pope, Joe L. Midgett, James Stallings, Jackie Underwood, R. Shannon Wills, and James E. Bush.

Most of the young men of Smith County entered the military the same way. They were called up by the local draft board run by Elizabeth Beasley on the bottom floor of the post office. In the morning darkness, they boarded a Trailways bus on Main Street, were handed a tuna fish sandwich and a Coca-Cola, and were sent off to the induction center in Nashville. Not all of them wanted to go. Phil Sloan had dropped out of college and was working at a grocery in Lebanon when he got the word from his little sister. "I got some news to tell you; three things," she said. "I'll start with the lightest one first. Your car burned up. Your little sister is sick. And Uncle Sam wants you." Sloan slumped against the wall of his garage apartment "and I sat there for four hours, except for getting up and going to the bathroom and drinking beer." He was not eager to join the military, but considered it his obligation. "It wasn't like you didn't want to go enough that you'd go to Canada, that wasn't considered," he said later. So he quit his job and went to basic training at Fort Campbell, Kentucky, where another local boy, Rooker Silcox Jr., was already there, running the mess hall. When Sloan complained about the spare servings of food one day, Sergeant Silcox slapped a heaping pile of mashed potatoes on his plate and stood over him until he had eaten it all. Soon enough Private Sloan was in Vietnam eating C-rations.

Stephen Claywell, who lived in Defeated and worked at a printing company in Nashville, was drafted the same month as Sloan. "Just about everybody around here was in," he said, except for "the stupid and the rich." Another Carthage-area boy, Jack Martin, said "they had to pull the splinters out from under my fingernails from where I was hanging onto the porch" at his family's grocery when he got the news of being drafted. His father, a World War II veteran, said to him, "If I could go in your place, I would." But everyone in Jack's family knew what his responsibility was, "just like I knew it." There were ways he might have gotten out, he said:

"I coulda gotten married.

"Gone to college.

"Had a child.

"Left the country.

"But you don't do that.

"You just don't do that. Period."

One of the names in Mrs. Beasley's registration book in 1969 was Albert Gore Jr. He might live most of the time in Washington or Cambridge, but Carthage was always listed as the family's hometown, and it is where he registered for the draft. He still subscribed to the *Carthage Courier*, where the military comings and goings of the local boys were front-page news. Thomas Bush was on leave. Garry Carter was in Vietnam. Sergeant Kenneth Bennett was awarded the Silver Star. Boatswain's Mate Walter G. Pope died leading a Navy SEAL team in the Mekong Delta. Jimmy Trainham got hit by shrapnel in his legs and eyes serving with the 1st Cavalry near the Perfume River. James Donald Stallings's jeep hit a mine and blew his body apart. Jackie Underwood came home to Pleasant Shade in a casket. Phil Sloan's mother attended the funeral. In a letter to her son in Vietnam she described how the bugler played taps and "it echoed all over the little old town that sets in a small valley."

In Cambridge, reassured by the prevailing sense that the war was evil and had to be stopped and that any means of avoiding it was acceptable, Gore allowed himself to consider other options. But it was impossible, he said later, for him to think of Carthage and not come back to the conclusion that he had to go. "The meaning of a decision to say, 'I'm going to get out of this by hook or crook,' " Gore said, "is very different in Carthage and in the eyes of the guys that I knew there, than it was among my peer group in Cambridge." And by registering in Carthage instead of Washington, he could not think of the process as the random doings of a faceless bureaucracy.

In the list of draft-eligible young men in Mrs. Beasley's registration books at the Selective Service office in Carthage, he said, "there wasn't a huge big number of people, few of whom I knew. There was a very small number of people, all of whom I knew. And the take each month was three, four, two, three out of four, five, three, four. And what was common in Boston and Washington was unheard of out in Carthage. Finding a way out. And there were lots of ways out. But not in Carthage."

The prospect of another Jackie Underwood being buried in his place, the political demands of his father's reelection campaign—even if he was taking Tipper's advice and turning the question around to *you, what do you think is best for you?*, he knew now, a few weeks before his graduation, that the answer was that he had to go into the Army and that he would have to go in as a private. As he told Neustadt during one of their conversations, he felt he "had to do what his father's constituents had to do."

There were other options if he wanted them. His cousin Gayle Byrne was in graduate school in Alabama. Her then husband, who was working in the state legislature, knew a top officer in the Alabama National Guard and played trombone in the Guard's band. According to Byrne, her husband inquired of the top guardsman, "This is Senator Gore's son, it's my wife's cousin, would you have a spot for him in the Alabama National Guard? He is just coming out of college." They had not discussed the plan with Al or his parents before they pursued it. Byrne said she was "thinking along the lines of, this would be wonderful, this would provide him with a way to avoid the draft and avoid going to Vietnam." The Alabama National Guard officer called back and said yes, they did have a spot for Al Gore. Byrne was ecstatic. Her husband thought he was "going to be a hero" and hailed by the family as "a wonderful guy" for saving young Al from Vietnam. "We then went straight to the telephone and called Al and said, 'We've secured a spot for you in the Alabama National Guard!' " Byrne recalled. "I don't remember if he thought about it for fifteen seconds or a minute and a half; it was no more than two minutes. He said, 'I appreciate all that you've done for me, and I know that this has been a lot of work for you, but I believe what I'm going to do is enlist.' "

The response floored them. Byrne's husband said he "almost felt little for having offered it to him. Like this guy is operating on a higher plane, and I feel bad that I even suggested it to him."

The question was settled, for the most part, but until the day Gore entered the Army there were constant tugs of doubt, he said later. "Somebody that age, with a decision like that, it's a little different from

a Cabinet officer or a president getting a typed memo listing the options with little boxes to check off and as soon as you check off the box
then all the different bureaucracies move into play. It's more like you
know, 'I think I'm going to do that. And the next day . . . aaahhhheer-
rrrrnnnn. Yeah? I think I'm going to do that! Uhhhhunnnnrrrrh . . . '
The process I'm trying to describe is one where you come to a tentative
conclusion and you double-check your feelings and where your heart
is and second-guess and then come back to it."

THERE WAS A SENSE of incompleteness to their final day at
Harvard, June 12, 1969. A bright summery sun shone down on the
Yard, where 1,115 seniors were to receive their degrees. Some of Al
Gore's motley crew were not even there. Tommy Lee Jones had gone
back to New York for an acting gig. Bart Day left early for Washington,
preparing for the Peace Corps, "disaffected" by the tumult of the final
months and the university's handling of it. Sixteen seniors, including
Jamie Kilbreth, were not allowed to attend, having been suspended
from school for their part in the University Hall takeover, though Kilbreth came anyway, slipped in by a Dunster roommate who was first
marshal for the class.

Albert and Pauline Gore were there, taking a suite at a Cambridge hotel, where they would hold a reception afterward for Al and
his friends, including Richard Neustadt and Marty Peretz, the two
men they believed saved young Al from Chaucer. Mike Kapetan's
mother and father, a school janitor in Wayne, Michigan, came as well,
and Mrs. Kapetan and Mrs. Gore delved into a long conversation
about the trials and tribulations of raising two young sons who had
made it this far, cum laude graduates of Harvard.

The commencement ceremony was a 1960s period piece, cen-
turies-old college pomp jarringly interrupted by the passions of the day.
A brilliant law student lured any law-and-order parents in the crowd
into a trap, reciting a passage lamenting the unrest and mindless anar-
chy of the students and the need for order—and then saying it was a
quote from Adolf Hitler. Whatever good cheer the red-armband-
wearing students got from that speech quickly dissolved in embarrassment when a sloppily dressed Students for a Democratic Society orator
took the stage, smoking and pacing and cursing, deriding Harvard administrators by their last names. As Don Gilligan listened to "this totally incoherent rant" from one of his classmates, he looked around

and watched many of his peers "try to discreetly slip their armbands off. I was one of those."

At an agreed-upon moment, just when President Pusey delivered his time-honored welcoming of the graduates to "the company of educated men," hundreds of seniors rose from their folding chairs, raised their fists in defiance, and walked out. John Tyson chose a different moment to make his exit—when the school gave an honorary degree to David Rockefeller, whose bank did business with South Africa. "I walked out in the style of the ghetto, with a swagger, on purpose, because of the symbolism, as an athlete," Tyson recalled. "I was basically saying, 'Harvard, you haven't taken out of me my people, even though you might see this as the lowest part of my people, the swagger, I know how to swagger!' " So swagger he did, right on down to Dunster House, where he picked up his degree, along with all of his housemates who had walked out earlier. Gore stayed in his seat for the entire ceremony, with his proud parents and Tipper watching, and then escorted them down to Dunster House. His friends always thought he was somehow different from the rest. He seemed to know where he was supposed to go.

CHAPTER SEVEN

PRIVATE GORE

THERE WAS A CURB, a kiss, and he was gone. He said goodbye to his fiancée, Tipper Aitcheson, slipped behind the wheel of his red and white Camaro, and drove south from Boston. It was August 1969, the month of Woodstock, the seminal rock festival that would embody the live-for-the-moment mood of his generation. Many of his Harvard classmates were bound for the farm in New York state; it was in fact a crew of former Dunster House techies who ran the Woodstock lights. But Al Gore had another idea and destination in mind. He was off to join the Army.

Gore could have enlisted in Boston or Cambridge, where he had just graduated cum laude from Harvard. He could have returned to Tennessee and signed up at his local draft board in Carthage, where he had first registered and where his parents had a farm overlooking the Caney Fork. Or he might have walked into a recruiting station in Washington, where he had attended prep school and where Albert and Pauline Gore, the U.S. senator and his wife, lived most months of each year. All logical, but none his choice. He went to Newark instead. Newark was a city where he had never lived and one that he barely knew, beyond what he had seen while speeding along the New Jersey Turnpike on the way to and from college, or on those few occasions when he and his Harvard pal John Tyson, from nearby Montclair, slipped down for a Portuguese meal. It was in part for those reasons that the location appealed to Gore. He believed that he had "a better chance of getting treated as myself" there. It seemed less likely that anyone in Newark would recognize him as the son of a liberal senator whose opposition to the war was making his reelection chances increasingly uncertain in conservative Tennessee.

Tyson was the only soul he knew in greater Newark, and when Gore reached town the two met at a downtown diner and talked for several hours about what they wanted to do with the next chapters of their lives. Gore told Tyson, whose football-wrenched knee had kept him from the draft, that he was signing up. He was doing so despite his misgivings about Vietnam. He still hoped to stay away from the war itself, and had in fact reassured Tipper several times that the Army was unlikely to send him there. Germany, maybe, but not Vietnam. "Are you sure you want to do this?" Tyson remembered asking Gore. "Yeah," came the simple reply. Their final discussion at the diner, Tyson said later, was "the culmination of touching all the points on the compass. I was the last one he touched, and then he went off. He jumped into the pool."

That moment in Newark marked one of the bleakest periods of Gore's young life. His faith in government and the American political system would be shaken as never before, but beyond that he faced a dilemma of a personal and ironic nature. Since his prep school days at St. Albans, his life had been inextricably bound to his father's. They pushed and pulled each other in ways that were often rewarding, sometimes frustrating, but the result always seemed to have them rising together. The father constantly pushed his son to keep learning lessons and occasionally pulled him back onto the track of public life. The son, in return, pushed his father to hold firmly to his progressive beliefs. They had several arguments in 1964, when Gore Senior opposed that year's federal Civil Rights Act, disappointing his son, and after that vote, which the senator called "the biggest mistake" of his career, he listened more attentively to young Al's advice. Six years of bold outspokenness made Gore Senior a folk hero among liberals and antiwar activists, but also a marked man back home.

Push and pull: The son had no choice but to go into the military to try to save his father from electoral defeat, even though he hated the war and suspected that his act would prove futile, which it did. On election day 1970, fifteen months after Al Gore's trip to Newark to enlist, his father's long political career came to an end with a bitter defeat to Republican Bill Brock, who portrayed Gore as an out-of-touch liberal opposed to God, family, and the Tennessee way. It was a defeat that taught the younger Gore an unforgettable lesson, one that he would follow six years later: that he should never venture too far from the center or from his constituents. But for now, it only led to this: Gore Senior departing from Washington, depressed, without saying goodbye to some of his closest friends, at about the same time that his son was shipped off to Vietnam.

SO MUCH FOR the incognito strategy: Gore was recognized the moment he announced his name at the recruiting station in Newark. "It was pretty much known that his daddy was a senator," said Sergeant Dess Stokes, the station commander. Normally one of five assistants would handle the papers for a new recruit, but in this case, because of the political connection, they handed him over to Stokes after the initial processing. And this was a good catch for an Army recruiter in an inner city. Gore had a degree in government from Harvard and aced his physical, except for eyesight. He signed up for two years, taking a preliminary aptitude test at the induction center next door. The examiner told Stokes that Gore "just about maxed everything."

By Gore's account, his military processing was left totally to chance, but there appears to have been some method to it. Before his trip to Newark, as he considered his options within the military, he had talked frequently with an older friend, an Army veteran he had known since his senior year at St. Albans. "He kept coming back . . . being a reporter," this friend said recently, asking not to be identified by name. A Harvard friend got the same message, saying that Gore told him he "signed up" to be a journalist when he enlisted. Even Gore's decision to enlist in Newark might have been influenced by his desire to be an Army reporter. His older friend said that he told Gore that he could maximize his chances of getting a reporting job by enlisting at a station near a large training center, such as Fort Dix in New Jersey, where there was a larger selection of job assignments. Army historians dismiss that notion as "urban myth."

Gore maintains that he did not go into his Army induction "with a clear idea" of what he wanted to do. "It was a surprise to me, a pleasant surprise, that the lieutenant who was there said at the end of the interview, 'I think you'd make a good journalist.' . . . I thought it was a pure gamble as to what I would get." Uncertain, perhaps, but not such a gamble, according to the recruiting officer, Stokes, who said, "I told him with his qualifications there would be more than an even chance that he would get" his desired job. According to Army historians, the fact that Gore enlisted, avoiding the vagaries of the draft, increased the likelihood that he would get the job he wanted. In practice, they said, the military favored those who joined voluntarily.

Whatever the lieutenant at the Newark induction center told Gore, he received his job assignment not there but during basic training at Fort Dix. His military occupational specialty was 71Q10—a journalist. How did he get that designation? According to his military file, he told a superior during the processing that he had worked as a "newspaper trainee" for the *New York Times* one summer. He had been a copy boy there, not a reporting intern, between his sophomore and junior years at Harvard. Apparently his superiors at Fort Dix were impressed enough to recommend him as a reporter trainee at Fort Rucker in Alabama, and allow him to take the relatively uncommon route to get there, skipping weeks of advanced training at Fort Benjamin Harrison in Indiana and moving directly from basic training to on-the-job training.

Before leaving for Alabama, Gore spent eight weeks in basic training at Fort Dix. He received "expert" scores in weapons training for the M-14, grenade, and M-16, and completed courses on the Geneva Convention, the code of conduct, and chemical and biological weapons. As he was about to board an armored personnel carrier one day, he encountered a friend from his class at Harvard, Paul Zofnass. Gore was surprised to see him. "Zofnass?"

"Al, gee, what are you doing here?"

Each was taken aback by the sight of the other in Army fatigues with shorn head and helmet.

"If there's one person in our class who probably could have gotten out of the war, it would have been you!" Zofnass blurted out to his friend.

"Yeah, I know," Zofnass recalled Gore telling him. "But I spent a lot of time talking to my dad about it, and we think it's an important thing for me to do." It was important "politically," Gore told Zofnass. "So I enlisted." According to Zofnass's recollection, Gore also told him that it was "important" that he go to Vietnam. Not just because it was "the most politic and appropriate thing to do" as an aspiring public servant, Zofnass remembered Gore telling him, but because it was the right thing to do. "If the country was at war, you may be against it or for it, but it was duty to your country"—that was the message Zofnass took away from the conversation. The exchange was brief but revealing.

Zofnass was impressed by his classmate's foresight—"pretty mature for a kid of twenty-one." It also reflected the more calculating side of Gore, the combination of principle and expediency that guides him, and finally how bound he was then and always to his parents, despite his assertion that they refrained from giving him direct advice on his military decision.

The most difficult part of this new life for Private Gore might not have been adjusting to the rigors of basic training at Fort Dix, but rather dealing with the way people reacted to him when he returned to Boston in uniform to visit Tipper. "It was like a Ralph Ellison–type experience," he later recalled. "It shocked me how big a difference it made to walk down the sidewalk with short hair and a uniform, compared to what it was like walking down the sidewalk a few months earlier, with longer hair and blue jeans. It was a real surprise, I guess. It was a real surprise . . . the extent to which you could tell, the many different ways that people could show their disapproval, their anger, their hostility."

AT THE END OF OCTOBER, Gore reported to Fort Rucker, a sprawling Army post deep in the wire grass of southeastern Alabama. The fort housed the largest helicopter training facility in the country as part of a virtual city, occupied by more than 21,000 people, with movie theaters, restaurants, officers clubs, and post exchanges. It also put out a paper known as the *Army Flier*, which was edited by civilian and military journalists. That is where Gore went to work. One of his editors there was Roy Mays, who had been drafted in 1968 while working for the *St. Petersburg Times*. When Mays first got there, he later recalled, the paper was filled "with a lot of . . . just crap stuff" like officers' wives' teas and officer graduation ceremonies. One note of reality, bitter but unavoidable, crept into the paper every issue. Death notices from Vietnam came in an endless stream, and some of the names were those of pilots who had trained at Fort Rucker.

Late in September 1970, General William C. Westmoreland, the Army chief of staff, appeared at Fort Rucker, and Gore was assigned to cover his visit. The day he arrived, Westmoreland went on a training exercise. As he was about to climb into a helicopter, he noticed the name tag on the reporter's uniform. "Gore," he said. "Are you any relation to the senator from Tennessee?" "Yes, sir," the private replied.

A few days later, Gore and Bob Delabar, his photographer colleague, went to a small airstrip to cover Westmoreland's departure.

Delabar neared the plane to take pictures. Gore, not intending to interview the general, hung back to observe the proceedings. The officers in charge of the flight school lined up on the tarmac. Westmoreland glanced at Gore, recognized him from their earlier meeting, and walked over to him. They exchanged greetings, and the general suddenly turned the conversation toward the topic of the war.

Why were so many young people against the war? he wanted to know. "I gave him my candid opinion, that I thought the war was a huge mistake," Gore said. Why? Westmoreland asked. The general challenged his answers, Gore recalled, and gave his own point of view. While he could not remember Westmoreland's exact words, the essence of the general's inquiry was "Why, when so many other people are expressing their opposition to the war by not serving, why are you serving?" It meant a great deal to Gore, he said later, that a four-star general would accord a buck private that kind of attention—"to have my opinions listened to with that kind of respect." There was no love lost between the general and Gore's father, the antiwar senator, opponents in the fight for public opinion on Vietnam. But Westmoreland gave Gore "a very positive feeling" about the fact that despite the father's views the son was serving in the Army.

Despite his views on the war, Gore was not a rebel at Fort Rucker. The dutiful son was now for the most part the dutiful soldier. He won a "special troops" soldier-of-the-month award, which came with a $25 savings bond, then the more exclusive post soldier-of-the-month award, with double the prize money. The winners were chosen for their knowledge of military subjects, leadership qualities, outstanding military bearing, and courtesy. He was also selected at least three times as "supernumerary of the guard mount"—which meant having the sharpest-looking uniform and the shiniest boots. The reward for that was being excused from guard duty. Nor was Gore all starch and spit-shined shoes. During that fall and winter, he bunked at Fort Rucker with seven other soldiers, to whom he was incessantly peddling books from his substantial library. He recommended that Gus Stanisic, his friend and fellow private, read *Dune,* a science fiction classic that Gore said "really influenced him," stirring the early traces of his environmentalism. Stanisic said he saw in Gore a likeness to the character Duke Paul, the son of the wise Duke Leto, who had an ability to see into the future. He lent Maurice (Marnie) Hendrick several books, more offbeat fare such as *The Beastly Beatitudes of Balthazar B.*

and *One Flew Over the Cuckoo's Nest.* "He'd say, 'Here, you need to read this,' " Hendrick recalled. " 'This will open your eyes.' "

Two of his bunkmates, Hendrick and Richard Abalos, bought a 1962 tan Chevy clunker and the boys would pile into it for getaway beach weekends at Panama City, Florida, only thirty-five miles away. For sixty bucks, they would rent a bungalow, pick up bread, cheese, beer, and cheap wine, play bridge and poker, smoke cigars and pot, and groove to Cream, Jimi Hendrix, and Led Zeppelin on Hendrick's eight-track tape deck. The totems of 1960s culture were everywhere by then, and could not be kept off the base. The movie house screened *Easy Rider, MASH, The Strawberry Statement*—films with antiwar or anti-establishment themes. "We all agreed with it," said Hendrick, a North Carolina native, who attended the movies with Gore and the others. "We were all a bunch of liberal freaks back then." Life at Fort Rucker was nothing if not irreverent. One of Gore's buddies, Private Barry Ancona, won a post talent contest with a song written to the tune of "Down in the Boondocks," which included this refrain:

> *Down in the barracks*
> *Down in the barracks*
> *I'm just a sucker 'cause*
> *It's Fort Rucker I live in.*

Some of the troops had a playful pejorative for the post: Mother Rucker. And was it just a newspaper typo that resulted in the reversal of the F and the R in Fort Rucker? All this in territory that was conservative and devout. "The roads were paved with Bibles around there," said Roy Mays. Gore and a few pals once went out dressed in civvies and ended up at a truck stop after a movie. Gore was the only southerner in the gang, recalled Ancona, a New Yorker who ran the post radio show. Not long after walking in, they realized that everyone in the place was looking at them, wondering who they were. Gore walked over to the jukebox, dropped in a coin, and "Tennessee Birdwalk" began to play. "That settled everybody down," Ancona remembered. "They thought that was neat."

By THE SPRING of 1970, public disenchantment with the Vietnam War had grown deeper. When American troops invaded Cambodia on May 1, another wave of protests rolled across college campuses, leading to the tragedy at Kent State, where National Guardsmen fired into a crowd of young demonstrators and killed four people. Two weeks later, the nation still numbed by those events, Al Gore returned to Washington to marry Mary Elizabeth Aitcheson at the National Cathedral. At the rehearsal dinner the night before the May 19 wedding, guests dined in a room under the Capitol Rotunda. Then Al, Tipper, and a band of friends went barhopping in Georgetown. Nancy and her husband, Frank Hunger, came along, as did Mike Kapetan from Harvard and Steve Armistead from Carthage. After everyone else went home, Armistead threw Gore in his car and drove him around all night, driving and talking in circles in the darkness of rural Maryland.

Al's mother was not pleased, but Gore turned out in fine fettle the next day, snappily attired in his borrowed Army dress uniform, an outfit that some found odd given that he was not a career military man. Tipper looked "stunning," a guest recalled, in a gown with a train of white lace and carrying a bouquet of orchids and white carnations. Canon Charles Martin, who had been Gore's headmaster at St. Albans, the boys prep school situated in the shadows of the grand cathedral, performed the service. Harvard roommate J. G. Landau (who died of a heart attack in 1997) was the best man. The newlyweds walked down the aisle and out the church as the Beatles tune "It's All Too Much" resounded from the pipe organ played by one of Gore's Dunster House friends, Warren Steel. The reception was held at Belle Haven Country Club in Virginia. Several of Gore's friends rode out to the swank reception on motorcycles, musician Steel hitching a ride on one, his vestments flying over his shoulder. Among the guests were Gore's Harvard seminar leader Martin Peretz, and his father's friend and cattle partner, the international financier Armand Hammer.

The newlyweds went from upper-crust Washington to a honeymoon in Hawaii and then on to their new home near Mother Rucker in the depths of Alabama, a trailer in a twelve-acre trailer park on the edge of the small town of Daleville. Tipper, with a degree from Boston University, did not take a job in Alabama, but spent her days, she said, as "a soldier's wife." They threw occasional fondue parties and guys from the post would come over and listen to music and play poker. Tipper was friendly and charming, but she had yet to develop the outgoing nature that she would show later in their political life. "She was," said Marnie Hendrick, "just a wispy little thing back then."

• • •

ALL DURING THAT SUMMER of 1970, Albert Gore Sr. was engaged in the toughest political battle of his career. He faced Bill Brock, a conservative Republican congressman from Chattanooga whose family ran a candy company. Gore still had a broader reach, a three-term Democratic senator with a national reputation in a traditionally Democratic state. But the times had changed, and so had Tennessee politics, turning more conservative in the wake of the civil rights and antiwar movements, and both state and national Republicans thought they had a real chance to defeat Gore. Brock sensed from the moment he entered the race that the incumbent was beatable, an impression underscored by the difficult primary challenge Gore faced from a relative unknown. "There were a lot of people angry at him in his own party," Brock recalled. The Dixiecrats thought Gore was too liberal, a perception fueled by his antiwar stance and his vote for the 1965 Voting Rights Act. Gore fully understood that his opposition to the war had placed him in particular jeopardy. "The popular support of the Vietnam War was perhaps as strong in Tennessee as in any state in the union. And yet I was at least one of the leaders in opposition to it. This created a reservoir of antagonism toward me on this issue," he said later. He was also, in Brock's opinion, even more vulnerable to a charge of neglecting his constituents.

"He gave the impression, whether fair or not, when asked questions, of responding sort of tartly, of talking down to them," Brock said. In that sense Brock thought of Gore as the opposite of the late Estes Kefauver, whose grassroots approach was one that Brock admired and emulated. Had Kefauver been alive, Brock thought, he would have found a way to hold on to the conservative Democratic voters who were now turning to the Republicans or George Wallace. Some of Gore's strongest supporters worried about the same phenomenon. "Kefauver was able to get those people who were basically redneck racist individuals and get their votes," said Ted Brown, who had worked for both Kefauver and Gore. "He took care of them. They knew if they had a problem they could call up there and get Estes." Even if Kefauver was ahead of them on civil rights issues, these "constituents thought they had a personal stake in keeping Estes in Washington. Senator Gore's constituents never felt they had a stake in keeping him in Washington."

To exploit the uneven public perception of Gore, Brock combined a well-organized grassroots effort with one of the first modern political advertising campaigns, hiring the firm of Harry Treleaven, who had done the ads for Richard Nixon's presidential campaign, and whose associate was a facile young consultant named Kenneth Rietz. Rietz, who later became entangled in the Watergate scandal and resigned his post with the Republican National Committee, moved to Nashville for the general election campaign, living out of a small apartment. He and Treleaven created a series of billboard, radio, television, and full-page newspaper ads aimed at reinforcing the image of Gore as out-of-touch and too liberal.

Bill Brock Believes.

The slogan is so stark it sticks in people's minds even today. It still riles James Blumstein, who was hired to teach law at Vanderbilt in 1970 and remembers driving from New Haven to Nashville to take his job and seeing, as he drove across the width of Tennessee, billboards proclaiming Bill Brock Believes—without saying what he believed. By the time Blumstein got to Nashville, he was so frustrated he launched a campaign to lower the waiting period required for new residents to vote.

Some of the billboards eventually did say what Bill Brock believed: "The Things We Believe In." It was the ultimate subliminal political slogan. Considered brilliant by Brock supporters and nefarious by his opponents, the campaign used a series of "snipes" or punch lines to convey to Tennessee voters that Brock was with them on key issues. " 'Believes' is a code word for" a racist epithet, wrote journalist David Halberstam in an article on the Gore-Brock race published a year later. "Against busing, for the war, for [conservative Supreme Court nominees] Carswell and Haynsworth." The pitch, Gore aide Ted Brown said later, was "almost calculated to send the subliminal message that Albert Gore may not believe in God, may not believe in the white race, may not believe in America the Beautiful, but by God, Bill Brock does."

The television ads were slick and well produced, showing a shirt-sleeved Brock shooting the breeze with working Joes in a parking lot; walking through a field and chatting with hunters; reassuring parents that he would not stand for school busing; and playing in his backyard with his wife and children. One particularly effective ad featured a disenchanted Democrat, good ole country lawyer Alf MacFarland, who turned against Gore because of the senator's support of gun control. MacFarland said he had written Gore a letter saying that his position on gun control was hurting him in rural Tennessee, but got "a right ugly letter back. He was not only going to get a bill to regulate that type of gun, but he was going to do long guns, hunting rifles, and shotguns."

Brock's negative ads ran late in the campaign, leaving Gore little time for a counterattack, which he was disinclined to do in any case, saying that he "never slung mud" in his life and was "not going to start now." But Gore did run some commercials, one of which stands out both because it was touching and because it appeared to backfire. It showed Gore playing checkers with a group of elderly men in front of the county courthouse in Carthage, a spontaneous scene that evoked the long-lost past, going back not just to Gore's first run for Congress in 1938, but even to his role model, Cordell Hull, who played checkers with old men on that very courthouse lawn. Gore, wearing a brown suit, the checkerboard balanced on his knees, jokes with his opponent, who is about to take another of his pieces, "I tell you, if you beat me two straight games, I'll cut you off Medicare!"

It was witty and humanizing, but also, according to Rietz's polling, raised enough concern about Medicare that Gore's numbers began to slip among seniors. "For a while we didn't know why until we started probing and found out that this commercial was having a great effect on seniors," said Rietz, who still uses the ad whenever he teaches a class on media campaigns. One of Gore's best-known commercials from that campaign attempted to counter charges that he was unpatriotic. It showed young Al in uniform sitting opposite his father, who instructed him, "Son, always love your country." That ad and others were shot at the family farm in Carthage by noted documentary filmmaker Charles Guggenheim, who considered Gore's antiwar position in the South "very brave" but probably fatal. Guggenheim hoped to diminish the animosity toward Gore by filming him in unposed situations. "My feeling was, right or wrong, that if people got to know him, that would be his strength."

Another ad, intended to evoke Gore's Tennessee roots and defuse the argument that he had become distanced from his state, showed father and son on horseback at the Carthage farm, Al on a bay mare, the silver-haired senator on his Tennessee Walker named Traveler. Gilbert Merritt, a family friend, recalled that the white horse ad was the subject of some joking, if not second-guessing, for while it portrayed a senatorial courtliness that the senator prized, to some it also conveyed a certain arrogance.

Brock's campaign spent about $1.25 million, a pittance by today's standards but one of the nation's costliest at the time. A significant portion of the money, by some reports as much as $200,000, was funneled into Tennessee through Operation Townhouse, an enterprise run by a Nixon operative out of a Washington town house. The effort was later determined to be illegal, although no one from Brock's campaign was implicated. President Nixon and his top aides were obsessed that year with the prospect of defeating Gore and other liberal senators. "It is imperative that our candidates call upon their opponent to repudiate what some of the leaders of the Radiclib have said—not just what the opponent himself has said," Nixon chief of staff H. R. Haldeman said in a September 26, 1970, memo to special counsel Charles W. Colson that was not made public until 1986. "In other words, Brock should call on Gore to repudiate specific statements made by McGovern, Hubert, or Teddy. . . . Another important issue that should be made is Cambodia. Hang all those who opposed Cambodia and ask if they still think it was so bad."

Another Haldeman memo, on September 23, included an analysis of the Tennessee race and noted: "Albert Gore can be expected to campaign against Brock with a never-ending stream of folksy gibes and populist economics, but Gore's cocktail party liberalism offers a chance to rebut his folksy image." The memo also suggested that someone research the society pages of the *Washington Post* back to 1965 for a complete list of parties attended by Gore, the menu ("the Frenchier the better") and the "society types and northern liberals" in attendance.

The existence of the Haldeman memos and Operation Townhouse was unknown to the Gores then, but they always suspected that the Nixon administration was manipulating the Brock effort behind the scenes, using it both as a battleground for the "southern strategy" of manipulating the race issue to their advantage and as an early training ground for the dirty tricks campaigns that were to follow. Years afterward, Gore Senior would refer to Nixon as "the vilest man." Family friends took note in the campaign's final months of how bitter the race was and how deeply it affected Albert and Pauline, Al and Tipper, and Al's sister, Nancy, and her husband, Frank Hunger. The race "got personal," Fort Rucker buddy Marnie Hendrick said. "And it bothered Al."

In late September, at the trailer house in Daleville, Tipper Gore answered the phone one afternoon and got the news she had hoped never to hear. It was Al saying that he had received notice of his next posting. It was not Germany, as he had promised her. He was going to Vietnam. That weekend, back in Tennessee at a fund-raising barbecue for his father, Gore told the reporter covering the event that he had received his Vietnam orders. The next morning a front-page article on the new military assignment for the senator's son appeared in the *Tennessean*, written by Andrew Schlesinger. It quoted Senator Gore: "I have not wished to bring my son's situation into the campaign and do not now. Like thousands of other Tennessee boys, he volunteered and has now received his orders for Vietnam. That is all I wish to say—except, like other fathers, I am proud."

Gore had thirty days' leave. He was to be ready to go by December 26. Later, in Vietnam, he told friends that the family believed his orders had been held up by the Nixon administration to deny the father any public relations advantage that might come with having a son in Vietnam. No evidence has come to light to substantiate that contention, which has been denied by then Defense Secretary Melvin Laird and others, but its existence reflects how personally the family took that political battle. "We all believed very strongly that Nixon operatives were involved in that campaign and watched it very closely," said Jim Sasser, a former senator and ambassador to China who helped run Gore Senior's 1970 campaign.

EARLY ON THE EVENING of November 3, Steve Armistead collected Gore at the Nashville airport and drove him downtown to the Hermitage Hotel, where his father was monitoring the returns. "Daddy wants me to write his victory speech," Gore said, but he knew that the race was lost, his father's career over. He had suspected it for at least two years, since that autumn day in Cambridge when he had encountered another Democratic politician's son, Don Gilligan, walking across Harvard Yard, and predicted that the same fate that befell Don's father in 1968 would happen to his own father in 1970.

The returns came in from east to west. The east went Republican as expected. Gore held his own in his native middle Tennessee, allowing the false hope that he might eke out a win. He had convinced himself that he was catching up, that his final-week barnstorming had energized the Democratic electorate and that Brock's negative ads had caused a sympathetic backlash. But at last the Memphis vote arrived and the mood in the senator's suite turned bleak. "Senator, it doesn't look too good," campaign manager Tim Schaeffer said. There were no tears in the room, and few words. The Gores were stoic. Twenty minutes later, the senator and his family went downstairs to the ballroom. His concession speech was brief and dignified and closed with a phrase ringing with defiance and hope. "The causes for which we fought are not dead," he said. "The truth shall rise again."

Those words carried a dual meaning. On one level, they conveyed Gore's belief that his controversial positions on the war and civil rights eventually would be vindicated. But they also hinted at the political rise of a younger generation of Democrats, a prediction that came true in 1976, when Sasser defeated Brock and reclaimed the Senate seat, heading to Washington along with a new congressman from Tennessee's 3rd District named Al Gore. That was six years distant. The day after the 1970 election, Gore father and son spent hours together in Carthage, paddling a canoe through the chilled waters of the Caney Fork. At one point Senior asked Junior what he would do if he had been repudiated by the voters he had served for so long. "Dad, I would take the thirty-two years," Al said.

There were farewell visits to be made before Gore shipped out for Vietnam. He and Tipper went to Baltimore, where they met Bart Day and Bob Somerby, two of the beloved motley crew from Harvard. Somerby lived in a spare apartment near Johns Hopkins. Both men were now teachers, jobs they had taken to avoid the draft, Day turning to it only after a brief and unhappy stint with the Peace Corps in Chile. Somerby and Day were dressed casually. The Gores looked pressed and neat, as though they had just been to church. The contrast struck Day as a symbol of how their lives were diverging. Al seemed mature and directed. He and Tipper seemed to know where they were going. "It was," Day thought, "as if they're grown-ups and we're not."

Perceptions are relative, of course, and what seemed like maturity to his Harvard suitemates appeared to be something else to his Harvard mentor, Richard Neustadt, when Al and Tipper paid a final call to the professor's home at 10 Traill Street in Cambridge that winter. Gore was dressed in his private's uniform, Tipper at his side, and they looked so young and innocent that it made Neustadt feel like their protective uncle. "I thought they were both scared to death," he recalled, "and determined not to let that show."

Christmas 1970 was dreary and depressing at the Carthage farmhouse. The election had sapped the family's spirits. Albert Gore was devastated, ashen. Not only had he lost his hardest-fought race, his only son was leaving for Vietnam. Pauline Gore was outwardly calm, but her disappointment was clear. Nancy and Frank Hunger alternated between anger and sadness. Tipper tried gamely to boost morale. "I remember trying to cheer people up, but it was a bleak Christmas, a time of great anxiety," she said later. "We were going to try to go on and be cheerful as if everything was fine. It was a close family time, but it was tough."

Then it happened again, the same scene as Boston. A curb, a kiss, and he was gone. This time bound for Seattle and the plane to Vietnam.

CHAPTER EIGHT

THE "SORDID CRUSADE"

AL GORE FELT as though he had been blindfolded and spun around for thirteen hours and then set down, staggering, in a strange land. He would never forget the moment his feet hit the airstrip tarmac after the endless flight across the ocean to a war that he hated. It was "a split second," he said later, "that I had known was coming for a long time." The first hot blast of air was overpowering, the scent bitter, fetid, smoky. He passed a ragged band of soldiers heading the other way, back to the States, who looked "faded and dusty and their hair was long . . . they were grizzled . . . their boots weren't new." Local mamasans casually hawked cartons of marijuana cigarettes on the street along with other black market staples.

Such was the young private's welcome to the intoxicating chaos of Vietnam in January 1971. And during his first week in Bien Hoa, after being issued stiff metal-plated boots, the straitlaced Gore went AWOL. At least that was the loose term he used in a letter to a friend back home to describe those first few days of free and easy movement. He was in no hurry to begin his public affairs job at the small Army installation on the edge of the massive air base. He wanted to soak in all he could of this besieged land, a place he found "interesting as hell." He hopped in the back of a truck and hitched a ride across the base to a hooch where he partied with some guys he had known at Fort Rucker in Alabama. Then he traveled to Saigon, where he joked that he would write "a feature on wine, women, and Tet."

But it did not take long on the new job before he acquired the typically sardonic voice of the disillusioned GI. He had read Joseph Heller's classic *Catch-22*, and now he echoed Yossarian's absurdist ennui. "Well, here I am," Gore wrote in the letter. "They put me in an Engineer Brigade, in a public information office in Bien Hoa. It's the most incredibly bull-shit operation I've ever seen in my life." During his first two weeks in the headquarters company of the 20th Engineer Brigade, he said, he did absolutely nothing—the same as everyone around him. "Basically the army has decided that the best public relations policy at this stage of this sordid crusade is to produce no stories at all," he wrote. "You know, maybe they'll forget about it."

The empty routine made him jumpy. "If I stay in this one small room with 10 people staring at each other, doing nothing, telling 'funny' stories back and forth 10 hours a day, I'll go stark raving mad," he wrote. So he took the advice of a new colleague, who told him in the jeep one day that he would have "a much better experience" if he left the compound whenever possible. From then on he traveled as often as he could in search of stories for the brigade newspaper and magazine, using travel passes given to Army reporters that allowed them to go wherever they wanted.

There was in Gore at age twenty-two a long-held cynicism about the war, but he tried to prevent that cynicism from devolving into mind-numbing detachment, a condition he saw in other soldiers. "You just wouldn't believe how outrageous some of these people are. They're stoned continuously. I mean, all the time. . . . It's just unbelievable. Actually, I suppose it's just a measure of how spiritually debilitating this experience is for a lot of people," he wrote. As for himself, he said: "I've been bombarded with sensory patterns from all sides since I got here. All I can say is it's astounding. . . . One reason I started traveling right away was to try to put the experience in some kind of perspective. For the same reason, I've decided not to smoke [marijuana]. Maybe once or twice, socially, but that's all." After one trip to Saigon, he sent another letter home to his old Harvard teacher, Marty Peretz, questioning another aspect of the American presence in Vietnam—an elegant party hosted by Harvard alumni in the CIA, a scene that Gore said gave him "the creeps."

Gore ended up spending five months in Vietnam, less than half the normal tour. He asked for and received an "early out" that May at a time when the 20th Engineers were standing down as part of a gradual

U.S. troop reduction. Even as he was bombarded with "sensory patterns" during his many trips around the country, his experiences were circumscribed by the nature of his job and his skill at working the military system. He was a reporter, not an infantryman, and while he was never fully out of harm's way, neither did he face situations where he had to kill or be killed, and he was spared the sight of seeing any buddies die. He had an M-16 rifle assigned to him, and photographs that surfaced during his later political campaigns showed him toting that weapon, though he carried it only on those few occasions when he drew perimeter guard duty. The rest of the time, the M-16 was checked in the armory while he moved about armed with his notebook and pen. Though he once told the *Washington Post* that he was "shot at" and the *Baltimore Sun* that he "walked through the elephant grass and . . . was fired upon," those war stories seemed enhanced in the retelling. He did not face direct enemy fire. He did arrive at a few combat scenes after the action, and several times base sirens warned of possible mortar attacks and he and his comrades scrambled for cover.

Gore was like most other Vietnam veterans in that his time there profoundly influenced the rest of his life. In his case the experience had a reverberating and contradictory effect. He had left for Vietnam disillusioned over his father's loss in the 1970 Senate race, the persistence of a war that he detested, and a general sense that the country had taken a wrong turn. He came back feeling the same way, even more so, determined once again to follow a career path outside politics, as a writer. Yet every decision he made during that difficult era — opposing the war, opting to serve anyway, and then finally shipping off to Vietnam — in the end did not irrevocably turn him away from the political life, but rather paved the way for his eventual return.

EVEN BEFORE GORE ARRIVED in Vietnam, word of his coming had reached Long Binh, headquarters for U.S. Army forces. Barry Ancona, a radio producer who had been stationed with Gore at Fort Rucker, was approached by his boss, a sergeant major, and told that the former senator's son was on his way. "Do you know him?" the noncommissioned officer asked Ancona, who had been working in the information office at Army headquarters since the previous summer. "Yeah, he's a nice guy," Ancona replied.

Gore touched down at Cam Ranh Bay on January 2, 1971, then

flew to Bien Hoa Air Base, where he took a short bus ride to an Army replacement station at Long Binh for processing. Ancona took a jeep
over to the station to meet Gore.

"What the hell are you doing here? You're too short!" Ancona
said, using military jargon to express surprise that someone with less
than a year to go in the service would nonetheless be sent to Vietnam.

"Yeah, well, that's what I thought," said Gore.

Ancona took Gore to meet his boss, but there were no openings in
the information office at headquarters. It was then, Gore wrote to a
friend, that "Major Ladue's letter went to work, and I was sent out here
to the 20th Engineer Brigade"—at the public information office at
Bien Hoa. Major Wade Ladue was his former boss at Fort Rucker. The
letter on behalf of Gore was an apparent act of military courtesy written
by an officer who had served in Vietnam for a soldier who impressed
him. Officers routinely performed such favors for soldiers they liked,
according to Army historians, helping them negotiate the fickle processing system, steering them to preferred assignments.

The 20th Engineers was considered a relatively comfortable posting. "Compared to what other people were doing in Vietnam, it was
like being on a college campus," said Mike O'Hara, who worked on the
newspaper. Ivin N. Marks, the chaplain, wrote a letter to parents of incoming soldiers offering them reassurance: "You will be pleased to
learn that our location is generally regarded as a safe area." Bien Hoa
was in the country's south, near Saigon, far from most of the combat,
and the troops had a name for soldiers posted in such safe havens:
REMF, or Rear Echelon Motherfuckers. At Bien Hoa, the men had
warm meals and hot showers. Mamasans streamed in every morning to
clean hooches and shine shoes. Each hooch housed ten men, two to a
room, some retrofitted for privacy and refrigerators. An outdoor movie
theater showed films twice a week. *Woodstock*, the documentary of the
1969 counterculture music festival, was the favorite. The hottest competition at the base involved not fighting the Viet Cong but battling another company in recreational basketball. Gore was welcomed as a
forward to the 20th Engineers' traveling team, the league champs.

The air base was a mile away, close enough to hear fighters,
bombers, and helicopters taking off in shifts twenty-four hours a day,
but separated by its own gates from the smaller Army base. Gore and
his fellow public information officers worked in the personnel building—drab Army green all the way, green linoleum, green walls, re-

lieved only by gray metal desks with rotary phones and manual typewriters. They wrote releases for hometown papers, along with articles
about the combat engineers. The dull routine was enlivened by the
slithering of a pet python named Moonbeam—which was kept in a
window cage at night but let loose to roam under the desks all day—
and by the daily mimicking of certain officers after they left the room.
No one was better at aping their mannerisms than Spec. 4 Al Gore,
whose earnest exterior masked a sarcastic humor that came out in his
dead-on impersonations of old characters in Carthage, parents of St.
Albans boys, professors at Harvard, and now brass in Vietnam.

Was Gore mocking the hand that protected him? There is no evidence that he sought special treatment in Vietnam. One longtime
friend said, in fact, that Gore was so concerned about being singled out
as the son of a senator that this friend asked General Westmoreland,
the Army chief of staff, for advice as to how someone in Gore's position
could avoid the spotlight. The answer, which the general provided
without being told Gore's name: Be yourself and people will grade you
on your output. But Westmoreland also said, according to Gore's
friend, that from "Day One" it would "be known to all elements of personnel" who he was.

The two superiors who worked most closely with Gore at Bien
Hoa recalled nothing out of the ordinary about his arrival or their response to it. "I had just come back from R&R and someone told me,
the word got around that a new guy was coming in and he was a
senator's son," said Joseph Colla, then master sergeant in the public information office and editor of the headquarters newspaper. "It wasn't a
big deal. He came up to me and introduced himself as Spec. 4 Al
Gore. I didn't say anything. He was just another soldier." Clayton Ryce,
a lieutenant with a journalism degree who ran the public information
office, said that when he heard that Gore was coming to work there he
recognized the name, but nothing more. "I . . . knew who his dad was,
but didn't know he had children," Ryce said, adding that Gore "did not
throw his weight around."

If Ryce and Colla were not briefed on Gore, the sergeant major in
the information office back at Long Binh certainly was, according to
Barry Ancona. "There is something which is colloquially called the
watch list, a list of sensitive people," Ancona recalled. "I knew that Al
was on the watch list even after his father lost the election, because the
sergeant major, when [Gore] came over, knew he was on the watch

list. These are presumably children of people who are in some way prominent. . . . It was people that you watched."

Another soldier at Long Binh said the brass's concern about Gore extended even beyond a watch list, though his story is disputed by Gore and not remembered in the same way by others. H. Alan Leo was a photojournalist who had served two tours of duty in Vietnam and knew his way around the country. By his account, a few days before Gore arrived, Brigadier General Kenneth B. Cooper, the brigade commander, called Leo into his office and told him that a senator's son was joining the unit. While the general did not use the precise words, Leo took his message to mean: This isn't an order, but keep an eye out for him. Leo said he was "elated" because the general trusted him with the assignment. "But I was also kind of pissed off at that point because somebody was getting special treatment," he said. If in fact it was special treatment, it was not sought by Gore. Cooper today says that he does not remember the exchange. "It may or may not be true," he said. The main point about Gore, he added, was that "he went" to Vietnam, while "other people were trying to get their sons out of it entirely."

When asked about Leo's claim, Gore said that he knew Leo but rarely traveled with him in Vietnam. He certainly never felt that he was being protected or watched over by Leo, Gore said. And he bristled at the suggestion. "As, uh, as the Vietnamese frequently said, 'Nev-ah hap-pen, GI!' "

OCCASIONALLY, being the son of Albert Gore made him the target of resentment by others who, like Leo, felt he received special treatment or who disliked his father's ideology. One night a soldier from Tennessee lit into Gore about his father's position on school prayer, an issue the Republicans had manipulated to help defeat Senior in the 1970 election. "He went on screaming a sermon about it," recalled Mike O'Hara, who became Gore's best friend in Vietnam and went on to a career as a sportswriter in Detroit. Gore sat quietly, listening, then got up and left, saying that his father had been "crucified" for his position by conservatives who did not believe in the separation of church and state. "Boy," said another soldier, "there've gotta be times when Al just wishes he was somebody else."

But he never lashed out. Along with his impersonations, he also took part in a few practical jokes, including once when he and his buddy O'Hara locked Lieutenant Ryce in a dark room and would not let him out until he apologized to O'Hara for something, using O'Hara's nickname: "I'm sorry, Mr. Moose. Sorry, Mr. Moose." Rare acts of that sort belied his utterly polite nature, which he discussed now and then in rambling philosophical reflections with O'Hara. Gore once told him that his politeness was not just a matter of good breeding, but also of family dynamics, his way of surviving. He said that the only way he could get attention as a boy was not by acting up, but by being polite. "He said one time, 'I was a real little politician,' " O'Hara recalled. "He said it as sort of self-analysis."

If he had once been a little politician, he told his Vietnam friends, he had no desire to become a big one. Michael J. Roche, editor of the Army engineer newspaper in Vietnam, the *Castle Courier*, remembered Gore talking to him about his early life in Washington and how he was not cut out for public service or government. "My dad, fine. But not me," Roche remembered him saying.

Gore had what Lieutenant Ryce called "a presence," and also a touch of public shyness, but he tried to be a regular guy. He seemed to open up especially around O'Hara, a street-smart city kid who called his new friend Brother Buck. They knocked around the country together, hitchhiking on jeeps and helicopters. They wrote stories, shot pictures, goofed around. Their most adventurous journey took them up near the DMZ, in Quang Tri province, where engineers were reconstructing an abandoned airstrip. They assigned themselves a story about the engineers, and pegged it to the landing of the first plane after the airstrip's reopening. This was a chance for Gore to see the war in full chaos, in a way that he had not witnessed before.

Moose and Brother Buck, armed with pens and notebooks and bulky Speed Graphic cameras, rode north on a troop plane that O'Hara recalled as "Dante's inferno in the air." Their first night in the province, they were housed with the international press at a media barracks. After checking in, they went off to an enlisted men's club to drink beer and smoke, and when they came back at nine o'clock, the barracks had been tear-gassed. "Think somebody's sending a message," Gore said. "It wasn't the Vietnamese, it was one of our own guys," O'Hara recalled. "The media was a little condescending to the soldiers. The soldiers were a little pissed off at them. Some guy let off a couple of canisters."

The next day they rode in a helicopter gunship armed with rocket launchers. The rockets had little messages plastered on them by battle-hardened soldiers. *Happy Birthday, Dink. Duck! Birth Control. Baby Killer.*

Boy, it's intense up here, said Brother Buck.

No kidding, said Moose.

They spent that night closer to the airstrip, eating C-rations in a makeshift foxhole. It was cold and miserable and things were exploding all the time, mostly outgoing, but still frightening. "Al was more frightened than I was," O'Hara recalled. "He started scavenging around the area and came back with these metal sheets that were used to build the tarmac and he put them in our foxhole. Once he started on it, he was highly motivated. He kept building it thicker. He wanted to make sure that if anything fell, it fell on that first." O'Hara, the less cautious one, had already been saved once by Gore. They had been swimming in the South China Sea and O'Hara had found himself being pulled out by a riptide, and for a second he was certain that he would die. "Al! Al!" he had shouted, and Gore had gone out and pulled him in. Still, this makeshift foxhole seemed a bit much. "Al, we're only staying overnight," O'Hara said to his pal. "You don't have to build a motel!"

The next day they started working the story like real newspapermen. The trick was to find out when the first plane would land. Nosing around with captains and colonels, they pieced together the estimated time of arrival. They thought this was their big scoop, and they cackled together as they waited in the weeds for the big plane to come in, their cameras and notebooks at the ready. As soon as the plane touched down, said O'Hara, "all of a sudden forty camera crews come out of nowhere. They had all been tipped off. We both just broke out laughing. All we had to do was be a couple of civilians and they would have told us straight out."

In many of their trips around Vietnam, O'Hara and Gore were struck by something: The further out they went in the field, the more black troops they saw. During this trip up to Quang Tri, they had seen some black soldiers playing basketball on a makeshift court near a Huey and a Cobra gunship. The contrast was stark. Gore wanted to take a picture.

One of the guys came over and said, "No pictures, man."

Gore said, "Hey, man, why not?"

The soldier: "No pictures!"

Gore to O'Hara: "Man, these guys are really angry."

Gore and O'Hara shared the perception that "the further away from safer spots, the higher percentage of black troops." That perception was only partially accurate, according to Army historians. Minorities enlisted in proportionately greater numbers in the Army as a whole, but they were not disproportionately represented in the infantry. Nonetheless, it all went into the bundle of guilt, despair, disillusionment, thrill, and boredom that Gore and his colleagues carried with them.

THE CULTURE in the hooches and foxholes of Bien Hoa by 1971 seemed no different from the cacophonous youth culture back home, just more intense, all music and noises and colors, image and reality merging in psychedelic jumble. Day-Glo posters of Jimi Hendrix and Janis Joplin hanging from the barracks walls, the fluorescent greens and oranges shimmering in black light, while in the distance tracers arc through the sky, red for the Americans, green for the Vietnamese. The boys sitting on lawn chairs bought at the PX, swigging whiskey and beer and passing around a joint. The campfire talk turning to home, the banter interrupted by the roar of a commercial jet overhead, little red lights blinking on the wingtips. *There it is*, someone saying, wistfully. *The Freedom Bird*, taking men home.

Three months into his tour, Gore began looking for a way to leave Vietnam. The 20th Engineers had begun standing down, soon to be deactivated as part of the gradual reduction of U.S. troops, and soldiers who were within ninety days of the end of their required service were allowed to apply for early outs for various reasons. Moonbeam, the pet python, found a new home at a zoo in Michigan. Some members of the brigade, even if they had served in Vietnam longer, were transferred to different units in country. But Gore knew what to do to avoid that fate. He applied to graduate school at Vanderbilt in Nashville, where Tipper was living. On March 9 the university sent him a letter permitting him to enroll in June or August.

His intention was to take courses in ethics and morality at the graduate school of religious studies as a way to recover from what he had been through. He never saw the worst of war. He did not see, as several articles written decades later would imply, bodies cut in half by machine-gun fire. He never saw a buddy die, or took live fire. But he did see "men who were shaken in the aftermath of battles, people in villages who were scared"—and at the office late every afternoon he saw the daily body counts coming over the Associated Press wire. And what he saw was enough to make him realize that he might have a difficult time adjusting when he got home unless he prepared for it.

"I felt that was a turbulent period for me," he said later. "I felt that I wanted to make extra certain in the immediate aftermath of that experience that I was grounded. And that I had a chance to have a systematic exploration of structures of right and wrong. . . . I had seen people come back from Vietnam and drift and feel rootless, and I didn't want that."

Nine days after receiving the letter from Vanderbilt, Gore filed his formal request for early release, and the Army soon granted it. He was let go seventy-five days short of fulfilling his two-year duty.

It so happened that he and one of his Fort Rucker pals, Bob Delabar, left Vietnam on the same day, May 22. Gore flew out on a *Freedom Bird* a few hours ahead of Delabar. They both landed in Oakland, then took a taxi across the bay to the San Francisco airport. As they waited for their final flights home, they shared a few beers in the lounge. One year earlier, at a going-away party for Delabar in New Orleans, Gore had scrambled out to a highway median strip and crawled around on his hands and knees until he found a four-leaf clover. Delabar carried the charm in his wallet all through Vietnam until it finally disintegrated. But his luck lasted, and they were both getting out in one piece. "We were feeling good when we left, no doubt about it," Delabar said.

Tipper Gore was waiting for her husband when his flight landed in Nashville. She drove him home, where he slept twenty hours straight.

CHAPTER NINE

A SUMMER'S TALE

THE OLD MAN had a thing about cars. He preferred to buy used ones, and the critical test was not taking them out for a spin or kicking the tires, but opening a back door (he insisted on four-door sedans) and settling into the back seat. He looked for comfort and space back there, enough room for a politician to stretch out and scatter papers and take a snooze if need be on the long rides from town to town in Tennessee. There were usually several old clunkers parked on the grounds of Albert Gore's farm above the Caney Fork River. He collected used cars the same way that Pauline accumulated antiques, more interested in the bargain than in the likelihood that he had a surplus of back seats. In late July 1971, one of those sedans, a black-and-white Chevy, rumbled down the dirt path toward the highway with Al Gore at the wheel and Tipper at his side.

The deep sleep that overtook Gore after his homecoming from Vietnam had been his last for some time. He seemed anxious and restless since then, searching for things to believe in. He had just signed on as a reporter at the Nashville *Tennessean*, while also enrolling in graduate courses in religious studies at Vanderbilt. He expressed no desire to be a minister, but told his professors and friends that he wanted to explore some moral questions he had confronted during his months in Vietnam. There was only one odd hint that he was thinking about public service of any kind: When Gus Stanisic, a friend from Fort Rucker, paid a visit to Nashville, Al told him that he had thought about becoming a policeman. Stanisic laughed, thinking his pal was kidding, but

Gore shot him a look and said seriously, "What's wrong with that?" The prospect of being a cop did not come up in conversations with Tipper. Around his young wife, Gore encouraged her idealized vision of their future by suggesting that someday soon they would buy the *Carthage Courier* and live out their days as artists, holing up in a rustic cabin on Center Hill Lake, where they could write books together. But before any of that, before facing the future, he and Tipper packed a tent, two sleeping bags, a cooler, a camera, and a backpack full of books, including a guide to the national parks, and took the old man's Chevy down the path and out to the highway for a free and easy camping trip across America.

First they drove north to the working-class town of Wayne, Michigan, where they picked up their traveling companions, Michael Kapetan, Al's Harvard roommate, and Kapetan's future wife, Karen Munson. Then they continued northwest toward Leland in Hemingway country on the Lake Michigan shore, where they pitched tents for the first time. It was a training maneuver, hardly Nick Adams stuff, since they camped in the protected backyard of a summer house in town owned by the family of another Harvard pal. As they left Leland behind and drove through the Upper Peninsula, stopping in the ancient dark of the Hiawatha National Forest, then through Wisconsin and Minnesota and on toward the Badlands in South Dakota, the foursome began to develop a sense of wonder about the continent, and Gore felt the stirrings of what would become his passion for the environment. *The land, the water, the air, the mountains, the rivers—it was fabulous, just fabulous,* he would say later of what he saw on that crosscountry trip. When a Styrofoam cup accidentally fell into the campfire and blackened specks of foam floated upward, Gore shook his head and muttered, "I call those things poll-utes."

He was not a skilled outdoorsman, but tried to look the part, wearing his Army-issue canvas boots and carrying a long, thin machete he had brought back from Vietnam, which proved most valuable on the day he locked them all out of the car. "He was able to reach through the window with that thing and somehow pry the lock up," Kapetan recalled. Tipper, a nascent photographer, was shooting pictures throughout the trip, Kapetan, a trained artist, was filling his sketchbooks with color pastel and black-and-white charcoal drawings. The Badlands presented what Kapetan called their first "astonishing experience"—a landscape so organic and barren that it enthralled them for several days. The eroded rock and sand formations had a way, Gore and Kapetan agreed, of "cleansing the mental palate"—what Gore needed most.

They stayed at a primitive campsite there, without running water, then drove west, reading aloud to one another in the car along the way. Gore brought along Alvin Toffler's *Future Shock* and Tipper had Dee Brown's *Bury My Heart at Wounded Knee*—early in their marriage, as later, their preference in books reflected the yin and yang of their vastly different sensibilities, the antiseptic futurist and the sensitive humanist. Kapetan wanted to see the Custer battlefield in Montana, but a group vote went against him, and instead they drove to Yellowstone, where they found a campsite on a bluff overlooking a meadow, then a few days later headed down through the Tetons and on to Salt Lake City, where they decided to forgo a freeze-dried meal of beef Stroganoff or macaroni and cheese and instead take an early dinner at a downtown restaurant. Would *thee* like coffee? the Mormon waitress asked.

Gore had made plans for them to spend the night in the Wasatch National Forest. They followed the directions on the map, wending through the forest until the road narrowed and turned from pavement to dirt, and they saw no campsites, not even signs for campsites, only what looked like a huge bonfire blazing up there in the distance, and they debated whether to keep going. *Bad vibes, man*, Kapetan said, and they turned around and stopped at a roadside café, filled the tank with gas and a thermos with coffee, and headed west again. Gore, a notorious leadfoot, steered the Chevy across the Bonneville Salt Flats in a windstorm and then on through Nevada, the headlights barely illuminating the road, the car doors locked, the windows rolled up, the smell of salt enveloping them nonetheless, the four of them still spooked by the Wasatch strangeness, battling their unease by screaming and howling and singing every Beatles and Rolling Stones song they knew in full-throated a cappella, until they made it through to dawn and eased toward the Sierras.

On their second day in California, they hooked up with two Nashville friends, John Warnecke and Nancy Chickering Warnecke, a reporter-husband, photographer-wife team at the *Tennessean* who had befriended Tipper during the months when Al was in Vietnam. In the colorful subculture of the newspaper, a menagerie of celebrity offspring and wry Tennessee characters, Warnecke was still one of a kind.

He had grown up in San Francisco and had become friends with the Grateful Dead, who often relaxed at a Sonoma ranch owned by his father, John Carl Warnecke, a noted architect who designed JFK's grave site at Arlington Cemetery. "Sugar Magnolia," among other Dead songs, was written at the ranch during a summer when Warnecke's father was away, he said. For three years, from 1965 to 1968, John was the ultimate Deadhead, their first friend and roadie. While he was never certain, Warnecke suspected that he might be the inspiration for the "Uncle John" referred to in the Dead's signature invitation:

Come hear Uncle John's band play to the tide
Come on along, or go alone, he's come to take your children home.

Warnecke came on along to the *Tennessean* in 1968 the way many young journalists did. He had connections to the Kennedy family, not only through his father, but in his own right, as a youth coordinator in the Bobby Kennedy campaign in California, and those connections proved irresistible to editor John Seigenthaler, who had worked for RFK in the Justice Department. In a newsroom of liberals, he considered himself the token radical, an engaging, opinionated, free-spirited 1960s creature who along with his leftist politics boasted of having the best stash of drugs in town. Nancy, who had known him since high school, was his opposite in demeanor, sober and responsible, and so protective of her friendships that even thirty years later she would not talk about her early days with Al and Tipper even to colleagues from her own newspaper. The Warneckes met the Gore traveling party at Nancy's family lodge on the north fork of the American River, and after a day of hiking in the high country they all drove down to Yosemite, stopping at a scenic turnoff along the way so that Kapetan could take in Half Dome, a sight that inspired what he called the best extemporaneous drawing of his life—"straight from brain to fingertips."

Warnecke remembers that he and Al were "smoking grass the whole time" they were together that week. Kapetan, in recalling the trip later, would not discuss the subject of drugs. His lasting memory of Gore and Warnecke, he said, was that they talked incessantly about politics and "how conservative the country was becoming." Less than a year had passed since Senator Gore's defeat, and the weight of anger and regret the family still carried was as heavy as the Big Rock in the middle of the Caney Fork below the Gore farm. Al talked to his friends about how disgusted he was by the way the Nixon administration had targeted his father with negative campaign tactics. Warnecke had covered that race occasionally for the *Tennessean,* and had a fondness for the old man. He had his own story to tell—the time when he was the only reporter on the campaign trail and the senator had run out of gas near Dayton, Tennessee, site of the Scopes trial, so the two of them had to get out and push the old man's sedan down the road.

These tales were told around a campfire in the back country after a long day of hiking up to the top of Yosemite Falls. When they retired for the night, Al and Tipper and Mike and Karen went inside their tents near the picnic table, while John and Nancy decided to sleep out under the stars in a clearing about a hundred yards away. Warnecke warned them not to take any food into the tents with them. "If the bears come and they smell the food, nothing's going to stop them," he said. The Gores failed to heed the warning, and took a half-eaten candy bar in with them. Kapetan later remembered waking up in the middle of the night to a loud snorting sound and turning on his flashlight, which "illuminated the face of a brown bear." Al and Tipper and Kapetan began screaming and somehow shooed the bear away. They shouted out to the Warneckes, who never budged and slept through the episode. In the light of day, they could see how close they had come to disaster. There were rips in the tent where the bear had mauled and clawed it. "The next morning they were both *ahhh . . . ddd . . . duhhh . . . ddd . . .* they were just absolutely terrified," Warnecke recalled. "That ended our trip to Yosemite." Years later, when Gore came out to San Francisco for a campaign fund-raiser, Warnecke urged him to tell the bear story, thinking it would add a self-deprecating touch to his earnest image as an environmentalist who in fact "didn't know anything about camping in the wilderness." When Gore resisted the entreaty Warnecke thought it was because "he couldn't stand to look bad in front of a group of people."

From Yosemite, Gore steered the old black-and-white Chevy toward the Bay Area, where the foursome spent a few days in Bolinas with a group of "hippie professionals." The water was polluted, the beach closed. Kapetan contracted a case of poison oak, which worsened as they drove south along Route 1 to Los Angeles, where they stayed with Kapetan's former thesis adviser at Harvard and visited an art museum and Disneyland. The return trip east a few days later was a hell-bent rush home, though Kapetan was in such agony on the way out of L.A. that they had to stop at a hospital emergency room for a cortisone shot. Two cops came into his room to interview him, thinking mistakenly that he had suffered a drug overdose. The next evening after a stop at the Grand Canyon, with Kapetan now recovered and taking his turn as driver, they discovered that the Chevy's gas tank had been ruptured. They barely made it to an all-night truck stop, where the attendant improvised by filling the leak with a cake of Ivory soap. There were few stops on the way back through New Mexico and Texas and on into Arkansas, except when Kapetan was pulled over and given a warning notice for speeding. When Tipper drove into Texas she wanted absolutely no part of the place—"Texas! Argh! I wanted to get through there as fast as possible," she said later. Leadfoot Al took the wheel again for the homestretch. "He had issues to deal with," Kapetan realized. "And he was going to deal with them like he drove that car. Flat out. And head on to the rest of his life."

CHAPTER TEN

THE STING

Here, for the young investigative reporter, was a rare moment of drama ready to unfold. Within the next few hours, if all went as planned, he expected to ensnare a public official in the very act of corruption. He would overhear and tape-record a local councilman asking for a bribe, then watch as his paper's photographers took pictures of the illicit transaction. It promised to be a major scoop, top of the front page guaranteed, the kind of story that inspires a proud newspaper to display a copyright notice under the byline. And it would be his byline, capitalized in boldface:

... BY ALBERT GORE JR. ...

The date was January 19, 1974, a midwinter morning so unseasonably warm that people strolled around downtown Nashville in shirtsleeves. Gore, in his fourth year as a reporter at the *Tennessean*, sat crouched in his little yellow Volkswagen, his profile a shock of black hair with fashionably long and stringy sideburns. He was parked just out of view of Haddox Pharmacy, a community drugstore owned by pharmacist Morris Haddox, a prominent black member of the Metro Council. Stationed nearby were officers from the Tennessee Bureau of Criminal Investigation, also there to monitor what was about to go down. The reporter and the state investigators were working together on a classic sting operation. Days earlier, a local developer had alleged to Gore that Haddox was hitting him up for a bribe to approve a zoning variance. Now that developer agreed to walk into the pharmacy, wired with a microphone hidden beneath his shirt, and see if he could get

Haddox to solicit the money again. This time it would be heard by Gore and the officers, who also had recording equipment in their car.

So excited was Gore by the prospect of the story, so certain were he and his editors that they were righting a wrong, that they participated as virtual adjunct members of the prosecution team, offering crucial assistance in every aspect of the case. Rather than pursue the story on their own, they went to the district attorney general and established a joint enterprise. The newspaper provided the cash (three hundred-dollar bills) that passed from the developer to Haddox later that day. Gore, with help from his wife, Tipper, transcribed the audiotapes and spent hours going over them with the district attorney general. He and three *Tennessean* photographers testified before the grand jury, and the paper held the story for three weeks, until Haddox was indicted. All for what seemed likely to be the young reporter's moment of triumph. But it was a moment that never came.

WORD HAD REACHED GORE even before he got home from Vietnam: The old man and Tipper both told him that if he wanted to work at the *Tennessean*, there would probably be a job there. All he had to do was drop in and talk to John Seigenthaler, who had covered Senator Gore, was a longtime friend of the family, and had already published "Fire Base Blue" and another of Al's pieces from Vietnam. Although Seigenthaler had the final say, and was known for his unabashed policy of hiring the sons and daughters of people he liked, Gore went through the normal rounds with other editors when he came in for his job interview on July 20, 1971. Frank Ritter, the city editor, prided himself on his opening question to every applicant: *What would you do if your editor ordered you to write a story that you knew to be untrue?* In a column he wrote years later, Ritter recalled Gore's answer: "I can't imagine that an editor would ever ask a reporter to do that. It would be unprofessional. But if it happened, I would resign before I violated my conscience." It was, Ritter wrote, "the best answer I've ever gotten."

The *Tennessean* newsroom Gore entered as a novice reporter covering night cops and obits was typical of the era, redolent of a time now gone forever, with cluttered rows of steel desks jammed together, the floors stained with ancient grease and littered with cigarette butts, desk drawers hiding whiskey and hard-boiled eggs, gruff editors barking orders to copy boys, reporters hunched over their desks banging out stories on manual typewriters and triplicate copy paper, some hidden behind fire-hazard stacks of newspapers, press releases, and long-forgotten notes. Newspapers were less homogenized then, each defined by its idiosyncratic politics and traditions. The *Tennessean* had a muckraking history, a sense of mission that was evident when David Halberstam worked there in the late 1950s and covered the early civil rights movement. "We all believed that the paper was of great value, that the paper really mattered," Halberstam said. "It had a moral legitimacy. Going against the conventional grain in Tennessee."

Seigenthaler, who had once been the paper's star investigative reporter before his stint at the Kennedy Justice Department, was now carrying forward that tradition while shaping the newsroom subculture in his own image. The place was a nonstop scene of practical jokes. The journalistic hazing of Al Gore, in which newsroom prankster Jerry Thompson called in a fake obit for a Swedish gynecologist from Carthage named Trebla Erog (Gore fell for it, and turned in the obit copy before realizing that it was his own name spelled backward), was a variation of the obit trick played on every new writer. When Carter Eskew, whose uncle was the city editor (and who decades later would serve as Gore's political consultant), came to the *Tennessean* as a summer intern, sitting at a desk near Gore, he was ordered to write an obit about a man named Wekse who died of a rattlesnake bite. A second call came an hour later with news that the sheriff who had found the dead man had now also died of a rattlesnake bite. Eskew's heart started pumping with the thrill of a certain front-page story—until he realized what Wekse spelled backward.

Gore the journalist was earnest and persistent in gathering facts, spending hours in the library studying clips, and hours more in document rooms at state and county offices, which he seemed to enjoy more than going out to interview people. He was slow and plodding as a writer, sometimes forcing exasperated editors to rip copy from his typewriter a paragraph at a time. While other reporters went home or over to the Brass Rail for a few drinks after turning in their copy, he would stick around, planting himself in a seat next to the night editor, waiting to see if there were any questions. At first he told his editors that he would write about anything but politics. "I didn't want anything to do with it," he said later. "I also didn't want to swim in the whirlpool that was left by the election wake of 1970. That was a bitter race, and there were people who played pivotal roles in that election I would have had to interview, on both sides, for and against my father. And I didn't want to try to perfect the craft of reporting while simultaneously trying to navigate in such turbulent waters. But the main reason was I just didn't want anything to do with it."

His first front-page story was about Hillbilly Days. But even as he avoided covering elections and government, Gore showed a strong and early interest in themes that could help him work through unresolved feelings about the cultural, political, and generational tensions in America. A story that particularly drew his attention involved an unlikely series of meetings between rural Church of Christ ministers and members of The Farm—a commune in Summertown populated by several hundred hippies and back-to-nature spiritualists and leftists who had moved by bus caravan out to southern Tennessee from San Francisco in 1971. "It began as a brave attempt by the churchmen to 'save' the souls" of their countercultural neighbors, Gore wrote in his March 13, 1972, front-page article. "Our first impulse was to associate them with Charles Manson, and theirs was to associate us with their unfavorable religious backgrounds," Church of Christ minister Bobby Williams told Gore.

But as Gore watched the two sides meet every Sunday afternoon and Monday evening for five weeks, he saw the encounters break down stereotypes and ease fears on both sides. "Overshadowing the disagreements, the real importance of the debates is that representatives of two groups of people who are natural enemies in many parts of America are learning to listen quietly to each other." The leader of The Farm, Steve Gaskin, said that his commune was based on spirituality, a sort of "coed monastery" whose members sought a purer life through simple, hard work, vegetarianism, and peyote and pot-smoking. The use of mind-altering drugs on The Farm—Gaskin and three of his followers were, at the time of Gore's visits, appealing convictions on possession of marijuana—had inspired the ministerial comparisons to cult murderer Charles Manson, but Gore saw them as less threatening and sought to explain them to his Tennessee audience. "He was our newspaperman," Gaskin said later. Albert Bates, one of Gaskin's lieutenants, said they came to think of Gore as "Clark Kent, kid reporter and divinity student," but they could always see "the Superman shirt"—his political ambitions—"under the shirt."

•   •   •

IF THERE WAS DISAGREEMENT among his peers at the *Tennessean* about Gore's future, it was about how long he would be able to resist politics. Few of them believed that he would remain in their profession forever. Six of his newsroom friends, including the political reporters, spent one night drafting a plan for Gore to be president, replete with timetables of when he had to run for the House and Senate. They had him in the Oval Office in the year 2008. One member of the cabal was Frank Sutherland, who sat across from Gore and became his closest friend at the paper. Decades later, when Gore was running for president, Sutherland, now editor of the *Tennessean,* said they had miscalculated when they plotted his political rise. "We didn't have the vice presidency in our plan," he said. As much as they teased Gore about it, he never seemed to think the 2008 plan was funny.

Seigenthaler, perhaps alone in this belief, had become convinced that his young charge would make journalism his career. But soon enough, the editor thought, he would lose Gore to a national newspaper or a network. The *Tennessean* would be his training ground. In December 1972, just after President Nixon's reelection, Seigenthaler sent Gore to New York for a seminar on investigative reporting. A dozen reporters sat around a room critiquing one another's stories, swapping tricks of the trade and discussing Topic A: Is investigative journalism dead? "The argument," Gore later recalled, "was that this was a medium that inherently requires so much complexity in the number of facts and the arrangement of facts that, in the age of television, people are not going to follow it. And Exhibit A was the work done to that point by Woodward and Bernstein on Watergate. It was ironic that at that time there were serious investigative reporters thinking this was a dying art."

This changed dramatically when the Watergate story consumed the nation and the tedium and complexity of investigative reporting suddenly acquired a glittery sheen. Back in Nashville, Gore started assuming the role of local gumshoe hero. His earlier cynicism gave way to curious skepticism: Now he was obsessed with how and why public officials made their decisions. Early in 1973 he began investigating the land appraisal and tax mapping industry, which was sloppily regulated and rife with petty cronyism and corruption. While apparent misdeeds gave his investigation appeal, what seemed to interest Gore most was not the potential scandal but lessons that could be gleaned from his findings about the unintended consequences of statewide property tax reform. Tennessee had undertaken property tax reform eight years earlier in an effort to eliminate regional inequities, but the reform had proved to be largely ineffectual and a gold mine for unscrupulous tax mapping firms.

In looking at the issue in its broadest policy implications, Gore seemed to be thinking more like a politician than a reporter. This mind-set was most apparent when he took a plane up to Washington and testified on May 3 before the Senate subcommittee on intergovernmental relations, chaired by Senator Edmund S. Muskie of Maine. The *Tennessean* investigation at the time was unfinished. In many newspapers, by tradition or ethical guideline, reporters are taught that they are not to take an active role in politics or policymaking, their job is to report and analyze the news. But there was no such line drawn at the *Tennessean*, where reporters were often participants in the news in various ways. They had used aliases to infiltrate and expose the Ku Klux Klan, a Teamsters local, a mental hospital, the county drunk tank. They had voluntarily testified as prosecution witnesses at various trials, and they had also appeared before the state legislature and Congress. If this seemed like unusual behavior to reporters elsewhere, Gore thought nothing of it. He arrived at the subcommittee table like someone who belonged there.

"It is a pleasure to welcome you, Mr. Gore, to testify," Muskie began. "Mr. Gore's father is, of course, a distinguished former senator, one for whom I think we have the highest respect, for his integrity and ability during all of the years he has served. I regard him as a personal friend and still do. It is a pleasure to welcome his son here this morning."

"Thank you, Mr. Chairman," Gore responded. "I appreciate the opportunity to testify, and I want to especially thank each member of the subcommittee for this opportunity. I consider it an honor, and I hope I can make some contribution to the legislation you are considering. Thank you for the kind words about the 'distinguished former senator.' A long time ago, when no one distinguished was looking, he and I used to play baseball out in that very hallway over there."

Senator Muskie: "There are other games being played there now."

Mr. Gore: "Right."

Gore went on to say that his newspaper was "in the midst of a continuing investigation" into land appraisal firms and tax mapping companies. "The bulk of my testimony this morning will deal with many of the facts I have found so far. As new information is developed, I will keep the subcommittee staff informed of it." Hardly the rhetoric of a young man disillusioned with politics. He was an investigative reporter in essence doing his work for a legislative committee (even suggesting an amendment)—an odd combination that appealed to him greatly, and one that he would later use to great advantage from the other side, as a legislator acting like an investigative reporter.

Gore's request that he not cover politics dissolved, and eventually he found himself attending night meetings of the Metro Council. Sometimes, when their sessions droned on late into the night, he was the only reporter there. He sat at a table in the middle of the room, surrounded by politicians arrayed in front of him on a U-shaped podium. The power he wielded in that situation made him feel giddy. When he picked up his pen and started writing, every council member suddenly wanted to talk. When he put his pen down, they would shut up. Something else started burning inside him: a sense that he could do what they were doing better than they were doing it. This reawakening did not lead Gore to befriend the local pols he was covering, but rather seemed to increase the tension between them. Some of the officials he covered began to think of him as a self-righteous political heir posturing as a journalist, trying to have it both ways. The prickly relations became most intense in November 1973, when Gore tailed a pack of junketeering councilmen to a convention in Puerto Rico, and mocked their trip in a front-page story, only to be found munching at their hors d'oeuvre table.

THE NEXT YEAR, Gore began picking up anecdotes from business sources about possible abuses of the zoning system. The city had a policy of councilmanic courtesy that allowed individual members to grant zoning variances within their districts. Gore started accumulating data on when and how these decisions were being made, and thought he saw a pattern of corruption. One day, he barged into the editor's office. "He came in with a stack of papers eighteen inches high," Seigenthaler recalled. "And he put them on the coffee table and began to break them down. I put my hand on them and said, 'Al, is there any way you could cut this short?' And he said, 'No, damn it! There's no way to cut this short!' He sort of scolded me a little bit, which took some guts, and so I went over and sat down, laughing to myself, 'You smart young prick.' " Gore spent an hour showing him the documents. Seigenthaler realized that there was a big story and gave Gore the go-ahead to drop everything else and dig deeper.

While covering the police beat earlier, Gore had helped break some stories about how police were abusing prostitutes and shaking them down for sexual favors. His key source was the foreman of a standing grand jury, a local developer named Gilbert Cohen. Now, as Gore was investigating the zoning system, Cohen came to him with a complaint that he was being shaken down by a councilman. "You're kidding!" Gore said. It perfectly fit his suspicions.

Cohen told him the story. He and his business partners needed a variance to close an alley, he claimed, but Morris Haddox was holding it up, yanking it from the council agenda and implying that it would take money to change his mind. Gore took the story back to Seigenthaler, who was not only an editor but a power broker in the Democratic establishment, a man who held a virtual veto power over the party slate of candidates. One of his friends in the party was the local prosecutor, district attorney general Thomas Shriver, who was also a close friend of Gore's sister, Nancy. "It's a small town, or it was then," Gore explained later. He and Seigenthaler both talked to Shriver, who agreed to work with the newspaper to see if Haddox could be caught in the act of soliciting and receiving a bribe. Gore brokered the contact between Shriver and Cohen. The sting operation was set.

Cohen entered the pharmacy on January 19, wired for sound, with Gore in his yellow Volkswagen and the TBI investigators in their unmarked cars listening nearby. Haddox was working at the back counter. The developer and the pharmacist talked for nearly two hours. Their discussion had a comic interruption once, when local promoter Abe Stein came in and joined the conversation, passing the time of day. Eventually, according to the tape recording, Stein left and Haddox got down to business, saying to Cohen, "It will take a grand to get it done."

Cohen left the drugstore, drove downtown, and called Haddox, saying he should meet him to pick up a down payment on the grand. He instructed Haddox to drive to the corner of Seventh Avenue and Union Street, where Cohen would be waiting. The location was selected because it was a prime spot for a stakeout. Three *Tennessean* photographers were perched above the corner, looking out from the offices of the newspaper's law firm. Also watching were Gore,

Seigenthaler, and the TBI agents. Siggy, as Seigenthaler was known, munched ferociously on an apple.

As Haddox's Lincoln Continental approached the intersection and came to a stop, Cohen stepped from the sidewalk outside the Downtowner Motor Inn. He was wired for sound again, and the conversation was again recorded by the TBI agents.

"Oh, you don't have to count it for me, Gibby," Haddox said.

"Okay. Well, there's three hundred here. That's all I got. Okay?" responded Cohen.

"All right," said Haddox. "I'll take care of it."

But none of that proved to be enough in court. Gore, after spending hours going over the tapes with assistant prosecutor Robert H. Schwartz, took the stand to testify about what he had seen and heard, providing a play-by-play explanation of the tape recordings. But Judge Allen Cornelius ruled that the tapes were of debatable accuracy and not admissible evidence. Haddox insisted that he had been forewarned that Cohen might be out to get him, and that he had no intention of keeping the bribe, but intended to report it to authorities. He just never got around to it before the indictment broke, he claimed. The first jury was deadlocked along racial lines and dissolved in a mistrial. At the second trial, Haddox's attorney, William C. Wilson, in his final argument, railed against entrapment, which he called "the meanest, vilest, sneakiest method of law enforcement." The jury voted to acquit Haddox after deliberating for four hours, determining that it was uncertain he intended to keep the money as a bribe and that the newspaper and prosecutors might have conspired to entrap him. Gore was outside the courtroom when he heard the verdict. He sat stunned on a bench, slumped down, head in hands.

The drama had profoundly different effects on its two central characters. Haddox was wiped out in the next election, then slowly worked his way back in local politics and returned to office two decades later. As a Democrat in a city where Gore, the erstwhile investigative reporter, went on to become the party's favorite son, Haddox felt some obligation to forget the past. When Air Force Two landed at Nashville one night during the 1996 campaign, he stood in the receiving line and greeted the vice president with a two-armed embrace. Four years later, a GORE FOR PRESIDENT sign could be seen in the storefront of the pharmacy. But in the privacy of his store, standing behind the back counter in his traditional white frock, Haddox still harbored a touch of bitterness about the reporter and the newspaper that pursued him. "They never admitted," he said in a whispery, high-pitched voice, "that they might have gone too far."

Gore's life was also changed by the case. "It was an outcome that amazed me," he said decades later. The verdict, in fact, helped put him back on the political track. When the trial ended, struck by the "unusual power of some words and phrases thrown around in a courtroom," he said to himself, "I need to know more about that," and enrolled at Vanderbilt law school. He soon begged off the investigative beat and began writing editorials for the *Tennessean*, then ran for office and began the long climb to the White House, where as vice president he watched his political patron, Bill Clinton, face an impeachment vote after being caught in a sex-and-lies scandal that relied on tape recordings and a variation of an investigative sting. But Gore never entertained a second thought about the way he pursued Haddox. "I thought a crime was being committed," he said. "I thought it was a big story. I thought I had an exclusive. And two out of three ain't bad!"

CHAPTER ELEVEN

OTHER LIVES

F OUR YEARS of graduate school in religion and law and not much to show for it. No degrees for Al Gore, even after all those classes and countless early mornings and long nights writing papers, reading coursework, and talking things out, stealing hours from a schedule already overloaded with obligations at the newspaper and home, and in the middle of it all, during the soggy-shirted Watergate-hearings summer of 1973, dealing with Tipper's pregnancy and the birth of their first child, Karenna. Here, during his Nashville days between Vietnam and Congress, it would be mistaken to define Gore by the stereotype later applied to him, that of the cautious plodder following a sure and narrow path to advancement. He was not so much an ambitious young man on the rise, doing what was necessary to attain the expected credentials, but more of a relentless if occasionally out-of-sorts figure trying out several lives in succession, or sometimes all at once, as newspaperman, ethicist, legal scholar, husband and father, pot-smoking escapist, and sober editorialist.

There are two ways to interpret this period of Gore's life. One is that for all the activity he was essentially marking time, waiting for the right moment to face the inevitable and begin the political career he had been groomed for since birth. His return to Tennessee in that sense was not unlike the homeward journey of his contemporary, Bill Clinton, who came back to Arkansas in the early 1970s ostensibly to teach law but in reality to prepare for his first run for Congress. From this perspective, the fact that Gore flitted from one interest to another at the newspaper and at school, and failed to complete his degree programs in either religion or law, only serves as evidence that he had politics in the back of his mind all along. He never worried about finishing his studies because he would not need them in the end, when he ran for office, even if it took him five years to reach the electoral starting line, compared to the one year it took Clinton. But whatever truth there is in that interpretation tends to overshadow another perspective on Gore's Nashville experience, one that better illuminates some qualities that he carried with him into politics.

The graduate degrees were not necessary to Gore in his scholarly pursuits because what truly mattered to him was whether he could convince himself, and everyone around him, that he *got* it, that he comprehended a subject both in minute detail and in the abstract and could make connections to related themes in other fields. If he had something to prove, it was not that he could advance; he took achievement as a given, a birthright, as certain as his acceptance into Harvard. But he had to prove that he had the worldly knowledge, not the grades or degrees, that made him worthy of achievement. Could he rid himself of the cynicism that had nipped away at him since college? Was anything he was doing meaningful? Those were his unresolved questions, the cause of his anxiety and insecurity, and he tried to deal with them in his own way, by taking the world apart and putting it back together again, piece by piece, until it made more sense to him, a characteristic response that was more intellectual than intuitive.

The chairman of Vanderbilt's graduate department of religion, H. Jackson Forstman, had accepted Gore into his program with what he later called "the foresense to realize that this young man was going to get involved in a lot of other things and likely would not complete his degree." And indeed Gore did not come close to completing his degree. His transcript indicates that of the eight courses he took as a part-time student in the master's program, he received credit in only three: American Church History (in which he received a B), Ethics (A-), and Primitive Religions (A-). In the other five courses, he was first given incompletes, meaning he did not finish all the required papers, and eventually those I's were crossed out and turned into F's. In later explaining why he dropped out of the religion program, Gore claimed that he stopped at the point where he would be required to take ancient Greek in the second year, a prospect that he said was beyond his level of commitment. That is an understandable explanation, but in recounting his own history, Gore is an unreliable narrator, and his account in this case is contradicted by the record. His transcript indicates that he was not doing all the required work in his classes during his second semester, when he received incompletes in Mysticism East and West, Social Factors in Christian History, and a seminar in Theology and Phenomenology.

It is still noteworthy that the professors who gave Gore those incompletes uniformly remembered him as an earnest and engaged student. The most obscure and intellectually challenging course he took was a seminar in phenomenology taught by Professor Edward Farley, which went through a series of complex questions on the nature of human interrelations, delving into the philosophy of the body and the philosophy of language. It was an advanced class that required some knowledge of the existentialism and semiotics of modern European philosophy, which Gore lacked. Farley discouraged him from trying it—"I remember saying to him, 'Look, I don't know what you have in mind for your future, but this looks a little too technical for you'"—to no avail. The texts by philosophers Edmund Husserl and Maurice Merleau-Ponty were so dense and difficult that Farley would spend an entire class going over a few pages, identifying "what seemed to be the central issue that the text posed" and asking questions about it. He remembered Gore as having a classroom personality much like his own. "Neither one of us was highly animated," he said. But he also remembered that "it was hard to find something too difficult" for Gore, who "seemed to know what he was up to." The few papers that Gore turned in left Farley "quite astonished" in that "they were of absolutely first-rate quality. . . . It was not the kind of work that was just woodenly reproducing the text. It was work that showed real thinking, engaging the text in a thoughtful way."

The graduate school of religion was overseen by Vanderbilt's divinity school, which had a long tradition of liberal activism. It prided itself in being the first previously all-white divinity school in the south to desegregate, and its moment of honor came in the spring of 1960, when the faculty threatened to resign over the expulsion of James Lawson, a brilliant black student who had been arrested in Nashville for an act of civil disobedience. During the Vietnam years, many divinity professors joined the peace movement, and the school became a safe haven for young men who opposed the war and wanted to avoid the draft. Some of them were still there when Gore arrived as part of a smaller number of students who had returned from Vietnam and were trying to come to grips with what they had seen. The activism was evident in other areas as well, including a seminar taught by Eugene TeSelle on theology and the natural sciences. TeSelle was a strong environmentalist whose central theme was the stewardship of the earth, the idea that "if the whole Earth is given to the human race, in stewardship, to keep it and tend it, then there are responsibilities not to exploit it or destroy it."

As his seminar moved through the material from Copernicus and Darwin to the Club of Rome's *Limits of Growth* report on population and food, searching for the common ground between science and religion, TeSelle was impressed by Gore's attentiveness and his obvious interest in the ecological issues. He was always asking questions, TeSelle said, pushing for precise details while trying to place them in a broad philosophical context. Many years later, when Gore emerged as a national figure on the environment, and used an overtly religious and moral vocabulary to frame his argument, he did not acknowledge TeSelle as one of his mentors. It was a point that the professor neither harped on nor ever quite forgot. While a multitude of experiences certainly shaped Gore's philosophy, TeSelle said later, "I think the course helped spark it."

The course that seemed at once perhaps the most religious and political in Gore's religion curriculum was taught by Walter Harrelson, then dean of the divinity school. It engaged the theme of community justice, or the lack of it, as seen through the prophets of ancient Israel, Amos, Hosea, Isaiah, and Micah. The subject had a timeless relevance, and though Gore never said so, and was still in his mode of repressing any political ambitions, Harrelson suspected that the senator's son, who sat in the back row of the large class of some eighty students, "wanted to know how religion related to politics" and was fascinated by the lessons of the prophets. He might have been especially taken by the professor's rendering of Hosea, who blamed the killing and stealing and bloodshed of his day on the leaders for not sharing their knowledge with the people; and Amos, who describes judges taking bribes and rich men pushing the needy off the road, "the kind of indictment that is so vivid and powerful of people in high places, the biblical material that is most straightforward and devastating about misfeasance and malfeasance."

As he watched Gore rise in later years, Harrelson became fascinated by the religious strains he saw in his former student. Gore often said that he was the product of a mixed marriage—Albert came from the free church side of the Southern Baptists, while Pauline was from the Church of Christ—but Harrelson saw more of Pauline's side in him, a frame of mind shaped by guilt. "He comes from that brand of religion that is informed by John Calvin," Harrelson said. "Calvin has this deep, deep sense of how human beings, none of them, can fully be trusted, precisely because we're not God. That one of the characteristics of human life is frailty, that human beings have an enormous capacity to deceive themselves and to always put the best face on anything they see or think or do. That . . . they can look at the right but do the wrong." In viewing Gore from this perspective, Harrelson said, he was reminded somewhat of Abraham Lincoln, "who never went to church at all, but what he learned, he learned out of the Calvinist tradition of Protestantism. He was a tortured human being. I expect Al Gore to be [like that] if he becomes president. In this regard it's worth thinking about. Of course Lincoln was so folksy and full of humor and so at ease with himself in public"—in contrast to Gore. "But with regard to life's meaning, he was one struggling always in every sense to prevent chaos."

Harrelson found Gore's religious sensibility different in important respects from the two Democratic presidents who came along after his Vanderbilt days, Jimmy Carter and Bill Clinton. Gore will "want to do everything" just like Carter, he predicted. "But Carter thought the world could be made *right*. Gore knows better than that. Gore knows the world can be made *better*." Bill Clinton, a Southern Baptist like Gore, represents the opposite end of the spiritual tradition. Clinton comes from the church of optimism and freedom, a tradition that draws him into the images of reconciliation and forgiveness. His spirituality, as Harrelson interprets it, allows Clinton to be "a pragmatic human being down to his toenails." He is always moving and adjusting to the situation, adapting easily to his surroundings and the people around him. Gore sees life in sharper contrast, good and evil, black and white. Along with the weight of guilt, he carries a constant notion of sin, and that burden makes encounters with him uneven. At times he can seem distant, at times he connects, and still other times he appears irritatingly moralistic.

• • •

GORE OFTEN STRUGGLED with the idealized image of himself as the good boy and good son. He seemed eager to live up to it, or at least not to disappoint his parents and other adults who thought of him that way, yet he also wanted to rebel when he could in minor ways: driving fast, sleeping late, telling tall tales. The tension between perfection and his sense of self produced a seemingly inexhaustible supply of the Calvinist guilt that Harrelson saw in him. Unable to integrate what he wanted to do with what was expected of him, he tried to ease the tension by leading several lives at once. It seems evident that John Warnecke, the engaging radical Deadhead at the *Tennessean*, was an important figure in Gore's countercultural life during the Nashville years, though whether Warnecke played the Mephisiophelean role that he claims for himself remains uncertain and debatable.

Nashville in the 1970s had the reputation for being an educated and relatively hip oasis in the middle south, a place where people of the same generation and class tended to know one another, connected through the newspapers, the city and state government, and the university. Within that subculture, the Gores had scores of friends, but there was a much smaller group of three couples who spent much time together: Al and Tipper, Frank Sutherland and his future wife, Natilee, and Warnecke and his then-wife Nancy. They were all connected to the *Tennessean*—eventually including Tipper, who took a bottom-rung job in the photo lab—and the paper dominated their conversations. "We talked mostly journalism and the *Tennessean* and stories when we were together," recalled Sutherland. "We were all interested in the same issues and we'd talk about everything from our editor Seigenthaler to the stories of the day to what we ought to be doing journalistically."

Within that intimate group, by Warnecke's account, he and Gore had a particular affinity that came from their intense interest in talking politics, listening to music, and getting high. Here is the scene as later depicted by Warnecke: His house was known as a safe house where friends could "go and smoke pot." He got his marijuana free from an old acquaintance in California, "really good drugs, imported from the Orient"—big, fat, and "so potent that after one toke you wouldn't need another." And since he acquired it for free he passed it along to his friends without charge. As Warnecke remembered it, Gore was a frequent visitor, coming by the house at least two hundred times during his Nashville days to smoke dope with him. They would sit in the living room, listening to Crosby, Stills and Nash, the Grateful Dead, and Janis Joplin on Warnecke's quadraphonic stereo, with Al using his own blue-beaded roach clip. The blinds had to be drawn and the lights dimmed, and every now and then Gore would rise from the couch and peek out the window. Warnecke considered him "extremely paranoid" and wracked with guilt. "It was like he knew he was wrong."

Whatever one chooses to make of Warnecke's account, there are several points of context to consider. Smoking marijuana, like dealing with the draft during the Vietnam War, is a subject that inevitably comes around and around again for every politician of the baby boom generation, usually with more attention paid to the nature of the confessions, denials, and rationalizations than to the ultimate importance or irrelevance of the events themselves. (It has come around for Gore in twelve-year intervals, in 1976, 1988, and 2000.) Warnecke did not tell his story about the dope den sessions until nearly a quarter century after the fact. Along with providing details to Gore biographer Bill Turque and to the *Washington Post*, he also gave an account to the *National Enquirer*, a supermarket tabloid. He seems to have a selective memory that puts him in the center of all the action. As an example, he insisted that Michael Kapetan and girlfriend Karen Munson were not with Al and Tipper during their western camping trip in the summer of 1971, and that he alone was there for the midnight attack by the hungry bear at Yosemite.

Frank Sutherland, who is now the editor of the *Tennessean*, has consistently refused to talk about his private life or those of his friends, rebuffing queries from his own paper. Warnecke's former wife, now Nancy Rhoda, has also kept quiet, saying only that Warnecke's memory was faulty and that he had lived a troubled life. Considering Gore's work schedule, plus family obligations and his on-and-off efforts at Vanderbilt, it seems almost unfathomable that he could find the time to smoke dope with Warnecke two hundred times or more over five years. Gore, when asked whether he smoked marijuana during his Nashville days, responded: "When I came back from Vietnam, yes. But not to that extent."

ANOTHER LIFE BEGAN in the fall of 1974, when Gore switched from reporting to editorial writing at the *Tennessean* and simultaneously enrolled at Vanderbilt law school. It often seemed as though his family wanted him to get his law degree more than he did. "He had absolutely no interest in going to law school whatsoever. I think his mother made him. She probably said it two thousand times," said Al's cousin Jamie Gore. That is certainly an exaggeration. Gore had become curious about the law since the verdict took him by surprise in the Haddox bribery case. And his mother was forceful but never so overt or obnoxiously pushy as to tell him exactly what he should do. Yet there is no doubt that Pauline and Albert, assuming that their son's adventure in journalism was temporary, hoped that he would get a law degree just as they both had decades earlier, and thought the credential would help him no matter what path his career followed. His brother-in-law, Frank Hunger, another lawyer, also nudged Al toward law school, with sister Nancy's encouragement. "I was very instrumental in that," Hunger said decades later. "I thought it was something he would enjoy, and he had a lot of characteristics that would be good in that profession."

So here was Gore at age twenty-six back at Vanderbilt again, not having attempted to make up the incompletes in his religion studies. He was now part of a group that called itself "the geriatric set," six first-year law students who had been out of college several years and were older than the rest. They sat together in the back of Contracts in Room 0-22 and formed a study group, though after a month or so Gore and two classmates broke off into their own smaller detachment in a polite difference over how and what to study. While the others turned to the study group for purely pragmatic reasons, as an efficient way to share detailed notes of class lectures and outlines of reading material, Gore, Tom Lindley, and Andy Shookhoff were more interested in holding wide-ranging philosophical discussions, searching for ways to relate legal issues to broader social and political themes. "Our concept looked extremely indulgent to the other three," Shookhoff recalled. "So they went ahead on their own." Again one could see Gore's motivation not simply to get through, but to prove to himself that he could master the material.

Three times a week, on Tuesday and Thursday nights and Saturday mornings, the trio met at Lindley's cramped one-bedroom apartment on 28th Street near the campus and Centennial Park on Nashville's west end. Each student had his own role in the study group. Shookhoff, from the Bronx and Bard College, was the most radical and most critical of American capitalism. Lindley, who had come from a poor farm town in central Illinois and had studied philosophy at the

University of Texas, approached the world in a constant search for philosophical truth. He thought of Gore, despite his Tennessee roots, as having the sophisticated East Coast sensibilities of "a Boston Brahmin—someone who is educated and capable and believes that it is critical to help make the world a better place." They often spent the first hour debating the role of law in society, then went about preparing for class. Lindley, sitting on his bed with class notes and heavy law books, suggested a preliminary outline. Shookhoff paced the room leafing through Horn's law narratives in search of relevant case histories and themes, and Gore sat at the desk, asking precise questions and banging out the outline on an IBM Selectric typewriter. Lindley's cats, Thucydides and Lilith, took it all in, perched on a shelf above the door.

Over the course of two years, his study mates saw Gore systematically using law school to work his way through difficult political and social policy issues, though he never hinted to them that he was preparing for a life in public office. For several sessions they had what Shookhoff later remembered as the "first really in-depth discussions I ever heard about the impact of AFDC [Aid to Families with Dependent Children] policy on families," with Al "in one discussion ranting about how federal policy was practically designed to break up families." Abortion had become a dominant political and legal issue again with the *Roe v. Wade* decision and was a frequent topic of discussion. Gore started out seemingly pro-choice. One night, when Lindley invited friends to a lasagna party, a Vanderbilt psychology professor argued that undergoing an abortion was so traumatic that it could not be justified under any circumstances as the lesser of two evils, even if the pregnancy was caused by rape or incest. "It was a very hot discussion that evening," Lindley recalled. "Al pretty much said that is absurd and went into why"—using both his legal and religious training in rebutting the professor.

In Constitutional Law, Gore struggled with the riddle of democracy that had puzzled him since his father's defeat: What is the role of elected officials in a representative government—should they be educating voters or reflecting voter attitudes? Lindley remembered Gore telling stories about his father's loss and how the senator had "gotten too far ahead of his populace; he may have been right, but was ahead of his voting base." When Shookhoff made sweeping arguments for political freedoms, Gore countered "that in the absence of any economic ability to take advantage of those freedoms, those freedoms are just as lost as if you never had them in the first place." His fascination with science and futurist issues also became apparent to his classmates. In his third semester he took a Communications Law seminar and could not stop talking about it. According to Lindley, he was "just absolutely bubbling one evening when he came over because of the new concepts rolling around in his mind on telecommunications. . . . He got into this long discussion about needing to find a way to open the bandwidth for additional options."

With the help of his study group partners, Gore plowed through the first three semesters of law school. He carried a heavy load for someone also working full time, seven or eight courses a semester, and completed all but one class (Law and Anthropology). His grades were satisfactory but utterly unremarkable, the highest an 81 in Legal Writing and the lowest a 69 in Civil Procedure II, with a cumulative average of 75.6. The lasting images of him from that period are of anything but a grind. Ted Brown, who had worked for Gore's father and was also studying at Vanderbilt law then, remembers seeing Gore in the evening "at one of the reading tables at the law library, in a red flannel shirt and jeans, his boots propped up on a table, reading like he didn't have a care in the world, he had everything under control." Along with their rambling study group discussions, Lindley and Shookhoff would not forget Gore's competitiveness and skill at games: his outside shot and sharp elbows in basketball, his agility with a Frisbee, and his unlikely talent as an acrobat. Whenever he got tired or bored at the typewriter, he would take out a tennis racket or umbrella and balance it perfectly on the bridge of his nose — an act he had perfected during the long lonely nights as a boarder at St. Albans.

Al Gore loose? That might be stretching it. He never could dance, Tipper was the dancer. But he loved to sing, and there he was one night at a party, dressed in his military fatigues, blaring it out: "They often call me Speedo, but my real name is Mr. Earl."

In his workaday life at the *Tennessean* during his law school days, Gore moved down from the newsroom on the third floor to the editorial board offices on the second floor. He attended most of the 10:00 A.M. editorial meetings and wrote on subjects that interested him, especially education. The newspaper had a fiercely liberal reputation, but Gore, though he was said to be "quite forceful" during the board meetings, wrote like what his colleague Jim O'Hara called "a raging moderate." He concentrated on local education issues and a few pet subjects, including the environment and climate change, that editorial editor Lloyd Armour found esoteric. According to Armour, Gore once wrote an editorial that prefigured his later warnings about global warming, but the piece never ran. "Frankly, no," Armour said, when asked whether he believed Gore's predictions. "You have people who are sort of backward like I was. . . . Global warming wasn't one of my most precious subjects." Gore struck Armour as "a better researcher than writer." His copy was sent back for a rewrite, but rarely to get more facts; Gore often interviewed a few dozen people before writing a single editorial.

Along with the climate change piece, Gore wrote another editorial in the spring of 1976 that never ran. It was a passionate attack on the state's education system that began: "Education in Tennessee is a damned disgrace." Even if this was a liberal newspaper in a relatively progressive city, it was still in the middle of the Bible Belt. The wry and gentlemanly Armour quickly struck out the "damn"—"I thought by removing that one word, it would improve the hell out of the editorial," he later joked—and then put it aside and misplaced it. By the time he found it again, Al Gore no longer worked at the *Tennessean*.

CHAPTER TWELVE

THE SON SHALL RISE

TIPPER GORE NEARLY HAD what she wanted in the spring of 1976. Her life was balanced between work and home, with a rambunctious two-year-old daughter and a job in the photography department of the *Tennessean* that gave her opportunities to shoot evocative pictures. Her husband had been saying for years that they would buy a country paper and write books and live in a cabin on the lake, and now he was starting to follow through on that idyllic vision. The *Carthage Courier*, the little 3,200-circulation weekly that "gave a whoop about Smith County," had been put up for sale by the widows of the two owners, and Al set about trying to borrow the money to buy it, exacting promises of loans from family and friends. He was one of four potential buyers, but his bid was underfinanced and he lost out to Hershel Lake, who already owned a weekly in Crossett, Arkansas, and had a better sense of what the *Courier* was worth. "I remember to the penny what I paid for it. It was $157,000. I had to mortgage my house to buy it," Lake said later. The negotiations began in January and Lake took control the first of March.

Three days earlier, on a Friday morning, Tipper's world had changed dramatically when her husband had come home from a law class and taken a call from John Seigenthaler. Everything came around and through Siggy sooner or later, usually sooner. As editor of the *Tennessean*, he was perhaps the best-connected figure in Nashville. He knew all the judges, lawyers, politicians, labor leaders, and financiers, and with his peculiar blend of disparate characteristics, part fearless investigative reporter, part old-style political boss, he could pick up rumors at their inception and move them along to those who needed to know, guiding the flow with the flair of a news virtuoso. Now he had definitive word that Joe L. Evins, the veteran Democratic representative from Tennessee's fourth district, would announce his retirement on Monday, creating a rare opening in the congressional seat once held by the senior Gore.

After trying unsuccessfully to interest young Gore in some political races in Nashville a few years earlier, Seigenthaler had become convinced that the senator's son wanted no part of politics and would play out his career in journalism. But there had been signs of a change of heart since then, with the move to the editorial board and enrollment in law school, so now Seigenthaler tried again. There was no need to make the case overtly; he just passed along the news and closed with the line, "You know what I think."

In that brief second, it all seemed to wash away, all the self-protective defenses that Gore had built up over years and years, his supposed cynicism and disillusionment, his determination to follow his own path, the promises he had made to his wife about living the writer's life. He hung up the phone and turned to Tipper and said, "I'm going to run for Congress." He just blurted it out, without his normal long and reasoned analysis of the pros and cons. Then he reflexively hit the floor and started doing push-ups, as if to prove to the old man that he had what it takes, that all those push-ups they sweated out together at the big house and in Suite 809 atop the Fairfax were in preparation for this challenge. Tipper figuratively headed for the floor as well. "I wanted to faint," she said later. "They would have to bring me back with smelling salts." The political life? She had seen very little to recommend it, only the bitterness of the 1970 race and how that loss had affected Al and his sister, Nancy, and Gore Senior and Pauline, followed by the corruption of Watergate. Politics was not part of the plan, and her first unedited reaction was one of surprise and dismay.

What would Al's parents think? They were not in Tennessee that weekend, but out in California with their friends and frequent traveling companions, Bill and Dorothy McSweeney. In the years since his forced retirement from politics, Gore Senior had been working in the oil and energy empire of Armand Hammer, his old Angus cattle partner, as executive vice president of Hammer's newly acquired Island Creek Coal Company and board member of Occidental Petroleum, sinecures that had brought him some measure of wealth for the first time in his life. ("When the voters put me out to pasture," he explained unapologetically, "I went looking for the tallest grass I could find.") McSweeney, a former Hearst newspapers journalist and White House aide to LBJ, was president of another Hammer subsidiary, Occidental International Corporation, and often invited Albert and Pauline to accompany him on trips overseas. During stops in Los Angeles near Occidental headquarters, the two couples stayed in their favorite suite at the Beverly Wilshire. It was there that Gore Senior received a call from his son late that Friday night. When he hung up the phone, he went back to Pauline and the McSweeneys and said dryly, "Al's going to run for Congress. I told him I'd vote for him."

It was a rare demonstration of understatement by the father, who was practicing the restraint that his son had urged on him during their phone conversation. Yes, Gore Senior had predicted in his concession speech six years earlier that the truth shall rise again, and yes, many took that to mean that someday his namesake son would avenge his defeat, and yes, Al admired his father and did not want to disappoint him, but still this had to be *his* race based on his personality and his issues. That meant his father had to give him enough room, at least in public. (Later, at a garage sale at the house of Nashville attorney James Neal, Gore Senior ran into Seigenthaler and confessed "how frustrating it was for him not to get back on the stump on behalf of Al," he so loved to campaign, but that he was trying to follow his son's wishes.)

The whole family, Tipper's shock aside, was all for Al running, of course, especially Nancy, who delighted in the political game and looked forward to escaping from Mississippi for a few months and working the county seats in middle Tennessee on her little brother's behalf. Pauline, who had been promoting her son's political skills at least since he was six, when she told a Knoxville correspondent about how he had outtalked his father the senator into buying him a more expensive toy bow and arrow, accepted his return to the family dream with only one regret. It bothered her that he would quit law school to make the race (so much so that she later privately inquired of the university chancellor if it was possible for him to get a degree by mail). There was some hope that he might at least finish that fourth semester, which ended in early May, since the congressional primary was not until August, but Gore wanted none of that, and politely rebuffed the pleas of his mother and a few family friends she had enlisted in her cause.

He had made the turn, finally, and now he was in a rush and wanted nothing in the way. This is what his friends had expected of him all along. *Politics was inevitable, just a matter of when,* thought Harvard friend Mike Kapetan. *Even during the dark days, deep down, if you got into his mind, he was politically motivated, he never really got away from it,* thought his Carthage pal Steve Armistead. *Al would never admit it but probably he always knew that he would go back into politics, the* Tennessean *job was just a sort of a sabbatical,* thought newspaper colleague Frank Sutherland. Now it all made sense to law school study mate Tom Lindley, both the way their discussions always came around to political consequences and something more telling: For years in his spare time, Gore had been "training his memory"—taking speed reading courses and reading books on mnemonics that "teach you to remember names and faces and places quickly." Lindley used to think of it as the kind of self-improvement that would make Gore a better businessman or lawyer. Now he realized it was all for this moment.

After an endless round of phone conversations, Gore summoned a few of his closest friends to dinner at the house in Carthage that Sunday for a long strategy session. Sutherland, as part of the newspaper gang that had already charted his rise to the presidency by 2008, now urged him on and offered advice on how to run and what to say. "What kind of advice have you got for me, Steve?" Gore then asked Armistead, and his childhood friend offered words of wisdom from the country boys who had once comprised the Snow Creek Gang. "I've got two things to tell ya," he said. "Get a haircut and buy some clothes. That's all I can tell ya."

In an instant, it seemed to the others, Gore had three new blue suits, new shirts, new shoes, no stringy sideburns, shorn hair, a new residence (moving from a Nashville apartment replete with beaded curtains and a waterbed to a suburban ranch house on eighty-eight acres across the Caney Fork from his parents; he had bought it from a Hammer subsidiary a few years earlier), a new political team—everything fresh and full of energy for the emergence of the prince of Tennessee. But even before he delivered his announcement speech, the first of many he would make on the steps of the Smith County Courthouse in Carthage over the years, there was one sign that this political life would be a struggle for him. As he was leaving the house with Tipper and little Karenna, he was overwhelmed by a sense of nausea and he rushed back inside and threw up.

• • •

HOW'M I DOIN'? *How'm I doin'?* It was understandable that Al Gore Jr., a candidate for Congress at age twenty-eight, would seem a bit insecure on the stump in the early days of his first campaign. He had not run for office since his freshman year at Harvard, and he had never given speeches in public like this. *How'm I doin'?* he asked his traveling aide after every event.

You're a little stiff, Larry Harrington answered. *But smart.*

Gore usually laughed at the critique. Then asked again, *How'm I doin'?*

When the campaign came to Putnam County for a courthouse rally, they ran an ad in the paper, someone brought watermelons, the crowd was ready for an old-fashioned stem-winder, and Gore in his blue suit and blue shirt and red tie leaped onto the flatbed truck and grabbed the microphone and—was pitiful. The body language, the message, the cadence of his speech, his choice of words, all wrong. Some supporters in the audience thought it was the worst speech they had ever seen in their lives and wondered why they had signed up to work for him. Even John Jared Maddux Jr., his county co-chairman, stood there thinking "this is not a very good speaker." Then Gore ended by saying that he wanted to "rekindle the spirit of America," and Maddux thought, *Well, that's pretty cool,* and decided his guy would win. Over the next few months, Maddux thought Gore's style improved, and so did Harrington, but others found him agonizingly formal and distant from beginning to end.

With Gore, it seems, it was always thus. He might have been born to politics, but he was not born to run. His aides quickly realized that not only was he shy and nervous about meeting the public, but he became carsick every time he read briefing papers while they were driving from town to town along the winding country roads, which meant he had an uneasy stomach nearly all the time. He just bulled his way through, though, fighting the queasiness day after day until eventually his body adjusted. Then, as always, his unease was counterbalanced by competitiveness, a sheer will to prevail that he had exhibited before mostly in athletics. One family friend remembered the fury with which little Al at age eleven had battled him in a life-and-death Ping-Pong match at the big house; another recalled the glee with which Gore the teenager at St. Albans had grappled with him when he visited one day to wrestle in the prep school gym. His friends could see a look in his eye; he had to win. If only you could win a political race by getting yourself into shape (more push-ups, better diet, longer morning runs) and then competing longer and harder (more predawn factory gates, more stops at country stores per day), Gore would not be outdone.

As he had explained to his father when they first talked about the race, he felt that he had to run on his own identity, not simply as the heir to a famous Tennessee name, but even though his parents obeyed his wishes and stayed on the sidelines most of the time, the presence of the old man and Pauline was everywhere nonetheless. In the morning, Gore Senior would drive the mile and a half from the big house to his son's new place, which doubled as the campaign headquarters. He would stand around in the little office back by the rear bedroom and strategize with whoever was there, then leaf through his battered old black leather book, calling out names of small-town mayors and vice mayors and judges and their wives and telephone numbers. The extent to which he influenced his son's policy positions seemed minimal, thought Ken Jost, who had taken a temporary leave from the *Tennessean* to serve as press secretary. One night they drafted a press release calling for the abolition of the congressional seniority system, only to find the idea spiked the next morning, with Gore suggesting that his father did not like it.

Pauline's influence was subtler but perhaps stronger. For lunch and at the end of the evening, many staffers would be invited over to the big house, where Gore's mother would feed them and gently interrogate them and guide them. *Did you call so-and-so over in Sumner County?* she would ask. Everyone was in awe of Miz Pauline, and more than a little intimidated, and the question was usually annoying, one aide recalled, because it was obvious that she knew so much more than any of them. You had to decide whether to lie to her and say that you had indeed called so-and-so, knowing that she had probably just talked to that person, or fess up and look like you were lazy or out of touch. There were times when it became apparent that it was his mother, more than the old man, who gave Al his will and determination. Once Pauline joined him for lunch at a café in Cookeville with the local organizers, who revealed that they were having a difficult time rounding up support. Gore, embarrassed, looked at his mother and declared, "Well, we'll just change that!"

Tennessee's fourth congressional district had been reshaped many times over the decades, and by 1976 it slashed through twenty-five counties across the middle of the state on an uneven diagonal from the Kentucky border to the Alabama line, but the heart of it was still the Upper Cumberland region that had first elected Gore Senior to the U.S. House of Representatives in 1938. The old man knew the territory, and if his old-time supporters were gone, he worked on the sons. Al Junior had tried to recruit John Maddux during an early trip through the Putnam County Courthouse, with no success. Maddux liked Gore, but was too busy, and also his law partner was the campaign manager for another candidate. Then Maddux got a call from Gore Senior, asking to come to his house. The old man arrived with a silver memento, a gift that Pauline had picked up at an antiques auction. Then he settled into a chair and told John, who was about Al's age, how much he liked his father, John Jared Maddux Sr., who had served in the Tennessee legislature and was part of the coalition that had beaten the Crump machine from Memphis. He reminisced about how the elder Maddux had placed Gore Senior's name in nomination for the vice presidency at the 1956 Democratic convention, and went on and on about their families before getting to the point.

"I want you to help Al," he said. "He's hurting here in Putnam County."

Maddux signed on as co-chair. Soon enough he was campaigning for Gore across the Upper Cumberland.

To be on the campaign trail as Al Gore Jr. had its advantages and disadvantages. His name recognition in the district approached 90 percent, three times that of any of his eight opponents in the Democratic primary, but that name recognition cut both ways. Some voters saw the son's campaign as a means of redemption for the father, whose defeat they now regretted, while others, especially in the more conservative counties on the southern rim of the district, wanted nothing to do with the Gore family and still felt sour about the father's final years in the Senate when he opposed the Vietnam War and came across to them as an aloof liberal. Those in the middle wondered whether Al had anything going for him other than his name, and watched to see if he would slip. Of the nine candidates in the primary, T. Tommy Cutrer, a country radio personality endorsed by the Man in Black, Johnny Cash, was the best known aside from Gore. The favorite, however, was neither Gore nor Cutrer, but J. Stanley Rogers, a well-financed liberal from Manchester who served as majority leader in the Tennessee House. Rogers, with a quarter-million-dollar campaign chest, was stunned by Gore's entry into the race and did not hesitate to pound away at the Gore family and its financial connections to Armand Hammer.

While Gore sought to portray himself as a populist who would protect the environment and fight big corporations, Rogers said that the Gore family's connections to Hammer made Al a "special interests" candidate who came into the campaign with "a tangle of conflicts" that he tried to hide. "The people of the fourth district should know that big oil and big coal are my real opponents in this campaign," Rogers said. He pointed out that Island Creek Coal was one of the three major suppliers of coal to the huge government-run Tennessee Valley Authority. And he demanded that Gore acknowledge that he received quarterly royalty payments for zinc mining rights on his land in a deal with another Hammer subsidiary, Occidental Minerals Corporation. Gore tried to finesse the issue. While his disclosure statement listed his assets in general terms, it did not name the company from which he received royalties. And because Occidental Minerals had recently sold its mining rights to another corporation, Freeport Zinc, Gore was able to argue that Rogers had his facts wrong, which was technically true. It turned out that Rogers was not aware of the extent to which Occidental had assisted young Gore in his acquisition of the land. The company bought it and sold it to Senior, who turned around and sold it to his son on the same day. The issue in any case became sufficiently fuzzy so that Rogers dropped it, turning instead to the argument that Gore was an interloper who came from Washington and wanted to return to Washington, that he had never really lived or gone to school or played football in Carthage.

The question of whether Gore was presenting himself as something that he was not took on another dimension during that campaign. Some of his friends in law school and at the *Tennessean* scratched their heads when they heard him on the campaign trail. They thought of him as a traditional liberal, yet here he was running to the right of Rogers and striking one conservative note after another, opposing gun registration laws, calling homosexuality "abnormal," pushing welfare reform, and saying that the courts had not found the "proper balance" between "a woman's freedom" and "the fetus's right to life." Did Gore believe what he was saying or was he trimming his thoughts to his rural constituency, trying not to get too far ahead of the voters, as he thought his father had done? Variations of that question haunt many politicians throughout their careers. It can be an especially troublesome proposition for ambitious young southerners trying to survive and rise from a conservative base. Bill Clinton, running his first successful race (for attorney general) in neighboring Arkansas that same summer, was also surprising friends and traditional allies by moving to the right. He refused to endorse organized labor's call for a repeal of the state's right-to-work law, a change from his previous position that he defended with the pragmatic explanation, "this is a bad time because our people generally are in a conservative mood."

Much like Clinton, Gore had been considering the conservative trend in the country for several years and often wondered aloud about the extent to which a progressive politician could or should adjust. He wanted to strike what he called "an ideological balance." Alan Carmichael, a reporter covering the congressional campaign for Gore's old newspaper, raised the question of Gore's rightward drift in a long account of a day he spent with his former colleague on the trail. "One of the more interesting questions in the race has been the surprisingly conservative views attributed to Gore," Carmichael wrote. He noted that the son seemed to be taking more cautious positions than his father had in his Senate loss six years earlier, then pointed out that the Nashville *Banner*, the *Tennessean's* conservative rival, had endorsed Gore and glowingly cited his conservative stands. "The young candidate," the story went on, "insists he is not taking these positions to get elected in the conservative district." "I believe what I say," Gore said.

There was one subject about which he wanted to say nothing. At one point during the day Carmichael spent with him, the reporter asked Gore whether he had a position on the legalization of marijuana. Gore said that he opposed legalization, but thought penalties should be reduced for first-time offenders. Then came the follow-up question: Had Gore ever smoked dope? The question, and Gore's response, did not end up in Carmichael's story, and in fact did not come out for another twelve years, when Gore was running for president and the *Tennessean* undertook a long story concerning Gore and drugs in which a few dozen people from his newspaper days were interviewed. While researching that article, reporter Jim O'Hara unearthed the unpublished conclusion to the Carmichael story. Gore and Tipper and another aide were in the car that day, and when Carmichael popped the question, Gore sat there speechless for a long time, then stopped the car and got out with Carmichael and asked him whether he really wanted to ask that question. Carmichael decided to retract it.

A perilous moment, but one that came and went quickly and was soon all but forgotten. It was July and Rogers still seemed to be leading. Rogers had money and the old Evins team behind him. The retiring congressman, who had served in Washington for three decades and was the dean of the Tennessee delegation, never made a formal endorsement, but it was clear that he wanted Rogers to win. He and Gore Senior had never gotten along, differing in politics and personality and patronage involving the TVA. The top people from Evins's staff were working the district now for Rogers, hoping to come back to Washington with him and keep their old jobs. Rogers was young and confident, a tireless campaigner. Gore had only one strategy, to outwork him. He rumbled through the district nonstop, sleeping between towns, getting bitten by dogs, climbing up ladders to talk to roofers, kissing his first collection of strange babies, attending cakewalks and fish fries, sometimes taking little Karenna along and weaning her on M&Ms, forcing his way through his shyness and the upset stomachs, bounding into stores and garages to talk to anyone he could find.

Once he stopped at a gas station near Tracy City on the way to Chattanooga. He shook hands with the attendant and asked if anyone else was there. Sure, came the answer, three or four guys in the back. Gore strolled through the garage looking for votes, and found a body shop out back where a group of grease-stained men were working on cars. Gore stuck out his hand to the first mechanic he encountered. Can't shake, said the man, my hands are dirty. Gore tried a joke. *That's okay, I'm a Democrat.* It usually worked, but this time it provoked only a cold look.

"I sure do want you fellows to vote for me," Gore said.

"You know who I am?" asked the mechanic.

"No," said Gore. "Tell me your name."

The name clanged. When Gore was an investigative reporter at the *Tennessean*, he had looked into a chop shop operation that stole cars in Nashville and drove them down to Grundy County. This was the place, and here was the ringleader. Gore was always boasting about how his experience as an investigative reporter would make him a superior congressman, but that line was useless now. He backed away, slowly, then sprinted for his car. It was rare that he ventured that far south anyway. Most of the summer he campaigned in the ancestral turf of the Upper Cumberland, leaving the less friendly lower counties to surrogates, especially his sister, Nancy. "Sister Baby," as the old man called his only daughter, spent the last month of the campaign working the territory down near the Alabama line, picking up gossip, learning the sensibilities of the local pols, flattering them, playing to their strengths, and then saying, "So, what are you going to do for my little brother, Al?" It was the considered opinion of the political set that Nancy Gore Hunger understood the complexities of human relationships and the unspoken rules of the game better than anyone in her political family.

WHEN BILL CLINTON LOST his congressional race in northwest Arkansas two years earlier, at age twenty-eight, everyone around him knew the defeat could not stop him. The very next morning he was working the town square in Fayetteville, sticking out his big fleshy right hand, thanking voters, laying the groundwork for his next race. He was a racehorse who ran for office again and again, as he once said, because politics was the only track on which he knew how to run. Clinton was not groomed for it by his family, he was a natural-born runner. With Al Gore, it likely would have ended right there, on the night of August 5, 1976. If he had lost to Stanley Rogers, he would have turned away from politics and reentered law school and pursued the writer's life. He used not the racetrack but sailing to describe his ambition. He was always looking, as he once said, for a life that would put the wind at his back. A loss would have had him tacking in another direction. It almost happened. The day before the primary, Larry Harrington made a pessimistic confession to John Maddux when they met at the town square in Gainesboro. "Looks like we may lose," Harrington said. "It's gonna be close."

There were no motels in Carthage large enough to hold an election night party, so Gore's supporters gathered at the Holiday Inn down old Route 70 in Lebanon, the seat of neighboring Wilson County. Gore took an early lead in the tabulations, but then results came in from the south, and Rogers moved narrowly ahead. Gore father and son kept everyone waiting in Lebanon. They were back in Carthage working the phones, taking results precinct by precinct from Wilson and Smith and Putnam counties. When Maddux called with the Putnam results, he started reading them off one by one, all nine candidates . . . "Dr. Larry Irby . . . Ben Hall McFarlin . . . T. Tommy Cutrer . . ."

"I don't want T. Tommy Cutrer!" Gore Senior screamed into the phone. "Just give me Rogers and Gore! Rogers and Gore!"

When Maddux gave him the results, the old man clucked and declared, "John, my boy, I think we've just elected ourselves a congressman!" Al was two years younger than Senior had been when he first won the same seat. This was the beginning. The *Tennessean* got the results at the same time and placed a bulletin on the top right of the front page. Frank Sutherland banged out the lead, which ran in boldface type: "Albert Gore Jr. was the apparent winner in the 4th district primary last night, leading Stanley Rogers in a close contest." Above it was a banner headline announcing that James Sasser had won the Democratic primary for the Senate and would face Bill Brock in the fall. Gore won by 3,500 votes out of 115,000 cast. There was no Republican opposition, only a fringe candidate running as an independent, so his election was assured. Sasser, who would go on to defeat Brock, was almost part of the family, his wife one of Nancy's closest friends. At the celebration in Lebanon, the young man in the blue suit was surrounded on stage by the old man and Miz Pauline and Sister Baby and Frank Hunger and Tipper and Karenna. "My family has known the bitterness of defeat," he said. Here was sweet revenge.

But what about Tipper? She had left the *Tennessean* darkroom to campaign for her husband. "If I have to go to one more tea, I'll die!" she had muttered to a friend near the end of the campaign, but she had been a trouper and done her part up through the final day, when she and Johnny Hayes, a good-old-boy friend who had a knack for raising money, went over in his '62 pickup to the largest voting box in the district, at a school in Hendersonville, and worked the place in the wilting August sun until the polls closed. But now what? Many congressmen lived in their home districts and commuted to Washington. If Al did that, she could still work at the paper and resume her photography career. "I had a job, there were some hard choices for me," Tipper recalled. Pauline, who tried not to assert her will too strongly around her daughter-in-law, took her aside for what Tipper later called some "very influential" advice. Thirty-eight years earlier, Pauline was a lawyer in Carthage, with two or three cases going on, but she decided to drop it all, believing that she could be most valuable at her husband's side. "Now, Tipper, you go right along with him," she said. "I don't think my son will do anything he shouldn't do, but you do everything he does. You grow as he grows. You grow together. And he'll have experiences that you should participate in. And you go and stay along with him."

CHAPTER THIRTEEN

THE INFORMATION MAN

H E WAS OUT AT DAWN the day after his election victory, shaking hands at a factory gate, and by the end of November, with his swearing in still more than a month away, he had revisited every county in his congressional district and had held thirty open meetings. Even before he recruited a chief of staff and other aides for his Washington office, he hired two secretaries to begin working on problems that were brought to him as he traveled from town to town in middle Tennessee. It would be hard for anyone to accuse U.S. Representative Al Gore Jr. of losing touch with his constituents, a charge that had hounded Senator Albert Gore Sr. when he was defeated in 1970. In the name of the father, the son was making amends.

Gore did not invent the congressional town meeting. It was the latest trend in the House when he arrived in January 1977, popularized by the class ahead of his, the so-called Watergate babies, who brought with them a new way of doing things, less beholden to party bosses and patronage. But Gore embraced the idea with a passion matched by few of his colleagues. Among the first assignments undertaken by his young chief of staff, Peter Knight, was to find out which congressional offices conducted the most efficient open meetings and report back on how they did it. Gore then set up five district offices and launched a proactive, if not hyperactive, schedule in which he invited himself, rather than waiting to be invited, to the gatherings of every garden club, civic organization, labor union, farm co-op, school association, and veterans group that his staff could contact. If a town was so small that it had no clubs or community centers, a meeting would be set up at the gas station or country store.

The symbol of Gore's operation was a large map on the wall of his cramped House office that resembled a war room map in the Pentagon, with pins stuck in every town that he had visited in the fourth district. A color code indicated the last time he had been to each place. It did not take long for the markings on the map to be obscured by a luxuriant swirl of pins. In a routine that he maintained for years thereafter, Gore flew from Washington to Nashville every weekend, then headed east toward Carthage and pounded through his district, holding an average of five town meetings every Saturday, morning to night, sometimes as many as seven or eight, spreading them out so that every meeting was in a different county. At this relentless pace he averaged 250 meetings per year.

Whether three people awaited him in a country store or a few hundred at an elementary school made little difference. Gore gave them the same amount of time and attention, using the first ten minutes to talk about events in Washington, then answering questions for forty-five minutes and staying afterward another twenty minutes so that he and his aides could respond to casework. Over time the operation became increasingly sophisticated. Gore used a computer to set up a rotation for which towns needed visiting, and he hired Roy Neel, a former Nashville newspaperman, to become his traveling expert on small-business loans and grant applications, a popular service that brought out more citizens when the Gore party reached town. Neel lent a down-home touch to the operation, in contrast to chief of staff Knight, who came from New England and had previously worked for congressman Torbert H. Macdonald, Jack Kennedy's old roommate at Harvard. How badly did Gore feel the need to appear in tune with the voters of middle Tennessee? So badly that he would not issue a press release announcing Knight's hiring because he did not want it widely known that his top aide was an easterner with connections to the Kennedy liberals. So badly that at first he instructed Knight not to answer the telephone in the office, lest drawling constituents become suspicious about an eastern infiltrator.

The open meeting became a variation of the permanent campaign strategy that Bill Clinton and consultant Dick Morris would begin refining in Arkansas a few years later, erasing any line between government and politics by finding ways to do both at the same time.

But the process was not one-sided; it had as much effect on Gore as it did on his constituents.

Gore had always been careful in his public speaking, talking in precise sentences, such a stickler that when his aides handed him a speech they knew he might grill them on grammar questions, demanding to know where the noun and verb were. But this discipline became even more pronounced, or took on a new meaning, when he began the town meetings. Andy Shookhoff, Gore's former law school study partner, attended several town meetings as the local Legal Services lawyer based in Gallatin, and noticed that Gore spoke in the same way whether he was addressing a luncheon of business executives or a few poor, rural, uneducated men eking out their livings in small tobacco patches or dilapidated car repair shops. It was a deliberative and earnest style that would provoke criticism later in Gore's career from people who thought he sounded patronizing, as though he were always talking to third-graders. Shookhoff observed that Gore's public style was meant not to be condescending but respectful. "He was developing an ability to talk about complex subjects that affect people's lives, and to people who did not have a high school diploma," Shookhoff said. "He talked to them with a level of respect—that they deserved to understand these issues, and they were capable of understanding them, and it was his job to find the words. I was sensitive to that, representing poor folks, many of them poorly educated, who were accustomed to being disrespected or not consulted."

The routine of going home every weekend and listening to the feelings and problems of his constituents also made Gore acutely attuned to the cultural sensibilities of his district. He began reliving, in a sense, the same push and pull that he felt in college between the society at Harvard, where military service was largely considered something to be avoided at any cost, and Carthage, where the boys were enlisting or accepting the draft as a fact of life. Now the contrast was between the liberal Democratic policies of the House and the more conservative mores of his home district. He knew it already, but the town meetings brought the point home week after week, that his constituents were essentially conservative on social issues. If during the first campaign Gore surprised his friends and former colleagues at the *Tennessean* by taking more conservative positions than they expected, that tendency only increased once he was in office, when he voted against federal funding of abortions and opposed stronger measures to control and register guns. A poll of Gore's own staff on those issues might have shown that he was in a minority of one.

Here again the experience of his father came into play. An unavoidable aspect of his political calculation was the memory of what happened to Senator Gore when it appeared that he had distanced himself from his constituency on civil rights, the Vietnam War, and school prayer. Gil Merritt, a longtime family friend and adviser, often discussed that dilemma with the young congressman. "I think he had a real question in his mind as to what extent he had an obligation to represent the consensus views of his constituents as distinguished from his own personal political views," Merritt said. "He was a young fellow then and had a question as to how to work out that equation. His father got beat because of the way he worked out that equation." Once, when Gore cast an anti-abortion vote, Merritt said to him, "Jesus, I thought that was a bad vote." Recalling the scene later, Merritt said it was apparent to him that Gore "struggled with it" because "he personally had a more pro-choice view than he thought his constituents had."

IN TAKING THESE STEPS to avoid the fate that befell Gore Senior, the son was not trying to repudiate his father but to honor him through his own success. He walked a fine line, sometimes turning away from the old man's ways, other times soliciting his help. He competed fiercely that first year for a seat on the Appropriations Committee, which had been the power base of his predecessor, Joe L. Evins. There was room for only two freshmen on the prized committee. "He went around and I went around," recalled Norm Dicks of Washington state, a fellow Democratic freshman that year. Dicks drew on the support of Senator Warren Magnuson and several veteran congressmen from the northwest, while Gore's chief lobbyist was his father, who came to Capitol Hill and worked the halls of the Rayburn, Cannon, and Longworth House office buildings on his son's behalf. To no avail—Dicks and another freshman got the coveted slots, while Gore was shunted off to Interstate and Foreign Commerce (later renamed Energy and Commerce) and its oversight and investigations subcommittee. "Al, I did you a favor," Dicks said at the time, asserting that the oversight committee would be more interesting and give him better opportunities for press coverage. But he sensed that Gore "was not thrilled" with those words of consolation.

In an interview more than two decades later, Gore said that he was the only member of the freshman class of 1976 "whose first choice for subcommittees was oversight and investigations." That is a partial truth; he was the first to request it *after* he lost out on Appropriations. In any case, whether his affection for O&I, as the subcommittee was called, came before the fact or after, Gore soon realized that Dicks was right. Largely because of that subcommittee, he came to regard his congressional work as an extension of his earlier career as a newspaperman, as Frank Sutherland of the *Tennessean* discovered when he visited that first spring. "We were sitting at dinner, just the two of us one night, and I said, 'Well, you've made the switch now and you've gone into politics. What's it like being a congressman compared with being a reporter?' " Sutherland recounted later. "And he said, 'It's just like being an investigative reporter, except for one thing.' And I said, 'What's that?' He said, 'You've got subpoena power!' "

The philosophy that Gore adopted then, at the beginning of his career, about his role as a public servant is one that he carried with him thereafter, even taking it into the vice presidency, and it has become so ingrained in him that it is a key to understanding what kind of president he would be as well. In Gore's view, everything came down to facts—more than parliamentary skill or emotion or personality or intuition or chemistry or poetry or even wealth, preeminent was the raw data that comprised information. It was always from that source that he believed his power would flow and that he could do the most to change the world. "I saw information as a strategic resource," he said during an interview later. "I had a way of thinking about this job of congressman that was based on the lessons I learned as a reporter. I felt then and I feel now that we are living in the midst of an information revolution, at a time when there is a surfeit of fact about almost everything. You may not have the key facts that you need, but you have the information out there about anything. So some of the skills that are most critical in this day and time are the skills that help people navigate through oceans of data, and then recognizing their significance, and arranging the significant bits of knowledge in priority order, and then communicating the package coherently. That's what reporters do, and that's also what congressmen do. Or at least that's how I did it."

The image that comes from that paragraph of self-explanation is not that of the effusive politician working the crowd but of a researcher poring over documents, or of a bulky old 1970s-style computer whizzing away in a temperature-controlled room, compiling and collating and "arranging significant bits of knowledge in priority order." That is where Gore started. He was the information man, and he played that role as efficiently as any congressman of his era, often for the better, sometimes for the worse.

That is not to say that Gore was a one-dimensional grind. The information man was always operating on several levels at once. From his earliest days on oversight, when his interrogation of a sweating oil executive involved in a worldwide uranium cartel became an iconic front-page photograph, he exhibited an uncanny knack "for what sells," as one aide put it. The tradition of the subcommittee, where aggressive staffers cultivated friendly relationships with investigative reporters, suited Gore perfectly. His pursuit of facts was matched only by his hunger for publicity. Had he won that seat on Appropriations, it would have taken him years to reach the point where his utterances were considered noteworthy. On oversight, with the right line of questioning, he could leave an immediate mark. After every hearing, he examined the newspapers and sat glued before the television set to see what was written or said and whether he received any face time on the national news. There seemed to be a bit of the knife in the sarcastic way he teased a staff member who got more publicity than he did or complained to a reporter who had interviewed him but not used his quotes in the story. He was constantly standing in front of the mirror in his little office bathroom, combing his hair so that not a strand was out of place before he went out to committee hearings.

It was obvious to his colleagues and the subcommittee staff that Gore was uncommonly diligent and competent as well as aggressive. John Moss of California, the revered First Amendment liberal who authored the Freedom of Information Act, chaired O&I during Gore's first term, and trusted the freshman so much that he virtually turned the subcommittee over to him during the months before his retirement. Even though, as one staff member said, "Gore was not the most huggable guy around," subcommittee aides clamored to work on his hearings. He shared their fascination with detail, loving, as colleague Dennis Eckart of Ohio noticed, "to drop down to levels C, D, E, and F of an issue." Staffers knew that if they filed a fifteen-page memo, Gore would actually read it overnight. Whatever topic he chose to investigate, infant formula or contact lens solutions or toxic waste dumps or nurse midwifery, would be sure to draw press interest. Although he never got his law degree, the precision and logic he used in his interrogations brought staffers out of the back room to watch. They did not feel the need to script his questions. He was known for doing his homework, often learning the material more thoroughly than the aides who prepared it.

Former aide Jerold Mande said Gore was constantly pushing himself and the staff to learn more. "He had a tireless thirst for really understanding an issue until he reached a critical point, like when you arrive in a new city and drive down a bunch of roads until at some point you get an understanding of how they all fit together. That's how he approached an issue. He'd go down various paths and would try to get to where he had not only all of this information in his head, but an understanding of how it all fit together to the point where he could put forward novel theories and policy ideas." The subcommittee staff was populated by a proud band of investigative warriors in that era, who considered Gore "our go-to guy," as aide Mark Raabe put it. Many of them also thought then that they were working with a young congressman who might someday be president.

The House was bubbling with Democrats who arrived in the classes of 1974 and 1976 and had a sense that this was their time, that the world had changed and they were going to change the House with it. Many of them shared the same characteristics as Gore: young, highly educated, hardworking, mentally and physically aggressive. Gore connected immediately with Tom Downey of Long Island when he heard Downey question a witness at a hearing. Downey then brought Gore down to the House gym and drafted him into the perpetual basketball game that served as a rite of passage for the new breed. Just as he had at St. Albans, Gore fired away from the corner, a long-range gunner who passed only if necessary. There were never enough balls for the ambitious young men of the House. Among those who had larger plans, Gore seemed matched only by Dick Gephardt of Missouri, who arrived with Gore, and seemed equally ambitious if more traditional. "That was classically it, those two, Gore and Gephardt," said Dennis Eckart. Leon Panetta of California, who was also in Gore's class, said "there was a sense that Al had perfected the new kind of approach to politics represented by those classes. The ability to take a few issues and to convert them into press interest and headlines" combined with the town hall format that "Al kind of took to the nth degree."

• • •

THE FIRST WORD Leon Fuerth ever heard used in relation to Al Gore was *global*. It was typical of Gore, Fuerth would later come to understand, that he would want to spend his time learning something of *global* importance. In this case it was arms control. Fuerth was the arms control expert on the staff of the House Permanent Select Committee on Intelligence. Gore, a new member of the committee, had gone to the chairman and asked for a tutor, and Fuerth had been sent his way. They met for the first time on the veranda of the Longworth Building facing the Capitol, this odd couple, Gore tall and broad-shouldered, Fuerth's modest height diminished by a slight stoop, with eyes that preferred furtive contact, reflecting the personality of a policy analyst who functioned in the shadows of power.

The two men retreated to Gore's cramped office in Longworth, an unprepossessing place where the staff desks seemed jammed together as though it were a basement storage facility. Every now and then a cockroach lazed across the floor like a corpulent landlord, confident that its species would survive the worst that Gore and Fuerth might imagine. The discussion went well. They talked generally about arms control issues — weapons, proliferation, verification, and deterrence. When Fuerth got up to leave, Gore said that he would like to continue the tutorial later. *Yeah, sure, that's what they all say*, thought Fuerth, who over the years had briefed many members of both parties and found that one or two meetings sufficed.

But Gore would prove to be different from the rest. Soon enough the two men began meeting once or twice a week, either in Gore's office or in the committee's secured quarters in the Capitol. Gore gave instructions to his staff not to be disturbed, except for calls from his family. For months, none of his ten aides knew who he was with, which suited Fuerth, if not Gore's staff. "For a staffer who was supposed to know where his boss was all the time, it was a scary proposition," recounted chief aide Peter Knight. "He would go for hours and hours and hours up to this hideaway in the Capitol and get briefed by all these CIA guys. Then, ten months later . . . he came out and said, 'I want to introduce you to the guy that I've been spending all this time with.' And that was Leon. But we on the staff hadn't met him, didn't know him, weren't supposed to ask, and we didn't until then."

The Fuerth tutorials were revealing in several ways. They reflected Gore's ambition to play on a national stage, his persistence in pursuit of subject mastery, and his determination to make a difference in an area so complex and important that it was treated with almost tal-mudic reverence. His partnership with Fuerth reflected his preoccu-pation with experts and his constant efforts at self-improvement. It was not enough to read up on an issue or hold one or two briefings. Gore wanted to be an *expert* on arms control, someone who could hold his own with the small tribe of policy elites who shaped America's re-sponse to the Cold War nuclear threat.

In his zeal to achieve prominence and to make the world a better place—which were never mutually exclusive enterprises with Gore—he underestimated the obstacles. With Fuerth's assistance, he ad-vanced an arms control proposal that won him a measure of acclaim, but in his desire to advance it, he and his allies struck a deal with the Reagan administration in which they were ultimately outmaneuvered. In so doing, Gore angered many of his Democratic colleagues on the Hill, even while burnishing his own credentials as a defense hawk. It was the classic Gore paradox: He was adroit at gaining command of a difficult subject and fashioning an impressive policy proposal that might help his party compete in an area that it had virtually ceded to the Republicans. Yet his utter conviction in the correctness of his posi-tion, which he characteristically arrived at through a process of fact finding, made him think that others would unavoidably see the right-ness of it. This led him to misread the degree of commitment, or un-derestimate the machinations, of those he was dealing with, in Congress and in the Reagan administration. He understood the sci-ence of politics, but failed in its art.

What had motivated Gore to learn the nuances of arms control? As the decade turned and the ominous 1984 loomed four years in the future, he began to sense increasing anxiety among his constituents about the threat of nuclear annihilation. The questions were being asked more often at his open meetings. *How can you stop nuclear war? What are we going to do?* The Cold War arms buildup was giving mo-mentum to its counterpoint, the nuclear freeze movement. Ronald Reagan was casting the world in Manichaean terms, ascribing to the United States the role of defender of what was good against what he later called the "evil empire" of the Soviet Union.

One summer day in 1980, Gore appeared at a Girls State conven-tion in Murfreesboro, the town where a half-century earlier his father had attended teachers college. One girl in the model legislature asked Gore about the arms race. Then, thinking of his own young children (three young daughters by then), he asked a question. *How many of you think you'll see nuclear war* in your lifetime? Nearly every girl raised her hand. *How many of you think we can change that if we really try?* Only a few raised their hands. The scene was one that he would not forget. He was struck, he told people later, by the "tremendous hopelessness." Not long after that incident, Gore said that he had a vivid dream in which a friend roused him to tell him that an atomic bomb had been found. Could he do something about it? He went outside, found the bomb ticking away, and realized that he had absolutely no clue how to defuse it. He gathered his family in a safe spot at their Carthage farm, and as they huddled behind a smokehouse they saw a flash of light and felt a shock wave. The dream, he told friends, tapped into the powerlessness he felt about controlling the threat of nuclear holocaust. The fatalism of the teenagers at Girls State and his dream of nuclear impotence became catalysts, spurring him to act in the manner he felt most effective, as the information man gathering facts and turning those facts into policy.

The tutorials showed another Gore trait that members of the O&I staff well knew already: He was a quick study. They began at an elementary level. ICBM is an intercontinental ballistic missile. Soon they were deep into the arcana of throw weights, warhead-to-silo ratios, and strategic stability. Gore never took notes. He was able to absorb information and then manipulate it, trying out ideas that were combinations of Fuerth's insights and his own. "I had an extremely intelligent individual . . . and someone who was an original thinker," Fuerth said later. "He remembers everything I say, more accurately than I remember it. It's unnerving. He'd just suck it in."

In superficial ways Gore and Fuerth seemed to have little in common. Fuerth was a New Yorker, the son of an ice cream truck driver and grandson of Russian immigrants. He was nearly a decade older than Gore, coming of age not in the 1960s but the 1950s, someone whose "every ounce of intellectual being was created by the Cold War," as one former Gore adviser described him. He was fluent in Russian and worked for eleven years in the State Department, focusing on planning and intelligence, before going to work for the House Intelligence Committee in 1979, when it was chaired by Democrat Les Aspin of Wisconsin. Yet for all their differences, Gore and Fuerth were intellectual soul mates. "They're really intense. They're very, very bright people who are very devoted to public service, and they get off on doing policy morning, noon, and night," said James Jensen, a former Gore aide. "I can recall sitting in the office at eight-thirty at night and calls would be coming in for these guys, and they're talking about what they're going to do, and you could tell there's nothing in the world they'd rather be doing than what they were doing right then, talking about how they're going to push the agenda for arms control."

Toward the end of the tutorials, which included a number of presentations from experts, Gore and Fuerth began to formulate an approach to arms control that centered on a shift from multiple-warhead to single-warhead missiles. The idea was to achieve a "strategic stability" in which neither superpower could gain an advantage by striking first. His concept was based on the assumption that it takes two warheads to destroy one missile. If the American warheads were grouped onto missiles at the rate of ten per missile, as advocates of the MX proposed, then the Soviets would be able to wipe out the American land-based arsenal with warheads to spare. But, Gore argued, if the United States positioned only one warhead on each missile, and furthermore spaced them out on mobile launchers, then the Soviets would not have enough warheads—using the two-to-one rule—to take out the American land-based arsenal.

This approach was, to use a favorite phrase of Gore and Fuerth's, "mathematically grounded." They had spent hours examining nuclear exchange calculations that Fuerth had ordered up from analysts at the Congressional Research Service. Once R. James Woolsey walked into the office to find Gore immersed in reams of computer printouts with calculations on them. Gore had asked Woolsey, who had just left his post as undersecretary of the navy, to explain to him the assumptions behind a Defense Department model that simulated a nuclear exchange, a line of inquiry that left Woolsey stunned by the level of detail the young congressman was seeking.

In March 1982, after fourteen months of work on the subject, Gore entered his own arms control proposal into the *Congressional Record*, replete with tables and an inventory of reduction schedules. It called for the superpowers to agree on a freeze on new weapons while they negotiated the gradual replacement of multiple-warhead missiles with single-warhead missiles. The single-warhead missile, which came to be known as the Midgetman, was an idea that had been around for years in the defense community. As a hedge against failure to reach an arms reduction agreement, Gore said, the development of another missile, the MX, could proceed.

"The objective would not be reductions per se . . . but reductions of those systems which contribute the most to strategic instability, and to the risk of nuclear war by reflex, rather than on purpose," Gore said in his speech. "The grassroots movement we are experiencing in this country is based on the fear that neither side truly appreciates the odds, that specialists and ideologists on both sides are thinking that a nuclear war would somehow be winnable. The people are demanding that their political leaders show that they understand what the specialists may not, and that these leaders will reach out and grasp their responsibilities."

Not long after the speech, Gore's office received a call from the Russian embassy, which had instructions from the Kremlin to acquire a copy of Gore's proposal. That was followed by a U.S. delegation visit to Moscow, where the group was surprised to be asked twice about a Gore proposal that the Soviets called "an interesting basis for negotiations." No elected official in the delegation, with the exception of Minneapolis mayor Donald Fraser, had even heard of the Gore proposal. That incident is now part of the Gore lore, and was chronicled as a sidebar to a longer arms control piece that Gore wrote for *The New Republic*, the magazine run by his Harvard mentor, Marty Peretz. "I thought—Bingo!" Fuerth recalled of the incident. "The concept that stability does not exist unless it exists for both parties, and that single-warhead missiles are the path, has just received its first echo."

From there Gore faced a political decision. Was he interested in merely establishing his credentials, or did he want to affect national policy? The answer was the latter, and he began to look for opportunities to spread his message. He asked his press secretary, Mike Kopp, to find national beat reporters who were interested in talking to a young congressman about arms control. Slim pickings, there, but he then began holding media briefings that were as instructive to his staff as they were to the few reporters in attendance. He tested and perfected his presentation at the open meetings he was holding every weekend back in Tennessee, seeing if he could simplify the Midgetman concept so that homemakers and farmers got it.

Kopp remembers traveling with Gore to a courthouse in Byrdstown, a remote community in the Cumberland plateau. There was a potbellied stove in the courtroom, a fire in the stove, and above it, hanging on the wall, a picture of Cordell Hull. As Gore stood before the small audience, he began to explain the concept of strategic stability. He pulled out three Styrofoam cups and placed them in a row on a wooden table normally used by the prosecution or defense. Each cup represented an underground silo containing a missile with ten warheads on it, and thus could be both a target and a weapon. He lifted the cups and moved them around like a street corner magician to demonstrate missiles launching and being hit. Then he explained how the single-warhead Midgetman missiles would be a more difficult target, since the Soviets would have to launch two of their missiles to knock out a single Midgetman. "And they got it! They understood it," Kopp recalled. "He could take a very complex subject that Leon Fuerth had immersed him in over several months and make it into a Styrofoam cup illustration that people would understand."

At the same time that Gore was explaining his proposal, President Reagan was calling for an arms buildup of unprecedented measure. He argued for the development of the MX missile, which he called the Peacekeeper—an ironic title for a weapon that arms control experts considered to be one of the most destabilizing weapons imaginable, since it envisioned ten independently targetable warheads in vulnerable silos, offering incentive for the Soviets to strike first. The tension was at an all-time high, giving momentum to advocates of a nuclear freeze, who saw the buildup as madness. In November 1982, freeze referenda passed in eight states, and the next year a freeze resolution passed the House. Liberal congressman Edward Markey of Massachusetts, a friend and colleague of Gore's on the Energy and Commerce Committee and in the House gym basketball games, began making eloquent speeches calling for a halt to testing and deployment of nuclear weapons. Markey and his allies felt the tide of public opinion was with them, that they finally had a winning issue that gave them the upper hand against the Reagan administration, which had been battering them since the 1980 election.

Gore had been moving in another direction. He became one of the leaders of a group of House moderates, also including Norm Dicks and Les Aspin, who considered the freeze advocates well-intentioned but naive. This group thought that the best course was to push the Reagan administration toward arms control by bargaining with them if possible. In April 1983, after the House had killed one measure to fund the MX missile, the administration came back with a report by the Scowcroft Commission, led by Brent Scowcroft, a former deputy to Henry Kissinger. The report called for the placement of one hundred MX missiles in silos, but also recommended the deployment of Midgetman single-warhead missiles and stressed the importance of arms control. Gore and his Democratic allies saw it as an opening. They wrote a letter to Reagan saying they would consider supporting the MX if the arms control rhetoric and the commitment to the Midgetman were serious—a position that was considered heresy to many in the Democratic caucus.

At the end of one of their strategy sessions, Dicks turned to Gore as they were stepping into an elevator. "I hope we're doing the right thing," the normally jocund congressman said. "Me, too," Gore replied. Their meetings with the White House were invariably frustrating. Reagan seemed distant and disengaged. After returning from one arms control discussion with Reagan, Gore remarked to a colleague, "You know, the president was asleep for three quarters of the meeting!" But minutes before the first critical vote in the House Appropriations defense subcommittee, Dicks received a letter from Reagan that seemed to offer enough to win over the moderates on the MX by promising to limit their number and undertake "a major effort" on the single-warhead concept. The subcommittee voted to release the money, and the full committee followed suit a week later. Many in the arms control community were outraged, believing that the Reagan administration was not serious and never had been serious about reducing arms. A House floor vote was scheduled for May 24, and the mood was fractious. Gore's basketball buddies, Markey and Tom Downey, condemned the direction he was taking, saying that it was politically shortsighted. Gore and Aspin and Dicks were selling them out and had become dupes of the Reagan administration, they fumed. The three were taking so much criticism that they sat huddled together on the House floor for protection and comfort. Dicks recalled one congressman, John Seiberling of Ohio, chastising him: *I hope your children will be able to forgive you for what you're doing!* Les AuCoin, a strong MX opponent from Oregon, took the floor during the debate and warned, "No strategic weapons system that has ever passed this stage of funding . . . has been permanently canceled. This, my friends, is the moment in which the genie leaves the bottle."

And so it appeared. The House voted to approve the funds, and then the Senate. Funding for the MX won vote after vote that year. But little seemed to come from Gore's grand idea. In the end, the Midgetman never went beyond the test-flight stage. As the arms debate wore on, it became a footnote in the annals of arms control history, overtaken by Reagan's futuristic Star Wars missile defense proposal, and eventually by the end of the Cold War. Leon Fuerth and Gore's loyalists maintain that the young congressman was not duped, that the precepts of Gore's idea were contained in later arms control agreements. But for arms control advocates such as John Isaacs, president of the Council for a Liveable World, the compromise that Gore and his allies tried to achieve "smacked of, shall we say, hubris."

Les AuCoin agreed. He said that he considered Gore, Aspin, and Dicks his friends. But he said they annoyed him by taking "it upon themselves to imagine that they were really negotiating with the guys downtown and wanted us to believe that if we gave up a few MX missiles to the White House that we would get somewhere on arms control. I just thought it was preposterous and a self-inflated view of themselves. And I think the years that have followed have found that. They were full of themselves. It's a kind of self-absorption, intellectual arrogance, to think that three members of Congress were going to turn around the entire foreign policy of the Gipper, who was bound and determined to throw every weapons system he could at the Evil Empire."

IT WAS EARLY IN 1983 that word started seeping out that Howard Baker would not seek reelection to the Senate. As usual, the rumor reached John Seigenthaler first, and he passed it along to Al Gore, his former reporter and favorite politician. Sure enough, within a few weeks, Baker formally announced his retirement. Gore was ready, and within two days had hired a fund-raiser and a field organizer for his next campaign. He had first turned to politics because he said it was the one endeavor where he felt the wind at his back, and here it was again, blowing him along almost effortlessly, moving large obstacles from his path, easing the way for the prince of Tennessee.

CHAPTER FOURTEEN

BO LOSES NANCY

ONE OF THE SHARED UNDERSTANDINGS of the people around Al Gore during his congressional years was that he tended not to take direct criticism well, and that anyone who challenged him too much might end up on the wrong end of an icy stare or sarcastic put-down. His big sister, Nancy, was the exception to that rule, or at least blithely unfazed by it, as she was demonstrating again here. *That's just a bunch of crap*, she said to her younger brother, and everyone in the room laughed. This was the dawn of the 1984 election season, and Gore had gathered his inner circle at the ranch house of Johnny Hayes in the little Tennessee town of Sideview to plan how he should run for the Senate seat being vacated by Howard Baker. One by one, aides and confidants had offered their advice. Then Gore took the floor with a dry and abstruse statement of his intentions, at the end of which there was silence until Nancy informed him, in her lighthearted yet direct fashion, that he had no idea what he was talking about.

That was pure Nancy, the most natural politician in the Gore family, the one who loved all of it, the give-and-take, the gossip, the inside story, the alliances, the odd hours, the earthy vocabulary, the drinking and smoking and scheming—all of it except running for office herself, which she left to the old Baptist, as she called her father, and a brother ten years younger who lacked her instincts but had the will and the expectations. She adored her brother, Bo, the nickname she used for Al all of her life, and had been one of his trusted advisers since his first race for Congress, yet she also was always reminding him that he was the younger sibling, "constantly on his case," as former aide Mike Kopp put it, "teasing him or pressing him, everything short of giving him noogies."

At the time of that meeting in Sideview, Nancy was already weakened by a cancer that had taken root in her lungs. She would be dead within a year, before she could celebrate the election in which her brother became the second-generation Senator Gore and in so doing redeemed his father's 1970 loss. Twelve years later, in accepting his party's nomination for a second term as vice president, Gore would tell the story of his sister's deathbed struggle with cancer in a speech at the 1996 Democratic National Convention in Chicago. That account remains the most vivid public image the nation has of Nancy, perhaps the only image. His words drew some criticism for sounding maudlin, a reaction that upset him, but he had not understood, as Nancy likely would have, that people could be offended by what might seem to be his exploitation of a deeply personal tragedy for political purposes.

In delivering that speech, Gore did not intend to reduce his sister's life to that of a convenient prop, an example of a smoker whose early death illustrated the evils of tobacco, yet that is what happened, partly because of his overdrawn rhetoric, partly because of the politics of the situation. Tobacco was the very crop that had once been the pride of the Gore farm in Carthage, as well as the source of federal subsidies for several years after Nancy's death. But to think of her only in those narrow terms is to greatly diminish her life, and in so doing to miss out on another way of examining the ways of her brother.

Bo was at once flustered by his sister and in awe of her, she was so unlike him. She was beautiful, languid, irreverent, endearingly messy, spoiled, unselfconscious about her family name, and seemed in the know without appearing studious or rehearsed. As wooden and pedantic as her brother could be in public, the type of person who once wore his trademark blue suit playing Frisbee on the beach, Nancy pulsed with imagination and intrigue. Where he seemed cautious, she courted adventure, if not in reality at least in style. It was as if in the Gore family gene pool, the daughter inherited the emotional intensity that the son would show only in flashes, and then in private among close friends. It is not completely fair, of course, to judge Gore by contrasting him with his sister. She was never burdened by the same weight of expectations; she had other burdens, but not those. She smoked heavily, drank abundantly, and eventually battled feelings of isolation as a married woman unable to bear children and living in a small town in Mississippi. But she filled out the human void that her brother often left, both within himself and with the public.

Women have invariably served that role for Al Gore in his life and career, generation after generation. Tipper connects with people at a level that her husband cannot, and so does their oldest daughter, Karenna, and both of them are part of a lineage that begins with the beguiling big sister, Nancy.

HIS LONGTIME FRIENDS sometimes talk about the sides of Al Gore that are lost in his public persona, Gore the daredevil, Gore the storyteller. These are traits he picked up from his big sister, in whom they were never hidden but there for the world to see. To use a word from her childhood, Nancy had moxie. She rode horses bareback and water-skied backward on one ski and shot skeet, all without anyone thinking of her as a tomboy. She told long and frightening ghost stories, according to Celeste Gore-Schreck, a cousin who visited the Gore farm as a child. Nancy's room at the big house was built on top of a graveyard, Schreck remembered. "And they had to move the bodies, so she'd make up these great stories about the souls that had stayed. I was always in a total panic." Celeste was much younger than Nancy, who during idyllic summers on the farm taught her how to drive a tractor, how to take a canoe out in the river in the cold Caney Fork and go for an early morning swim off the big rock. She was an instructor in how to live, as Schreck recalled, "with the world at your feet."

In the early summer of 1958, while the old man was campaigning for reelection against a racist opponent in Tennessee, Nancy took off for Europe to work as a tour guide at the World's Fair in Brussels. Her little brother, who idolized her, kept up with her doings through her letters and postcards home and an occasional picture of her in the *Tennessean.* Once, after seeing a photograph of her at the fair, he gushed, "Why, Mom, she looks just like you!" She indeed had her mother's looks and brains, but a knack for doing the unexpected or goofy that was all her own.

One weekend while visiting Germany she ended up at a car factory, and though she barely had enough money for a return ticket to Brussels, she acted as though she were in the market for a Mercedes-Benz 190 SL, which she described in a letter as "the most beautiful car I have ever seen, not an ordinary car but really a work of art." In short order she had three salesmen vying for her attention and a driver at her service for the entire morning. "I played the rich bitch," she gaily recounted in a letter she wrote while sitting in a beauty parlor getting her hair done. She urged her parents to look up the resale value of the Mercedes in the States, noting that "Daddy can buy it (VIP passport) for 15 percent discount factory price"—an idea that the frugal Senior ignored.

Even in these situations, when she could sound most spoiled, there was something about Nancy LaFon Gore that separated her from other southern belles, a sense of self-deprecating humor and detached irony. In one letter, she told her parents and little brother about an encounter at the IBM exhibit at the U.S. Pavilion. A Russian woman, an interpreter who spoke exquisite English, asked Nancy "some very probing questions" about the RAMAC machine, the world's first computer disk storage system, an invention that could answer questions about world history in ten languages. With a sneer, the Russian woman asked, "Can your clever machine tell me what will happen in 1959?"

"Yes, madam," Nancy answered, and typed in 1959. Looking at the machine, she pronounced, "It says you will be one year older, as in each subsequent year."

"Her feathers fell," Nancy wrote, relishing the memory. "A well-trained Russian—but still a woman."

Nancy would pretend to be frugal, but she appreciated fine things, like the fabulous Tennessee marble bathtub next to her room at the big house in Carthage. During her grand tour of Europe, she asked a friend in Germany to find her "the cheapest room at the nicest hotel in town." And while her brother as an adult never seemed to care much about his attire, wearing the same blue suit with the pants hitched slightly too high, she was always on the search for sophisticated clothes. She favored Donald Brooks dresses—they were "very Jackie." If her mother was not going to wear that fitted Jablow tweed spring coat, she wanted it. And would they also send over the white lace Larry Aldrich dress? Yet she never took herself, or her apparel, too seriously. Her friends noticed that there was always a hem hanging down or a seam coming apart or a bit of slip showing. She would put her hair up in a French twist, which was very becoming, but stray wisps were always flying loose.

Once, while driving with a carful of friends from Carthage to Chattanooga, the fan belt broke and Nancy slipped off her Christian

Dior leather belt, had it wrapped around the car fan, and got the group to their destination. Another time, the senator's daughter was supposed to make her debut in Chattanooga at an event called the Maid of Cotton. She asked her childhood friend, Bill Ray, to be her escort. When they arrived in Chattanooga after a long drive, she announced, "I'll be damned, I left my shoes in Carthage!" This "didn't bother her one iota," Ray remembered. "She had on this long dress. She went across the stage barefoot."

NANCY TOOK SOME of her most appealing characteristics from her parents. From Albert a zest for life and from Pauline a warmth and caring for people. What she did not inherit, her little brother did, such as the drive to achieve. Nancy lived in a family of high achievers: Pauline among the first women to graduate from Vanderbilt law; Albert up from Possum Hollow to the U.S. Senate; and little Al from his St. Albans days onward always seeming headed for similar heights. Nancy would rebel by refusing to be measured by their standards. While her little brother counted the cost of his conduct and calibrated his behavior to satisfy his parents and prep school advisers, Nancy, in the words of her friend Fred Graham, the prominent legal correspondent, "didn't care if people thought she was bossy or being a brat or whatever."

She was only thirteen when she picked up the smoking habit. She was a student at Holton Arms, an exclusive girls school then located on S Street NW not far from the Gores' Fairfax Hotel suite. "We were smoking our tails off, smoking Pall Malls one after another," said Barbara Howar, Nancy's close friend and classmate. "We came to Holton Arms smoking. They allowed it then. We smoked with white gloves on. We smoked longer and stronger. I can see the long red package, no filters, no nothing. Nancy was a real smoker. It mattered to her more than anybody I know. . . . She always had cigarettes in her pockets, so if she was anywhere near the smoking room, she was smoking. She had a nicotine addiction long before anyone else did."

Her parents did not approve, but she kept smoking anyway, lighting up as soon as she was out of their presence. She also started drinking at an early age, and hanging out at the Empire Drug Store with a fast crowd. Her parents tried to bend her to their will. They tried taking away her car privileges, withholding her pocket money, even sending her briefly to a strict Church of Christ private school in Nashville. But the more they pressed, the more she resisted, without fully turning against them or their way of life. She lived in dread of her father's disapproval. At night she often slipped over to her young aunt Jill Gore's house and the two women would stay up smoking and talking about Senator Senior. Once, as a young woman, she drank too much at a Washington party, yet was still aware of the consequences if her father saw her in this condition. *I can't go home,* she said. *The Baptist will be there!* She spent the night sleeping on a sofabed at her friends' house. The old man liked to think he was setting guidelines. "Now behave yourself, young lady," he would tell her. One weekend Bill Ray and his brother took Nancy out for a ride to Charlottesville, Virginia. "Now, Sister Baby, don't forget your hat for church on Sunday," Senior told her.

"Oh, yes, Daddy," she said. And they set off, her hat in the truck, though, as Ray recalled, "she never got within forty miles of the church on Sunday."

Her little brother was always trying to show off his prodigious memory and his facility with facts and foreign languages. Nancy was more interested in enjoying life and bluffing her way through if necessary. One summer the old man sent her to Mexico to study Spanish, one of the many self-improvement projects he imposed on his children. Nancy went to Mexico and had a marvelous time but picked up little of the language. Later, when a Spanish-speaking delegation was in Washington, Senior, wanting to show off his multilingual daughter, arranged to have her give a little speech in Spanish. Nancy approached the head of the delegation. "May I have a word with you? My father sent me to summer school in Mexico to learn Spanish. All I can say is *'cuatro mas cervezas'* and *'dónde está el baño?'* " The official loved it, and gracefully covered up for Nancy, praising the senator and his daughter and making sure that she would never have to give the speech.

THE BOYS AT VANDERBILT considered her "the best looking freshman" to hit the Nashville campus in the mid-1950s, according to Fred Graham, who met her then and was one of her many suitors. "She had a very rebellious, smoky way about her." She was straight out of Faulkner, like Joanne Woodward in *The Long Hot Summer*. She stopped men in their tracks to look in wonder, her sultry looks so enticing that at one time or another she had all three of the Graham brothers dreaming about her.

First came Fred, who had just arrived back in town from the

Marines and was working at the *Tennessean,* sharing an apartment with colleague David Halberstam. Nancy was one of them, someone who loved to talk about politics and the changing south. They would get together and stay up late, drinking whiskey, with Nancy always smoking. "We'd talk for hours about who was going to win the sheriff's race," Graham recalled. His brother Otis Graham had a friendly rivalry with Fred over who first caught Nancy's attention. Once, after Otis had managed a few dates with her, Fred remarked dryly, "You're out of your league, kid." So, too, was the third brother, Hugh Graham, who was older than Nancy but always felt like her worshipful junior servant. He would forever remember the time she dragged him from one shoe store to the next for an entire afternoon. "She'd ask me what I thought of every pair of shoes she tried on, and I'd say, 'I like this one,' and she bought another one. It wasn't contrariness. She was just comfortably independent in her own thinking."

Nancy was a dazzling presence on the Vanderbilt scene, the stories about her etched in campus lore—how she once had her picture taken with a pet lion at a fraternity house, and how she ignored the prudish rule that forced women to wear raincoats over their Bermuda shorts. "She wasn't big on rules," said Jim Gilliland, another friend and occasional date from those days. "She wasn't big on doing things other people's way. She was always out there, going out of her way to be sure she had more fun than anybody else did. She just had her priorities in life, which did not involve taking life that seriously." Nor gym, for that matter. Though she was a good athlete, she could not be bothered to finish her physical education requirement in college. She considered it a complete waste of time. "By the time her mama and papa found out, she had managed to duck PE for four years and she was not going to get her degree," Gilliland said. Her parents said that would not do, so Nancy, with typical single-mindedness, finally got some warm-ups and gym shoes and took four years of gym in one summer.

There was another young man she met at Vanderbilt. He first caught sight of her as he waited in a car outside the women's dorm, waiting for a hometown friend. The bobby socks, the red-and-black scotch plaid skirt, the white blouse, the hair and cheekbones and smile—Frank Hunger could not take his eyes off "this devastatingly attractive girl" walking toward him. He was an Air Force pilot readying to ship out for Taiwan in the spring of 1959 who had come to say goodbye to his friend Jane Holmes, a close friend of Nancy's. He introduced himself and walked her to class and said goodbye, thinking he would never see Nancy Gore again.

To be young, liberal, idealistic, and connected in 1961 meant there was one Washington address above all others where you might want to work—not 1600 Pennsylvania Avenue but 806 Connecticut Avenue, headquarters of the Peace Corps run by Sargent Shriver. Bill Moyers, a brilliant twenty-six-year-old protégé of Vice President Johnson, came in as the associate director for public affairs. William S. Haddad, a talented and volatile former Kefauver aide who had also worked for Bobby Kennedy, was there to head up the inspection and special projects shop. Charles Peters, a West Virginia lawyer and state legislator who had helped organize Kennedy's important primary win there, was brought on to work under Haddad evaluating the Peace Corps programs. It is not surprising that the attractive and politically sophisticated daughter of a senator who sat on the Foreign Relations Committee would find a job there as well. The only question was where to put Nancy Gore, who was talented and engaging but somewhat unfocused and disorganized. She was capable of hard work, but would not grind it out all the time. The solution was Special Projects, where she could float from one task to another without title or portfolio.

Though Nancy was never a Peace Corps volunteer in the traditional sense (as her brother later described her in speeches), she did forgo paychecks in the first few months and often forgot to cash them when she became a paid staffer. It was certainly not the money that appealed to her, but the energy of the place and the sense of community. She knew everybody in Washington, or so it seemed. The phone would ring and Nancy would pick it up and blurt out, "Hello, Angie!" It was the chief of protocol, Angier Biddle Duke. The president and first lady were Jack and Jackie when she was talking about them to her friends. She was "the resident Scarlett O'Hara and female political sage," as Coates Redmon described her in her book about the Peace Corps, *Come As You Are*.

Haddad might once have been a street-wise investigative reporter for the *New York Post*, but it was Nancy Gore who patiently schooled him in the politics of Washington. "I found I could ask her questions that I would be embarrassed to ask anybody else," he said. "She knew the system." In a first draft of a report he had written on the Peace Corps, he had included the organization's mistakes as well as its triumphs. *Should I take them out?* he asked Nancy. *No,* she said, *the Peace Corps is unique and can thrive with criticism.* He left them in and the report went over fine.

It was in this era that friends noted how much of a surrogate parent Nancy became for her brother. Moyers remembered her bringing him over to the Peace Corps headquarters, where he sat quietly waiting for her to finish, always polite and respectful. Sometimes she would put her coat on in the middle of the afternoon and take her leave, saying that she had to go over to St. Albans to watch little Bo play basketball. Senior and Pauline were too busy to attend his sporting events, which added to her sense of obligation. Once, when she asked for an afternoon off to watch Al play football, Peters questioned her dedication to the job, but Nancy persisted. *My parents can't go and I have to,* she said. "So I understood," Peters recalled. "Her mother was a very good woman, but she was a pioneer career woman. I think Nancy filled some of the maternal gap for Al." Phil Rosenbaum, one of Al's St. Albans classmates, remembered an afternoon when Nancy came to visit, and was struck by their relationship. "It was the warmth of it that came across."

The extent to which Nancy filled in for her mother was not lost on Pauline Gore, who battled her own feelings of guilt. Years later, after Nancy's death, Redmon commented to Pauline how she and Nancy had gone to watch Al play basketball, and Pauline seemed mortified. *Oh, that makes me feel just awful. Albert and I weren't really around enough. We traveled. We were busy. We went out a lot, which left Nancy to look after him.*

That is not to say that Nancy was a homebody. She had scores of men after her during her Peace Corps days, but took a disaffected view toward most of them, figuring that they were interested in her because she was the senator's daughter. There were always two or more men eager to be her date for the evening, including Indiana congressman John Brademus. She was also very close friends with Jay Rockefeller and his roommate, Bill Wister. The Peace Corps was a sociable place where drinking was part of the scene. Several times a week, at quarter to noon, Nancy would look up and say, "Chez?" And a group would head downstairs to Chez François for lunch and a Bloody Mary. After the first one, Nancy would want a second. *Oh, come on, have another one!* she would urge her friends. There were early signs of what would become a serious problem as Nancy grew older and left Washington.

• • •

SISTER BABY left the Peace Corps in 1964 to head back to Tennessee to run her father's campaign. By then she was back in touch with Frank Hunger, who was out of the military, studying law at Duke University, and determined to win the girl who had taken his breath away in her plaid skirt and bobby socks. Hunger was a tall, attractive man with politics in his blood. Their romance bloomed while she was in Tennessee. Her cousin Celeste Gore-Schreck remembers making fun of Nancy talking on the phone with Frank. "When Frank would call, she would really light up, and she was always in a good mood after that," Gore-Schreck said. "Aunt Pauline really liked Frank. Everybody just really liked Frank. He was down to earth. Very athletic. He liked animals. He liked the farm." Nancy told friends, *Well, I certainly never thought I'd marry a man named Hunger from Mississippi.* Better than marrying a man named Mississippi from Hunger, one joked back.

The couple got married in the summer of 1966 at the big house in Carthage, Nancy's favorite place. Just as her mother had done three decades earlier, she decided to follow her husband—this time to Greenville, Mississippi, where Hunger a month earlier had joined the elite law firm Lake, Tindall, Davison and McGee. In a sense she was moving from one small southern town to another small southern town, but Greenville during the civil rights era was a far different world from Carthage. It was a racially divided town in the heart of the delta in the deep south, and life there could be more interesting than in middle Tennessee, but also more difficult and stifling. Greenville had cultivated a vibrant literary tradition; it was said that among its forty thousand residents it had more authors per capita than any town in America. The writer David Cohn had lived there, as did the historian and author Shelby Foote and William Alexander Percy, who wrote *Lanterns on the Levee*. (His relative Walker Percy sometimes passed through.) Perhaps of most comfort to Nancy was the family of Hodding Carter III, who would become assistant secretary of state under President Carter and later a PBS journalist. Carter's father had founded the *Delta Democrat-Times*, a liberal newspaper for which his editorials on the racial, economic, and religious problems of Mississippi had won him a Pulitzer Prize in 1946.

Nancy held out hope that Greenville would be a nurturing environment, but over the years it became clear to her that the town's literary reputation belied a conservative core. Greenville, said one friend she made there, was "too conservative to be utterly reactionary, but more like Kenya in the days of the British raj," highly stratified and lubricated by liquor. The Hungers first moved into the former home of Hodding Carter Jr. and Betty Carter (known as the big house, like Senior's place in Carthage), out on Highway 82 West just beyond the city limits, then eventually settled in next door to Hodding Carter III and his wife, Peggy, on Kirk Circle near the center of town. She and Frank befriended the Percys. William Percy was on the school board, in an era in which the schools were being desegregated by court order, and though she and Frank had no children, she believed in the public school system and grew increasingly dismayed as white flight took hold. Nancy was not a churchgoer, but occasionally attended synagogue for high holiday services with her friend, Jay Stein. "She had the curiosity," Stein recounted. "Nancy was as much Jewish as anything else. She related to our issues. She was very sensitive."

With her history degree from Vanderbilt and a strong interest in politics, why did Nancy not have a career of her own? Some friends say she never wanted one; others felt that she wanted to become politically involved, but adjusted, or submitted, to the realities of that time and place and followed a course that she thought would be most helpful to the career of her husband, who was working eighty-hour weeks to move up at his conservative law firm. Though she never begrudged Frank his career, she began feeling that her life was circumscribed in Greenville. She grew bored there, one friend recalled. There were so many mosquitoes in the summertime, she told Coates Redmon, that the first thing you have to do is slather yourself with all the insect repellent you can and then dash out the door and throw yourself in the pool before they get you.

Boredom turned to melancholy. There was no university to keep her occupied. No government program like the Peace Corps or the War on Poverty where she could use her talents. There were times when she thought "it sure would be nice if I had some kind of business to be involved with," that according to friends she could find nothing of that sort that held her interest. She kept up with politics in Washington by subscribing to the *Washington Post* and "read it avidly," according to Hodding Carter. She took up gourmet cooking. She traveled often, to Washington and Nashville, Colorado and Mexico, and volunteered at the Boys Club and helped create a day-care center and a state park to preserve the ancient Cahokia Indian mounds. She was a stalwart defender of civil rights, once writing a column for the *Delta Democrat-Times* calling for domestic help to be paid the minimum wage before it became federal law. She opposed the Vietnam War, daring to express a minority view in the small delta town by protesting, along with her friend and philosophical soul mate, Anne Percy, in front of the federal building in Greenville. Her husband admired her "unique way of being able to disagree with people and do it in a way that they still like her," a trait that made her beloved by nearly everyone in town, from the attendant at her service station to the mayor.

By the 1970s her unhappiness was becoming more apparent to people who knew her. One longtime friend was taken aback when he ran into her after not seeing her for years: her nails were bitten down to the nub and she looked haggard, not the vibrant woman he had known. She was coping with a difficult situation, made worse by the fact that she and Frank were unable to have children. She was utterly loyal to her husband. "She promoted me," Hunger said. "That was the bottom line. She was my wife and my best friend and loyal supporter." At times she would broach the subject of moving to Washington, but Frank had wanted to establish his own life on his own terms in a state that he hoped to influence and in a town that he thought was more liberal than it was. Hunger came from Winona, Mississippi, an even smaller and more stratified town, where Fannie Lou Hamer had been jailed for entering a whites-only dining room at the bus station in June 1963. He had come from "just that side of the tracks" and had scrapped to get out, and now he was making partner in his law firm and serving on committees and becoming active in the state Democratic party.

In the social scene in Greenville, drinking was an accepted practice, so pervasive that a heavy habit was easy to hide. As Nancy grew older, her drinking became more of a problem. It weighed on the marriage and distressed her parents. By the early 1980s, she began to show signs of ill health. She had high blood pressure, continued drinking and smoking, and the tips of her fingers had begun to swell. In October 1982, she went to Vanderbilt University Medical Center to have the swelling checked and the doctor diagnosed a more serious problem. She had lung cancer.

WHEN AL GORE LEARNED that his sister had cancer, he came out to Nashville and met with his mother and Frank at Jim and Nancy Fleming's house. Jim Fleming, who had spent time in his general surgery residency doing cancer work and knew Nancy Gore's doctor, sat down with Al.

Let's talk about what's wrong with Nancy, Fleming said.

Gore interrupted, presenting himself as an expert.

Well, look Jim, there are ten cancers of the lung, he said, and then proceeded to name them all, small cell lung cancer, squamous cell carcinoma, adenocarcinoma. Which one does she have? He had gone to the National Institute of Pathology in Washington and studied the disease before coming out to Nashville. This was quintessential Gore, compulsively memorizing the specific cancers. It reflected his impulse to be in control, Fleming realized later, and masked a deeper insecurity and fear of losing a central figure in his life. Fleming, who had battled his own alcoholism and identified with Nancy, saw in the Gore siblings different manifestations of compulsive behavior. Al, he said, overachieved "to prevent the pain of shame. Just like Al memorized all the tumors of the lung. Al, he'll one-up you. You learn that this behavior gets you places and does things for you. Nancy rebelled against this. Nancy said, 'To hell with you.' "

As she battled the illness, Nancy traveled back and forth from Greenville to Nashville, going in and out of Vanderbilt hospital, where she received chemotherapy. The disease at one point went into remission and the family briefly took heart. But when it returned, her doctor had a frank discussion with Nancy and Frank and Pauline and Senior, saying, as gently as he could, that perhaps one option was to make peace with her illness. Pauline would hear none of it. *That's not an option,* she said. "That's the family," Jay Stein said, recalling that discussion. "They didn't step out of character." Nancy wore a wig and maintained a brave front, constantly calling to check on her brother's Senate campaign, offering advice from the sickbed, and when possible making public appearances for him. "I wouldn't say that she was in denial the whole time, but she would never let you talk as if this thing was never going to be whipped," Bill Percy said. "That was never part of the equation."

Three days before she died, she called Anne Percy from the hospital. I'm going to resume my treatment, and then we're going to take a trip, she said. One day before she died, she called her housekeeper and friend, Rosie White, from her hospital bed. It seemed to Rosie that Nancy sounded well. *Oh, you sound real good this evening,* Rosie told her. *And I feel good,* Nancy said. *I'm coming home tomorrow.*

Hours later, her brother, Al, was headed to Memphis for a campaign fund-raiser when he got the call from Frank Hunger. Nancy had taken a turn for the worse. He sped back to Nashville and found his sister lying weakly in bed. As he walked in, someone said, "Al's here." Nancy was in a fog from a powerful dose of painkillers. "She looked up and from out of that haze her eyes focused intensely right at me," Gore later recounted in his speech about Nancy at the convention in Chicago. "She couldn't speak, but I felt clearly I knew she was forming a question: 'Do you bring me hope?' . . . All I could do was to say back to her with all the gentleness in my heart, 'I love you.' "

The funeral was held on a brilliant July day at the farm in Carthage, as Nancy had requested. There was no music. Her casket was in the living room, cleared of furniture. Anne and Bill Percy drove up from Greenville, bringing along Rosie White. When they emerged from the car, Anne escorted White toward Senior, the old Baptist, who was standing at the door. In paying respects to the woman who had looked after his daughter, he said, *You all just step back. Miss Rosie will be the first one to come in.* Pauline, mourning for her daughter, turned to Anne Percy and asked softly, "What will we do?" To which Percy replied, "We will pray to have the kind of courage she had." The pallbearers carried the coffin to the backyard. Bo stood there, the stoic little brother, part of him gone forever. He looked down the slope to the cold Caney Fork and the big rock where he and Nancy had taken so many early morning swims. Then they were singing "Amazing Grace," and saying the Lord's Prayer, and Jane Holmes Dixon was reading from the first letter of John, Chapter 4—and that was Nancy, with all of her spirit and sorrow, the essence of the idea that a person cannot live if she has not served her sisters and brothers.

CHAPTER FIFTEEN

HUBRIS ALERT

IN THE DETRITUS of a long gone campaign, inside an old box sagging with daily schedules, telephone lists and internal memos describing events that once burned with urgency but now evoke the melancholy emptiness of political things lost, there is a handwritten note that reveals an illusion of greatness. When Al Gore Jr. ran for president the first time, he and his aides might have thought they were graced by fate. This artifact of political archaeology consists of a single legal-size page of ruled paper that on the top carries the underlined words "A 28 Year Cycle." A yearning to attach Gore to twentieth-century presidential history flows from there in the easily decipherable shorthand of American politics.

TR—04 FDR—32 JFK—60 AGJ—88

The Roosevelts and Kennedy and Al Gore Jr. all in a line.

Great presidents, the paper says, and with more in common: *Harvard grads. Prep schools. Political families, controversial fathers. Aggressive foreign/domestic policies.*

Young (oldest was FDR—50). And all touched by personal tragedy. *1) TR—death of his wife (1886). 2) FDR—polio. 3) JFK— death of sister and brothers. Retardation of sister. His own end. 4) AGJ— death of sister.*

If AGJ and his advisers spent an evening drawing out these parallels, a sort of political numerology, they might not admit it later. At least not the full conspiracy of greatness going back to the Roosevelts. But the notion that Gore thought that he could be like Kennedy is obvious and indisputable. Almost every young Democratic politician who grew up with Camelot sought to reenact it somehow, and Gore was no different. He mimicked JFK from the moment of his announcement in the spring of 1987, when he stood in the same Senate Caucus room where Kennedy had stood a generation earlier performing the same ritual: a boyish senator, surrounded by family, proclaiming himself ready for the White House. Modesty did not restrain Gore from drawing the comparison. "After eight years under Ronald Reagan, the oldest president, Americans may well feel as they did in 1960 that it is time to turn to youth, vigor, and intellectual capacity," he said, a shaft of brilliant April sunshine slashing in through the French windows and reflecting off the crystal chandeliers.

Gore's Kennedy affinity was more than Harvard, prep school, and twenty-eight-year cycles. The Kennedy mystique framed his political life. As a child, he had eavesdropped on telephone conversations between Senator Gore and President Kennedy. As a college student, he had been tutored by Kennedy's favorite government instructor, Richard Neustadt. When he reached the Senate, he hung his shingle in Room 393 of the grand Russell Senate Office Building opposite Kennedy's old suite. In drafting the formal announcement speech that he would deliver in Carthage following the coming-out party at the Capitol, he even sought the advice of the Kennedy wordsmith himself, Theodore Sorensen, who offered Gore another turn of phrase to herald the generational theme: "Twenty-seven years ago, the voters of America, looking for the strength and hope of a new generation, replaced the oldest man ever to serve in the office of the presidency with the youngest ever to be elected to that office. I believe they are ready to do so again."

The comparisons were predictable, audacious, and naive. The presidential campaign that Al Gore waged in 1987 and 1988 ended not with the elation of an inauguration but in a political theater of the absurd that found him at times hating his own campaign and what it stood for, though even he was not always sure what that was. His first presidential run was not a disaster because it conditioned him for much of what was to follow in later years and helped establish his national presence. But considered on its own, it had the markings of a troubled endeavor, with a staff and candidate often appearing to compete to see who could seem more inept or uncertain, and in that sense it foreshadowed the worst of Gore's 2000 presidential campaign.

It was in fact two of Gore's children, the *next* generation, who demonstrated at his announcement press conference that perhaps they had the wisest take on their father's overreaching. The oldest daughter, Karenna, showed up at the event dressed entirely in black: black shoes, black socks, black pants, black fringe top. *Karenna, why?* Gore had moaned when he saw the thirteen-year-old's outfit, but Tipper shushed him quickly. They both knew why. Karenna was a rebellious teenager. ("I was fascinated by the D.C. punk scene and bands like Fugazi, the Holy Rollers, and Minor Threat," she would say later. "Part of my atti-tude was a general antiauthoritarianism and a sort of shrill questioning of anything that might be imposed on me.") Black for mourning, a silent protest against what was sure to come. Tipper had already brought the public glare to the family with her crusade against obscene rock lyrics, and now this, at least another year of it. When the press con-ference was over, the staff and family marched back to the Senate of-fice, where Gore's namesake son, not yet five, innocently posed the most penetrating question of the campaign, one that the candidate and his staff would ponder, and fail to answer, time and again over the fol-lowing months, the same question Robert Redford asked in the closing scene of *The Candidate.*

"Now what do we do?" asked little Albert.

THESE ARE THE BASICS: Age, thirty-nine. Experience, two years in the Senate, eight years in the House. Political network, virtu-ally nonexistent beyond Tennessee.

How do you decide from there to run for president? It helps to be part of the curious tribe whose members think they can and should live in the White House, which Gore certainly was, though that did not dif-ferentiate him from perhaps half his colleagues in the Senate. It also helps to look at the field of candidates as it takes shape and see a possi-ble place for yourself, which Gore did, not just because he thought he was smarter than the rest, but also because he was the only one from the south. (The northward tilt was such that Senator Joseph Biden had been hoping to stake his claim as the southern candidate—from Delaware.) But in the end it was the old man, and other older men with money, who wanted Al Gore to run for president in 1988, and they kept telling him what he wanted to hear.

Gore Senior began "putting the bite on him," as one family friend put it, during the Christmas break in 1986. Father and son went down to the basement of the big house above the Caney Fork and had a talk. *Son*, said the father, *I want to see you elected president before I die*. The old man was seventy-eight and had no way of knowing he would live another twelve years. *Daddy really wants me to do this, really wants me to run*, Gore told friends and associates when he got back to Washington. In this case, the pressure from the father was not unwelcome, not in conflict with the son's ambition. With the help of a former party finance chairman, Peter Kelly of Connecticut, Gore drew up a list of about eighty important political and financial people to consult to see if running made any sense. The canvas, according to Kelly, revealed "a great deal of excitement." Gore had already received some flattering mentions in the national press, including a cover story in *Washington Monthly* that presented him as "the longest shot" but an intriguing possibility nonetheless. And back in Tennessee, Governor Ned McWherter, an old family friend, who knew exactly what Senior hoped for, started saying that he would welcome a "favorite son" candidacy by young Gore.

Then along came the rich old men from Impac 88, a group of forty-five Democratic financiers who wanted to become decisive players in the nomination of the next presidential candidate. Their plan was to find a candidate with moderate views and a vigorous personality and put their money behind him, hoping not to repeat the debacle of 1984, when Walter Mondale lost all but one state. The organizer of Impac, Maryland developer Nate Landow, already had his eye on young Gore. They had met the year before when Landow came to the Hill for a birthday party for one of his financial pals, Bill Crotty, a backslapping Florida operator who was the lawyer for the Daytona Speedway (and later, under Clinton, would become ambassador to Barbados). It was once said of Gore that he was an old person's idea of a young person, and that phrase never seemed more apt than now. When Landow first caught sight of him, he said later, he was instantly struck by Gore's all-American good looks, his erect carriage, his voice. "I had a feeling the first time I got to know him that he was presidential material, period," Landow said. "He was a smart man. I just always thought he was a shining star."

Right there, at Crotty's birthday party, Landow had urged Gore to think about running, a remark that Gore remembered months later when he invited Landow and Crotty to meet him for lunch at his parents' antique-filled apartment in the Methodist Building not far from his Senate office. Landow could tell that Gore was starting to take the suggestion seriously. Mario Cuomo, the popular governor of New York, had announced that he was not running. Sam Nunn, the senator from Georgia, and Bill Clinton, the young governor of Arkansas, had not jumped in and seemed reluctant to do so. Still, there was a sense of urgency. The two money men liked Gore, but some of their compatriots had already begun to commit to other candidates — the early favorite, Senator Gary Hart of Colorado, Biden of Delaware, Missouri congressman Richard Gephardt, and Michael Dukakis, the governor of Massachusetts. If much more time slipped by, Landow said, "there wouldn't be much left to make a significant contribution." He offered to bring Gore in to meet the group.

His audition came on March 19 in a conference room at the Grand Hotel at 25th and M streets in Washington. The money men flew in from every section of the country for cocktails and dinner and an informal presentation by Gore followed by questions. No reporters were there to grade his performance, but by all accounts the big guns were impressed. There was no decision on either side, and no direct talk of money. The next day, Senator Dale Bumpers of Arkansas, another potential southern candidate, ended speculation that he would run, and Gore swiftly called Landow and asked for a return visit before the group. Landow told Gore that he would do what he could to get his boys on board, but this time it had to be for real. "If we bring them together, you're going to have to make a decision," he said in his soft, gravelly voice. "It won't work with these guys if you're going to string it out and say you're going to have a look-see, exploratory committee, forget about it. You gotta cut the mustard."

The same room in the same hotel was reserved a few days later, and this time only seventeen Impac members made the trip. Again, they were impressed, and they pushed for a commitment. "You're dealing with a group of political junkies, none of whom want to be left at the station," explained Impac member Jerome Berlin, another Florida fund-raiser and former DNC official. Landow put Gore on the spot: *Okay, Senator, we're all together. What is your commitment to this? When will you decide?*

Give me a week, Gore said. When he left, Landow canvassed the group. Some said they could raise as much as a quarter-million. If they came through, the total would be about three million. One week after the second meeting, Gore walked into his Senate office, called his young staff together, and announced that he had slept on it and had decided to run for president. An impulsive act demanded immediate action: He wanted to hold his press conference that very day. Not even his closest aides, Roy Neel and Peter Knight, were aware of his decision beforehand. They knew he was thinking about it, but were still unprepared. "It seemed," said Neel, "like an improbable adventure."

It hardly took a push, but the old man and the old men had done it. Not until months later would Gore realize that for a multitude of reasons, some his own doing, some not, he was getting less than half of what had been pledged. The start was emblematic, in a sense, of the rest of the enterprise: He had been encouraged into a race that he was not fully prepared to run by the prospect of millions that never materialized. It is also worth remembering, when considering the finance-related troubles Gore faced years later as vice president, that his era of White House ambitions began not so much with a groundswell of popular support but with rich people promising him money.

GORE KNEW SOMETHING was wrong from the start. Most of the political pros had signed up with other candidates by the time he got in. "We had no first-round draft picks," said one aide. He barely knew his campaign manager, Fred Martin, a soft-spoken fellow five years younger than the young candidate. Martin had worked as a speechwriter for Mondale and policy aide for Cuomo, but had no experience running a national campaign. Gore had hoped and expected that he could bring in the consulting partners Bob Squier and Carter Eskew to help him shape the campaign, but they declined to take a public role, since their firm had previous consulting relationships with three other candidates. Gore ended up talking to them on the telephone nearly every day, but it was not the same. And he had jumped into the race having spent far more time worrying about whether to run than about what he was going to say. During his first trip to New Hampshire shortly after the announcement, he was driving from one event to another with Tom Grumbly, a former aide who had moved to Boston, when he let loose with a bleak assessment of his own prospects.

"You know, we're not going to win," Gore said.

"Oh, yeah?" asked Grumbly.

"We don't have a message yet," the candidate confessed.

There were at least parts of a message, not fully formed, that went back to his work on arms control, and even further back to those days at

Harvard when he role-played as President Kennedy dealing with the Cuban Missile Crisis. He wanted to be considered the candidate who knew the most about foreign policy in the nuclear age. "He had in his head what the next president needed to do. It was to negotiate arms deals," said one of his admen, Thomas (Doc) Sweitzer. Encouraged by the centrist Democratic Leadership Council and by his increasingly hawkish college mentor, Marty Peretz, publisher of *The New Republic,* he presented himself as the one national defense hard-liner in the Democratic field, a right flank that might serve him well in the Super Tuesday primaries, which were weighted with states in the conservative south.

Al Gore, tough guy, was the image by the fall of 1987. In late September, six of the candidates appeared at an old theater in downtown Des Moines at a debate sponsored by the nuclear freeze advocates, Stop the Arms Race Political Action Committee. The large crowd buzzed with approval when Jesse Jackson gave an impassioned plea for world peace and former Arizona governor Bruce Babbitt charged that the Reagan administration had a "soldier of fortune mentality." Then Gore, in the words of his aide Paul Risley, "caught the ire and the fire of the crowd" by stating that he was against a unilateral freeze and that he would take a tough stance with the Soviet Union on arms control. "The American people have been given the impression over the last several presidential elections that the Democratic party is against every weapons system that is suggested, and is prepared to go into negotiations with the Soviet Union on the basis that we will get something for nothing," he declared.

It was during that part of his first presidential campaign that Gore displayed a contradiction in his political character that would be repeated and become more pronounced in later years. From an early age he had cultivated the image of a polite and cautious young man, sometimes to the point of being dull and artificial, yet once he was in a competitive race nothing could bring more juice to his personality than competition, and when he was in a competitive situation his instinct was to go on the attack. At the Des Moines debate, he took special aim at the front-runners, Dukakis and Gephardt. He accused Dukakis of advocating a pullout of U.S. troops from South Korea, which prompted the governor to snap, "Get your facts straight!" And he went after Gephardt for supporting a ban on missile flight tests, which he called "a really bad idea."

The more the crowd booed, the more Gore and his staff seemed to enjoy it. "It was like music to our ears," said one aide. But the utterances from Gore sounded increasingly grating to his opponents and their staffs. Gephardt's campaign manager, Bill Carrick, compared Gore to "the little boy who comes to the first grade and pulls his pants down. We're hoping he will wake up and discover he's embarrassing himself instead of just attracting attention." The old man, Senator Senior, as the staff called him, was not quite sure what to make of his son's attitude. The antiwar orator wanted to think of his boy Al as an arms control expert, not as a hawk.

At a staff meeting in Iowa, Gore Senior expressed his befuddlement at the way his son was being received. "These people should *love* you. You should be their hero," he said to Junior, referring to the nuclear freeze supporters. Gore's aides kept quiet, wondering where Senator Senior got that idea. Finally, as his father went on, Gore interrupted him and said, politely but firmly, "No! Dad, no!" As pollster Mark Mellman remembered it, the staff adored Gore Senior with all of his idiosyncrasies, and "nobody wanted to be the first to say, 'Well, you are so far out of date, it's not even in the same world.' "

Gore did meet privately with members of the peace movement. Late one night in Des Moines, he and a few members of his staff sat down with ten members of the board of a nuclear freeze group known as Beyond War. The session took place in a church basement, the blue-suited candidate face-to-face with ten gray-bearded activists in sweat-shirts and sandals who denounced war in all its variations and supported a pacifist American foreign policy. Gore began by recounting the progress civilization had made against slavery, from Babylonian times to the present, even mentioning the notorious ancient slave rings in the basement of the mansion in Carthage. It was possible, he said, that humans could make similar progress against war.

His audience wanted him to denounce war entirely, but Gore argued that there were sufficient reasons to use military power in defense of progressive ideas as long as there were dictators and Hitlers in the world. Then, ever the professor, he pulled up a blackboard and began to draw diagrams of missiles and silos, and missiles with multiple warheads, and missiles with single warheads. He explained his theory of mutual deterrence, how if both sides had only single-warhead missiles, neither could take out the other's silos in a first strike. This was dense and technical and it had Gore fully engaged. Every ten minutes or so, someone from Beyond War would raise his hand and say, "Would you sign our declaration to be against war forever?"

As aide Paul Risley later remembered it, Gore "mumbled something about how he had to make a phone call" and went into a little room next to where the meeting was taking place, where he expressed his frustration silently, looking up at the ceiling, his eyebrows raised, "as though he's asking God for help."

Throughout that fall, Gore moved further right to distinguish himself from the pack, claiming that he was in "the mainstream" of public opinion while his rivals were drifting to the left bank. He and his staff knew they could be seen differently, as having crossed over into Reagan territory, as internal notes and memos from the campaign reveal. One campaign note worries that Gore's support of humanitarian aid for the Nicaraguan contras could be confused with military aid, "and make Al look like a crypto-Republican." For a debate in Miami in October, the Democratic Leadership Council hired Stan Greenberg (who would later become Bill Clinton's pollster) to conduct an admittedly unscientific focus group of randomly recruited volunteers, paying them ten dollars to watch the televised debate and record their impressions. "Most of them took the money and ran," according to DLC founder Al From, but those who bothered to take part found Gore's performance most impressive.

It was there that Gore widened his hawkish credentials, saying that he was the only one to back nonlethal aid to the Nicaraguan contras, that he supported Reagan's decision to invade Grenada in 1983, and that he was also in favor of putting U.S. flags on Kuwaiti ships in the Persian Gulf. He tried to present himself as the "raging moderate," looking past the fact that any attempt to rage as a moderate was likely to fall flat, since the essence of moderation is temperance. After the debate, Gephardt accused Gore of "pandering to the right wing of the party" and archly suggested that the next debate be between "the old Al Gore and the new Al Gore." This was a fair and predictable fight, Gore v. Gephardt. They had entered Congress together in 1976, two moderate Boy Scout types, and had seen each other as rivals ever since, each with one eye on the prize. At a debate in Williamsburg, Virginia, Gore called the 1981 tax cut package the "Reagan-Gephardt tax bill" and asked Gephardt if he thought it was fair. As Gephardt started to answer, Gore broke in.

"Is it fair? Is it fair?" he demanded.

"Are you finished? Are you finished?" Gephardt shot back.

"If you'll answer," Gore said.

"I thought they taught you manners at St. Albans," came the reply.

After the debate, Gore and Gephardt bumped into each other in the men's room. *Dick, you think we'll get through this?* Gore asked, indicating that his hostility was just an act. *Oh, yeah,* Gephardt replied. *I'm sure we will.*

But it only grew more heated. Dick called Al *Al Haig.* Al called Dick *Dick Nixon.* Gore, showing a studied viciousness that he would later perfect as a tool to irritate and badger opponents, accused Gephardt of a string of flip-flops on issues ranging from the minimum wage to abortion (ignoring his own evolution on the latter issue). Gephardt's campaign manager was so fed up with Gore's tactics at one point that he spilled out his hostility in an impolitic rant to *Washington Post* writer Tom Edsall for which he would later apologize. "I hate all of them," Bill Carrick said. "I think they are the phoniest two-bit bastards that ever came down the pike, starting with Al Gore."

With all of the heat coming down on his son from progressive voices, Senator Senior came to his defense. He said that Al was "playing hardball" as part of a larger strategy to get the Dixiecrats back into the party. After Al won the nomination, Senior explained, "people will see the other side of his record come through: his work on the environment, on chemical waste, on standards for infant formula, on the ozone layer. It will be clear he is a very progressive, forward-looking candidate."

But Gore rarely seemed that surefooted. In the early stages of the campaign, he talked incessantly about global warming and other environmental issues that fascinated him, sometimes even to the dismay of his most ecologically minded aides. Deb Callahan, who worked for Gore that year and later became president of the League of Conservation Voters, was perplexed despite her credentials when Gore would talk to senior citizen groups not about Medicare or pension benefits but about the ozone layer. "You'd be sitting in the back of the room as a staffer," she remembered, "thinking, 'What are you doing?' " His absorption with the details of global warming was such that during one debate Jesse Jackson wryly observed, "Senator Gore has just showed you why he should be our national chemist."

• • •

THE NEWS BROKE on a Thursday in early November 1987. Supreme Court nominee Douglas H. Ginsburg admitted that he had smoked pot as a Harvard law professor. As soon as the story hit, all the candidates for president knew that they would be getting the same question. For some, the issue was easily dismissed. "We've had the sex test, the plagiarism test [Biden had been ousted from the race after acknowledging that he had ripped off swaths of a speech from a British pol], and now the marijuana test," said Jackson. "I use neither cigarettes, liquor, or marijuana." Dukakis said he had never used drugs of any sort. But Gore squirmed.

At an airport in Mobile, Alabama, on Friday morning, before leaving for an event in Miami, he said that he had never smoked marijuana as an adult, or within the last fifteen years, and that it would be "inappropriate" to question if he had done so in college. "I personally feel there are some lines that should not be crossed," he said sharply to reporters standing on the airport tarmac, adding later, "You're not going to find saints who are running in either political party." His staff then privately counseled him to cancel his Miami appearance so that he could return to Washington, where he might collect his thoughts and prepare a statement. Gore overruled them, saying they should proceed to Florida.

In the lobby of the Fontainebleau Hotel in Miami Beach sat Jim O'Hara, the campaign reporter for Gore's hometown paper, the *Tennessean*. He hoped to get in a question or two before his deadline: *How much had Al smoked? When?* Seven o'clock. Eight. Nine. O'Hara's deadline came and went, and he gave up and headed to his room. Around ten Gore finally arrived at an upstairs suite, where he and his father and a few aides convened a meeting that stretched on until three the next morning. It was, to say the least, an uncomfortable session, one in which the Gore generations, Senior and Junior, not only argued about how to run a campaign for president but also confronted the limits of their knowledge of one another.

Senator Senior was upset on several levels, concerned about the fallout that could result from an admission that his son had smoked dope, and also upset as a parent that he had apparently done so. It was a subject that he had never expected to face with his dutiful son. "Here he was, having to confront a very difficult issue that, it was apparent to me, he and his son had never talked about," Mike Kopp, the campaign's deputy press secretary, said later. "His father was still trying to get around this issue and how his son had gotten himself in this position." Senior advised silence—say nothing more about it. Junior thought he should make an admission—to a point—and then move on. Back and forth they argued. Two staffers asked questions and kept notes. It seemed surreal, something out of a movie, the confrontational scene between father and son. "It's two o'clock in the morning. . . . Gore Senior was really upset," recalled Kopp. "It was as upset as I've ever seen him." Senior kept raising his voice, Junior kept cutting him off. It got so intense at one point that the staffers felt embarrassed and left the room.

As the night wore on, the group debated the nuances of what Gore could say, how far he should go, what impression he wanted to convey, what he needed to avoid. They finally worked out a statement, scrawled on a notepad, that read in part, "Like many others in my generation, my life reflects the times. The 1960s and early 1970s were a period of change, of a nation growing up, maturing, coming out of the Cold War, trying to come to grips with Vietnam, a nation in search of itself. We made mistakes, but learned from those mistakes. As a nation, and as individuals, the experiences made us stronger."

Below that was another scribbled line:

"Want to avoid: Life out of control, pothead, addicted, offending others of his generation by being hypocritical."

Gore, with his need to seem in command, an impulse intensified by his desire to project a presidential demeanor, did not want to convey that his life had ever been "out of control"—which he feared pot smoking might imply to the older generation, as it seemed to imply to his own father. But at the same time, he did not want to appear to be a moral prude hypocritically lecturing his generation about the evils of drugs. He spoke at the Florida event, a state Democratic convention, and made his short announcement. "There were people who said, 'Ugh, that's the end of it. He's finished!' " said Jerome Berlin, one of the Impac fund-raisers. But then in quick sequence Senators Lawton Chiles and Claiborne Pell and Congressman Newt Gingrich revealed that they had tried pot, and Berlin and others felt relieved.

Gore's next destination was Des Moines, where he attended the annual Jefferson-Jackson Day dinner. O'Hara followed him to Iowa, and late that night, in his hotel room, the reporter began thinking that the real question was not whether Gore had smoked dope, but "whether he was being truthful or not. . . . You know, he had clearly minimized his smoking. Was that the truth?" Early the next morning, O'Hara called his editors in Nashville and said that they needed to do a follow-up and call everyone who worked with Gore during his days at the *Tennessean* and ask them "what they knew about Al's smoking." There was some resistance to the idea, O'Hara said. "Siggy [editor Seigenthaler] was not enthusiastic." But he prevailed by noting "if we don't do it, the *Globe* will do it, the *Post Dispatch*, the *New York Times*, the *Post*. Your call." He and political reporter Larry Daughtrey agreed to divide the newsroom list and start phoning.

O'Hara's first call was to the Gore staff. "I need to talk to Al," he said. Word came back to him that Gore had checked out, but that he had not left the building and would stop by O'Hara's room at the Hotel Fort Des Moines. When the two former colleagues, who had worked in the editorial department together, met that morning, O'Hara kept asking Gore questions, and Gore kept trying to push him away from the story, saying it wasn't an issue, a variation of the technique he had used with former colleague Alan Carmichael during that car ride in the 1976 campaign. But the story was already out there, and all Gore could do was try to make it fuzzy. O'Hara got no new answers from him, and was left with only one overriding image of his old colleague, an image that had nothing to do with the question at hand yet revealed something about how Gore handled pressure. In the middle of O'Hara's interrogation, Gore picked a clothes hanger off the bed and started balancing it on the bridge of his nose, keeping the hanger up there, not letting it fall, lightening the moment, and gently ridiculing it, while delivering his nonanswers.

O'Hara and Daughtrey eventually interviewed forty people for their article, which ran the next Tuesday. Of that number, three declined to comment. One, John Warnecke, old Uncle John, said that he knew of one instance when Gore got high, adding that it seemed Gore did not enjoy it. That was the end of it—for nearly a dozen years, until Warnecke's conscience started wearing on him. In the thick of the 1999 Democratic primary season, Warnecke went public with the story that he said he had kept bottled up for too many years. He readily admitted that he himself had been treated for drug dependency and depression, and said that his therapist had urged him to get his story off his chest, which he did by telling first biographer Bill Turque and then others about his version of Gore's extensive drug use and of some measure of pressure to keep quiet he felt from Gore and his staff back in 1987 and 1988.

According to Warnecke, the first person to call him was Peter Knight, who advised him that he might be getting some calls from reporters and that it would be best to deflect them by saying it was a private matter. "I said, 'This is stupid,' " Warnecke said later. He said he would not hurt Gore, but nor would he say what Knight wanted. An hour later, Tipper called with a similar message, then put Al on the phone. "I kept telling him, 'Trust me. I wouldn't hurt you,' " Warnecke remembered. Then Gore hung up and Warnecke never heard from him again. O'Hara called soon thereafter. Warnecke asked him what Gore had said, and when O'Hara said Gore was acknowledging that he had smoked dope a couple of times, Warnecke went along with that version. "I said, 'Yeah, he tried it a couple of times. And he didn't like it. He liked beer instead.' And that killed the issue."

GORE'S CAMPAIGN made a decision early on not to campaign in Iowa. He was not popular there; it was Gephardt territory. He barely reached 5 percent in the polls. With limited money, the plan was to focus on states he had a chance of winning. In what he hoped would be regarded as a bold and daring stroke, he planned to pull out of the Iowa caucuses on the very night of the Jefferson-Jackson Day dinner. He had put together a speech brimming with righteous indignation over how the caucuses were undemocratic. But that was the same day that he held a press conference on marijuana use, and by the time he delivered the speech at eleven that night, the last of six candidates to talk, hardly anyone was listening. Few were listening to him anywhere late that fall and early winter. The hawk message was not catching on. Some of his advisers wanted him to recast himself as a populist, the posture the old man always preferred. As the Iowa vote approached, the Gore strategy devolved from the audacious to the gimmicky. Why not completely insult Iowa and advertise a trip to sunnier climes? They printed up a press release aimed directly at the traveling press, drawing on the rhyming phrase that the old man and Pauline had come up with in the 1952 race against McKellar: *Think Some More and Travel with Gore.*

"Today's weather forecast in Iowa is calling for more of the same — just another typical wintry day; more snow or sleet expected, windchill temperatures in the minuses. . . . Why not let your imagination drift off to sugar-white beaches, or stroll through gardens where flowers bloom in February. . . . We can make your dreams come true. . . . break away from Iowa for a couple of days and join us down south. . . . Paradise is waiting for you."

In early February, while the other candidates were trudging through snowbound Iowa, the campaign chartered a plane and flew some three dozen reporters to Florida. The plane had some trouble along the way and broke down in Chattanooga, provoking the press corps to dub it *Old Sparky*. But everyone made it to Florida. Gore jogged at sunrise on the Fort Lauderdale beach. He met with condo leaders at a catering hall. He wandered through the marshes of Tampa Bay with environmentalists. All of this won him some attention, but it did not move his numbers. New Hampshire a few weeks later treated him no better. He came in a weak fifth, with barely 7 percent of the vote, behind Jackson, Paul Simon, Gephardt, and Dukakis. The campaign was foundering. Nate Landow, who still had high hopes for Gore, put in a call to Ray Strother, a media consultant who had worked for Hart in 1984 and had met Landow on a junket to China. There were only a few weeks before Super Tuesday, the day Gore had been aiming for all along, but he had to break out somehow.

Strother got on the plane and traveled with Gore for a few days to assess his strengths and weaknesses and see how he dealt with people. Standing at a podium, Strother quickly decided, Gore was awful — wooden and not believable. Yet when you sat next to him on the plane, he was a very affable, agreeable person. When he waded into a crowd and had one-on-one conversations, he could also be very effective. The image maker wondered how to translate the better side of the personal Gore into the public Gore. First he attempted to shoot Gore speaking without a script, but that did not work. "What he was giving me wasn't believable," Strother said. "It was a rote recitation of issue decisions. He wasn't making the connection with the heart. He was just interested in making the connection with the mind. He was all intellect, no heart, telling people what was good for America, not what was good for them."

One week before Super Tuesday, Strother decided to film Gore talking to real people. He went to his old union, Local 23 of the AFL-CIO in Port Arthur, Texas, and rounded up some workers, dressed in jeans and baseball caps, to talk to the candidate. He met Gore at the motel, took him out of his blue suit and put him in a plaid work shirt (the early version of his 2000 earth tones). There was no script; he knew that if he gave Gore the words he would put the punch line in the wrong place. And no podium, nothing to hide behind. *What are we going to do?* Gore asked nervously.

The issue of the day was jobs and how they were being lost to foreign investment. Strother placed Gore in the middle of the men and had them fire questions at him, then picked up his camera and started to shoot, walking slowly around the group, quietly warning them that if they looked at the camera the film would be ruined. It was not perfect, but the difference was substantial; Gore seemed as loose and as natural as he could be. At the same time, it became evident in other ways that the decision to focus on Super Tuesday was starting to work, so much so that the campaign took out a loan to push for more. Gore started drawing boisterous crowds, the first he had seen. Local sheriffs were providing escorts. For a few brief shining moments, in the days before the vote, Gore allowed himself to entertain the fantasy of that "28 Year Cycle" idea. AGJ in the White House. On one campaign flight, he looked at tracking polls that showed his strength. He could envision the states falling into his column: Tennessee, Arkansas, Kentucky . . . was it possible? He stopped himself short. An alarm was going off in his head. "HUBRIS ALERT! HUBRIS ALERT!" he shouted, to no one in particular, or to himself.

CHAPTER SIXTEEN

REPORTING GORE

T HE MEMO was dated February 15, 1988.

> To: AL
> From: ARLIE
> *This is very important.*
> *As I've mentioned to you the past couple of days, Nolan Wal-*
> *ters of Knight-Ridder has been nosing into your past.*

NOLAN WALTERS, a polite, soft-spoken reporter from Georgia, was covering his first presidential campaign. His bureau chief in
Washington was intent that year on doing in-depth pieces on all the
candidates, and Walters, the southerner, had drawn Gore. He caught
up with the candidate on a commercial flight between campaign stops,
and thought, naively, that they might strike up a conversation. After a
perfunctory hello, Gore "went off and sat by himself . . . and he put on
one of those little night masks and was trying to catch a few winks,"
Walters recounted. From then on, it seemed to him that he never
found Gore relaxed. "He always seemed *on*. When he tried to tell
southern anecdotes to show that he was a man of the people, it was
kind of awkward. I never really felt he was at ease with us."

Start with what is in front of your nose: Walters listened to Gore
on the stump and studied his campaign literature. Besides touting him
as "one of the leading experts in Congress on arms control," and "co-
author of the Superfund law" to clean up hazardous waste sites, and

"an important voice in the field of health care" and proponent of "tougher cigarette warning labels," the press kit biography also said that Gore operated a small homebuilding business and owned a small livestock farm near Carthage. It struck Walters that Gore made much of his rural roots, bragging in Iowa that he was "the only farmer" running in the race. He decided to look into some of Gore's claims, especially his experience as a homebuilder.

The development was called Tanglewood—a name as susceptible to ironic interpretation as Whitewater, the now infamous Arkansas real estate venture that launched a presidential investigation that led through an unlikely series of twists and turns to the impeachment of a president. Unlike Bill Clinton, who was preparing to take over as the governor of Arkansas when he became swept up in Whitewater, Al Gore was barely twenty-one, a senior at Harvard preparing to enlist in the Army, when his father helped him take out a $45,000 low-interest loan to buy twenty acres of land, already owned by the old man, and start a small business, Tanglewood Homebuilders Incorporated. His partner was Walter King Robinson, the brother of Senator Senior's longtime aide Jack Robinson. The corporation built nine homes between 1969 and 1973, during a period when Gore was either in the service or working as a reporter and attending graduate school at Vanderbilt. They were split-level traditional models with family rooms and landscaped yards situated on a gentle slope on the edge of Carthage.

As soon as Walters started looking into Tanglewood, he became a pest to the campaign. He questioned whether it was appropriate for Gore to have received a loan from the Federal Farm Credit System, which supposedly was set up to help farmers finance their crops, not split-level subdivisions. He wanted to know what role Gore and his father played in getting the loan, and also how involved Gore was in building the houses. Gore's press secretary, Arlie Schardt, sent a memo to campaign attorney Todd Campbell laying out Walters's argument: "His line is that even if the loan was technically legal (which he doesn't concede), there is an appearance of impropriety. You have a powerful senator saying, 'I want a low-interest loan for my son to start a housing development.'"

The staff scrambled and came up with documents establishing that Gore had apparently acted within the law. One bank official's letter noted that the son was eligible for the loan because "the entire deal was within the family," which was headed by a farmer, Gore Senior, and that the loan "in effect helps the son get started financially."

Walters persisted. Just how involved was Gore in building the homes? The reporter did not know it at the time, but the campaign staff feared that his suspicions were dead on. A note from lawyer Campbell to press secretary Schardt noted: "Last week Nolan Walters called the homeowners to ask them how much 'hands on' work Al did on the houses. One theory he seems to be pursuing is that Al has exaggerated his 'homebuilder' occupation (which is true)."

By then Walters had contacted six of the nine original home buyers and none of them said they knew that Gore was involved in the subdivision when they bought it. They all said they dealt with Robinson. A flurry of staff notes culminated in a memo Schardt typed up for his boss that day, alerting the candidate to his weakness:

> Walters . . . has made many calls to people in Tennessee and plowed through lots of records. He is therefore very familiar with your past activities and will undoubtedly ask you about them in hopes of catching you in an exaggeration. Therefore . . . do not overstate your degree of involvement as a farmer or homebuilder. . . .
>
> BOTTOM LINE: You should say, "I didn't drive all the nails or pour the concrete, but I did put together that business venture. It was up to me to see that it was a financial success because if it wasn't, I was the one who would lose money."
>
> The main point is to be careful not to overstate your role. . . .
>
> RE YOUR ROLE AS A FARMER:
>
> Your staff has never exaggerated your role as a farmer. The campaign bio we distribute everywhere says only "He owns a small livestock farm near Carthage where he and his family reside when Congress is not in session". . . . You did say near the end of the Iowa race something like "I'm the only farmer in this race."
>
> Conclusion: As I see these two subjects, your main political pitfall is exaggeration. Be careful not to overstate your accomplishments in these two fields.

There was, in these cases as in others, a factual basis to every claim Gore made, but it seemed to Walters that "none of it really rose to the level of what he was claiming." He had a financial connection to a homebuilding enterprise, but he was not a homebuilder. He owned farm land, but he was not a farmer. Just as, in Congress, he had publicized the issue of hazardous waste in a series of hearings, but it was his colleague on the Energy and Commerce Committee, James Florio of New Jersey, who actually authored the Superfund legislation. The symbol of this tendency, what Walters believed was Gore's "résumé enhancement," actually came from the presidential announcement event in Carthage back in the summer of 1987. The picturesque scene reporters encountered that day included cattle grazing near the fence of Gore's country house. "Except the cows weren't Gore's," Walters wrote in the lead of his profile. They actually belonged to Senior and normally grazed in the old man's field on the other side of the Caney Fork. Judd Key, a former farm hand for the family, had been ordered to take them over to Junior's place for the special occasion. "They'd be easy to look at there," Key explained to Walters. "We just tied them to the fence."

Schardt and others on Gore's staff were clearly nervous that their candidate tended to overstate his accomplishments. He had already been forced to acknowledge that he had exaggerated his record as an investigative reporter for the *Tennessean*, once being quoted as saying that he "got a bunch of people indicted and sent to jail." In fact, two officials had been indicted on charges that stemmed from Gore's investigation, but no one went to prison. This tendency to stretch reality is one that persisted with Gore long past 1988, nibbling away at his credibility as he ran for president again a dozen years later.

What explains it? He always had a need to live up to expectations, first those of his parents, then those of the larger world. He had a competitive instinct that made him want to be able to show that he could do anything and know everything. In a broader sense, manipulating reality is an inherent aspect of politics. Some politicians are deft at it, Gore seems especially clumsy. His exaggerations are clunkers and he is a bad liar, without the nuance or fluidity of Bill Clinton. There is also a cultural context, a country storytelling style that he inherited from his father, built on grandiosity and hyperbole. It was in Senator Gore's nature to claim that he had built the nation's Interstate system almost single-handedly, and in his day that sort of boast, when pronounced in the

middle of a long and loud stump speech, seemed expected and acceptable. When Junior used the same style a generation later, he often
came across as an insecure figure trying too hard.

IT TOOK RICHARD BEN CRAMER one meeting with Gore to
reach that unsympathetic conclusion. Cramer, who trained his uncanny political ear listening to the Runyonesque cadences of the ward
heelers of ethnic Baltimore, was working the campaign trail that year
for a book that became *What It Takes*, a chronicle of the lives and psy-
ches of the men who wanted to be president. He was out there early, in
Iowa, picking off the candidates one by one for preliminary interviews
in which he hoped to prepare them for the depth of his endeavor while
at the same time starting to take their measure. The Gore staff slotted
him for face time with their man during a long car ride "from this town
to that town" in Iowa. It was an interview doubleheader, with Jules Witcover, the political columnist and author, also crammed in the back
seat. Witcover went first. "I don't remember what Jules asked him, but
Gore talked about his plan to reshape a missile system," Cramer recounted. "Gore was so proud of himself and to him that was interesting." It struck Cramer that Gore went on and on, never considering the
fact that he could talk about that subject forever and "it was never
gonna make a line in Jules' column—but still he wouldn't shut up."
    When Cramer's time came, he opened with the "base level" ques-
tions he asked every candidate as a means of deciding, as he put it,
"who I could do something with"—meaning which ones would be
willing to go beyond constricted political rhetoric and provide him
with the juice of real life. His first questions were variations on this
theme: *What were the last things you had to figure out before you got in
this thing? What did you have to settle in your mind?* When he asked
Gore that question, Cramer recounted, "I think he wanted to get back
to that missile thing. He said there were *thousands* of people—that was
the honest-to-God number he used, *thousands*—writing to him,
telling him he ought to be president, that he ought to run, so that made
his decision to run easier, that he wouldn't have done it without that
kind of public chorus."
    Cramer's self-described "truth-o-meter" started clanging. "I
sensed that probably didn't happen. I had never seen someone trying to
pull that line off. I said, 'Okay, Senator, thanks much. What were the
issues for Mrs. Gore? What did she have to settle?' He said she had no

problems at all. No issues. Now, I wasn't married then, but I knew that wasn't so. So I thought to myself, life's too short to talk to this guy anymore. It wasn't the fact that he wasn't telling me the truth, it was the pallid bankruptcy of the lies, all in service of a picture of himself that wasn't even interesting. He wasn't even an interesting liar. That really was the kiss of death for me. His lies were in service of the smallest common denominator correctness. When I tried to indicate that I wasn't satisfied with the answers, he went back to that missile thing."

JIM O'HARA, covering Gore for the *Tennessean* that year, became preoccupied with another political trait, a tendency to trim responses to the audience and seemingly change positions. O'Hara was with Gore at a Des Moines debate on a Friday when he declared that "there should not be any public subsidy for tobacco at all . . . in spite of the fact that there are 100,000 tobacco farms in my home state." And he listened to Gore the next day, at a press conference in North Carolina, say that "as long as it's legal and is going to be grown and sold . . . we have a right to structure the marketplace and say the money that is earned growing tobacco should go to the small family farmers." Noting his family's reliance on tobacco and federal price supports over the years, he then delivered an ode to tobacco that became one of the better known utterances of his career: "I've plowed the ground, put in the seed beds. I've planted it, hoed it, wormed it, suckered it, cut it, spiked it, put it in the barns, stripped it, and sold it. I know what it's all about, how important that way of life is."

For that Monday's paper, O'Hara wrote an article contrasting Gore's Iowa and North Carolina statements. The story then was spread along the campaign network on *Hotline*, the then fledgling daily news bulletin for political junkies. It was Headline No. 7 on Tuesday: "Gore Walks a Tightrope on Tobacco Subsidies." What O'Hara captured was Gore's awkward attempt to articulate a nuanced position that conveyed sympathy for farmers as well as concern about the health risks of tobacco, which he knew only too well after the death of his sister, Nancy, from lung cancer four years earlier. "There wasn't any real inconsistency in his two answers," O'Hara said later. "But clearly the answers had been calibrated to the crowd in Des Moines and the crowd in North Carolina."

It was also O'Hara who broke another story about the Gore campaign using a loophole in federal election laws to take out loans for

Super Tuesday based on matching funds that he had not yet received. The tendencies he was seeing in Gore prompted him to write a column on the *Tennessean*'s op-ed page suggesting that his old colleague was not living up to his announcement speech promise to be truthful and straight and honest. That column prompted an angry midnight call from Gore to Seigenthaler, who then called O'Hara in a foul mood. *What was wrong with holding a politician to his own words?* O'Hara responded. *That's what you expect from a reporter at the* Tennessean, *God damn it!* That was the end of the conversation.

LEAP-FROG IN TIME, momentarily, beyond the rest of the 1988 campaign, to reach the codas for these three hard-nosed reporters, O'Hara and Cramer and Walters, and their relationships with Al Gore.

Soon after the election, Gore hired a new press secretary, Marla Romash. In one of her first visits to Nashville, she encountered O'Hara, and had dinner with him. All she knew about him at that point was that he "gave Al a horrible time" and "had a reputation for being the meanest sonofabitch in the press corps." When Gore asked suggestively about the dinner, Romash snapped, "Al, there are a lot of things I would do to get you good press, but that's not one of them." Five months later, she walked into her boss's office and announced, "Jim O'Hara's not going to be covering you anymore." *Why?* Gore asked. *Well, we've kind of fallen in love,* she said. At the same time, O'Hara told John Seigenthaler that he need not worry about any more late-night telephone calls from a nervous Al Gore. Romance had taken him off Gore's trail.

Richard Ben Cramer talked to Gore only one other time during the period he was researching his book, at a corn festival, and came away as empty as he did the first time. He wrote *What It Takes* without Gore, excavating iron ore from the rock of other candidates, Bush and Dole and Gephardt and Dukakis and even the ill-fated Biden and Hart, smelting their stories into narrative steel. He never went back to Gore, not even for his near-moment of Super Tuesday. Cramer was intrigued by Senator Senior, though he thought the old man had done Al "a terrible disservice by making him go out there. It was like bringing a rookie up too fast." His lasting impression of Gore was that he could not give a true accounting of his motivations and feelings because "he was scared. He was scared of his own self."

Nolan Walters's last encounter with Gore came at a post-election campaign party at a Washington nightclub known as the Vault. Here was a side of Gore many reporters had not seen before. He had a beer or two and seemed "loose as a goose," Walters remembered. So loose that at one point he called Walters over and put his arm around him.

"Nolan, we've had our differences in the past, but I've always liked you," Gore said.

"Senator, I would have voted for you," the reporter responded.

In revisiting that scene twelve years later, Walters laughed and said softly, "We were both lying."

CHAPTER SEVENTEEN

BLOWN
TO SMITHEREENS

IN THE EARLY HOURS of the big primary night, at the Opryland Hotel in Nashville, all you had to do was look at the old man to gauge the mood. Eighty years old and pumped like a high school kid. Everyone in the campaign was excited, but Senator Senior found a state of delirium all his own.

I want to see you elected president before I die, he had told his son back during the Christmas break in 1986, and ever since he had been working as hard as anyone to see his wish come true. He was the definition of irrepressible, this white-maned old pol, the one member of the Gore team who had visited every county in Iowa before his son had decided not to compete there, so proud of his accomplishment, so determined to hit each and every courthouse in the Hawkeye state, that he had put "the pedal to the metal" as he roared through the last untouched stretches, counting off ninety-seven, ninety-eight, ninety-nine—done! During debate preps, Senior was there with a catalogue of old country tales, reminding his son to put things in personal terms that voters could appreciate. With the pressure of his own career gone, the once-formal senator was feeling free and easy in his old age, and urging his son to relax as well. *Get him to laugh,* he would tell the staff. *Get him to laugh.* F. Guthrie Castle, a "Gore Corps" volunteer from Memphis, watched one late night Texas debate in a hotel room with Gore Senior and felt like he was watching a college football game, with the father cheering wildly whenever his son made a point. The next morning, at six-thirty, there he was in the lobby, ready to roll.

All, it seemed, for this moment at the Opryland. The calls were coming in from the networks, a sign that they were taking his boy seriously. They hadn't paid much attention all year, why now? wondered Skila Harris, a family friend and volunteer. Then she saw the results. Gore was winning Oklahoma, Arkansas, Tennessee, North Carolina, Nevada, Kentucky. Now here came the candidate, bouncing onstage, engulfed by balloons and banners, the crowd roaring as he shouted in exultation, "This is a Super Tuesday!" Arlie Schardt looked over at Gore's father, who threw up his hands in a victory gesture and shouted, "Arlie! Arlie! Do you realize that boy is going to be president!"

But the thrill did not last long. An hour later the spotlight started shifting away from Gore. How do you interpret a night when Dukakis wins the big states of Texas and Florida, along with Maryland and Massachusetts, and Jesse Jackson beats Gore and the rest of the field in the cradle of the Confederacy, sweeping Alabama, Georgia, Louisiana, Mississippi, and even Virginia? Maybe if Gore had won one of those states it would have been different. But now, he and his supporters watched with dismay as *Nightline* focused its attention on the governor and the reverend. The story was not Gore coming out of nowhere to make such a strong Super Tuesday showing, but Dukakis accumulating more delegates and Jackson becoming the first serious black contender in history.

The lights burned late in two separate suites at the Opryland that night, as little Albert's announcement day question once again came to the fore: *Now what do we do?* In one room sat Fred Martin and his campaign team of pollsters and schedulers and advisers. In another room was the family, Junior and Senior and Tipper and Miz Pauline and Frank Hunger. "There was a family meeting upstairs and a staff meeting downstairs," said pollster Mark Mellman. "It was the upstairs downstairs metaphor in this case." They might as well have been considering two totally separate campaigns, so different were their conclusions. The staff was worried about money, or their lack of it, and thinking that they had to be careful about where they went next. Spurning Iowa and neglecting New Hampshire had almost paid off, at least the victories on this Super Tuesday night had kept them in the race, and they felt it was even more important to be precise in picking the next target. Michigan and Wisconsin made sense to them, then on to New York.

But up at the family session, the Gores were in full throttle. Senator Senior had never liked his son's decision to bail out of Iowa—had he barnstormed through ninety-nine counties for nothing?—and he believed that if you are running for president you run, and if you have momentum, you go where the next contest is. Al agreed. Next on the calendar was Illinois, so on to Illinois. When members of the staff heard the news, they were stunned. Illinois made no sense to them. There were already two favorite sons in Illinois, Paul Simon and Jesse Jackson. Even if everything broke right, the best Gore could do was finish third. Why waste time and energy and money on another losing proposition? The Gores were not listening. "This decision has been made," the candidate said.

The next morning they were in Illinois, where the entire local staff seemed to consist of one or two volunteer drivers. They eventually spent a quarter of a million dollars there and won 5 percent of the vote, then limped through a few more third-place finishes toward what was seen as a last stand in New York.

THE FIELD HAD WINNOWED to three: Dukakis, Jackson, and Gore. Some in the campaign had nonetheless abandoned hope and thought the goal now was to find a graceful way to lose. Why not lose in New York, where at least you could go to a Broadway play after a bad day on the streets? Gore was entranced by New York, by its big-name players and big-time publicity machine. He was increasingly concerned about the thinness of his staff ("We were always letting him down," said one), and worried about the gap between what he wanted to say and what he was saying, but he believed that perhaps his troubles could be smoothed over if only he could attach himself to the right New York star.

For months, Gore had hoped that star would be Mario Cuomo, the eloquent but exasperatingly vacillating governor. In 1988, almost anyone who placed his hopes in Cuomo came away disappointed, and Gore was no exception. Would he run himself? Would he endorse another candidate? The melodrama of Mario played out week after week in the early days of the campaign. In a late-January swing through New York state, Gore had made a stop at the state capitol in Albany, his last leg on a four-city swing, where he met with a group of state legislators. It had been a freewheeling session that had gone well, with one state senator describing Gore as the "most electable" candidate. But all the press corps wanted to know was whether Gore would be meeting with the governor. The campaign staff had been trying to arrange a visit for days, but kept hearing that Cuomo was busy. At the capitol, as Gore was winding up with legislators, press secretary Schardt ran into Cuomo's office to find out what was going on. Why were they stonewalling? Surely the governor could come out for five minutes to have his picture taken with Gore. An aide reassured Schardt that Cuomo would appear. After waiting around until late afternoon, with no luck, Gore finally left.

In his car on the way to the airport, the cell phone rang. It was Cuomo, saying that he was sorry that he had been too busy to work Gore in, but next time they had to get together. The papers the next morning reported the snub. How much did Cuomo care about Gore? He had been too busy to meet with the candidate, but not too busy to greet the visiting Syracuse football team. An omen of troubles to come. As the New York primary approached, Cuomo could not restrain himself from serving as an informal adviser to anyone who called, and Gore was one of those who called, still believing that Cuomo might endorse him. During one conversation Cuomo suggested that New York was unlike any other place and that Gore needed a media adviser who understood its idiosyncrasies. Gore chose David Garth, a bombastic consultant with a personality as large as the candidates he had helped elect—Cuomo and New York City mayor Ed Koch. Though out of cash, Gore scrambled to try to raise a million dollars to pay for Garth and his television commercials. The idiosyncrasies of David Garth, if not of New York, were made immediately apparent to Gore's pollster, Mark Mellman. "I've never met you before. The rumor is that I'm going to fire you," Garth screamed upon meeting Mellman. "But I'm not! You're Gore's guy, so you're here." Mellman had never heard the rumor. He did not know what Garth was talking about.

Mellman and the other staffers were still there, perhaps, but not of much use to Garth, who had his own ideas about marketing the candidate. He would talk about Gore in a stream-of-consciousness rataplan. *Okay, the guy was in Vietnam. Great. Great. Does he have his fatigue jacket? Okay. Get him at the Vietnam Veterans Memorial tomorrow. We're going to film him right there because he's the only goddamned veteran in the race. So let's get him out there with that jacket. I want it now! I want that jacket! Get the jacket!*

Some Gore aides suggested that this might not be such a good idea, dressing the now forty-year-old candidate in a scruffy jacket he had worn two decades earlier.

Shut up! Get over it! Get the jacket! And get me Koch now! I want Ed Koch! Now! Koch, I want you down there with Gore tomorrow!

Mayor Koch was the other half of the bargain. On April 14, five days before the primary, Gore was in a plane with an aide and his daughter Karenna, taxiing down a runway, headed to New York to attend an AIDS event, when the call came in. Koch was on the line announcing that he was going to endorse Gore. The immediate reaction was one of jubilation. This was a big catch. Both Dukakis and Gore had gone fishing for Koch, so if nothing else it seemed like a victory over Dukakis, as well as another possible way to win the city's heavy Jewish vote.

IF AMBITION AND BOLDNESS had combined to get Gore to this point, they conspired against him in New York. This was his introduction to the inimitable ethnic cacophony of the five boroughs, the Irish and Italian Catholics in Queens and Brooklyn and Staten Island, the Jews of Manhattan and Brooklyn, the blacks of Harlem and Brooklyn, the West Side liberals and Village gays and lesbians. Gore came to this complicated scene trying to differentiate himself from Dukakis, first, but also Jackson, worried about the Dukakis camp's argument that a vote for Gore was in fact a vote for Jackson. The implication was that the white vote would split, perhaps throwing the primary to Jackson, whose 1984 reference to New York as "Hymietown" had been neither forgotten nor forgiven by a significant number of Jewish voters. Jackson was hot, finishing second in Illinois and winning Michigan, which forced Gore and his aides, belatedly, to take his candidacy seriously.

After developing a friendly relationship with Jackson over the long campaign year, Gore now found the need to attack the reverend in an effort to salvage his own troubled campaign and to prove that a vote for Gore was indeed not a vote for Jackson. His first attack was indirect, charging that Dukakis was being "absurdly timid" in his treatment of Jackson. Then he began his own broadside, asserting that whatever talents Jackson had, he was not White House material. "We're not choosing a preacher," Gore said. "We're choosing a president."

With his hawkish defense position already established, Gore aggressively courted Jewish voters. He criticized the Reagan administration's proposal for a peace conference because it included China,

Russia, and five Arab states, as well as Israel. "It doesn't take a genius to figure out that Israel faces a stacked deck," he said in a television ad shot by Garth. "I believe Israel deserves a better chance to achieve peace." He also drew a contrast with Dukakis, who had supported a letter signed by thirty U.S. senators in which they said they were "dismayed" by the Israeli prime minister's rejection of the American peace proposal. And he saved his strongest language for another disagreement with Jackson. "I categorically reject his notion that there's a moral equivalence between Israel and the PLO," he told one Jewish group. "And I am dismayed by his embrace of Arafat and Castro."

Although Gore came from a state with a small Jewish population, his support for Israel was deep, informed by his father's experiences and by his own trips to Israel, some with his longtime mentor from his Harvard days, Martin Peretz. He had also clearly established a reputation in foreign policy circles for being more of an interventionist than the liberal Democratic norm. Yet his tendency to come across as hard-edged if not outright nasty, to speak in harsh and seemingly moralistic terms, did not help him in the already hyperbolic world of ethnic New York. Was he pandering? Yes and no. He accomplished the nearly impossible and put himself in the unattractive place of being a panderer in politics while also simultaneously sincere in policy. And he was so clumsy in his efforts, so black and white in his presentations, that he seemed divisive as he "lurched from issue to issue," as one magazine described his campaign.

At a debate on April 12 at Madison Square Garden's Felt Forum, he lurched to crime, bringing up a prison program in Massachusetts that granted unsupervised weekend furloughs to inmates, including some serving life sentences. Dukakis had inherited the program from his Republican predecessor, but had kept it going despite the controversy attached to it since a 1987 incident in which a man named Willie Horton, who happened to be black, stabbed a Maryland man and twice raped his girlfriend. The program had first come to the Gore team's attention through an unsolicited sheaf of news clippings that arrived at headquarters one day. Thurgood (Goody) Marshall Jr., Gore's issues director, had asked a young opposition researcher named Victor V. Cooke to look into it , and the information found its way into a debate briefing memo to George Shipley, his preternaturally aggressive political consultant, known in some quarters as "Dr. Death." From there it found its way into the Felt Forum ring.

In mentioning the program, Gore noted that two convicted killers had killed again during their unsupervised furloughs. Would Dukakis support such a program on the federal level?

"Al," Dukakis replied, "the difference between you and me is that I have to run a criminal justice system. You never have."

Gore never mentioned Willie Horton's name, never held up his picture, never mentioned race. But his attack did grab the attention of advisers to Vice President Bush, who would lob it back again at Dukakis later. With the help of Lee Atwater, Bush's junkyard dog tactician, the campaign created the now famous ad showing inmates going in and out of prison, and an independent group promoting Bush launched a separate ad campaign that directly evoked Horton, turning him into a symbol of white America's fear of black crime. Did Gore thus introduce Willie Horton into the lexicon of American politics? The charge seems overstated. In his desire to look tough on crime and embarrass Dukakis, he might have made Horton possible, but Gore himself always focused on the policy, not the symbolism. "It was a stupid policy and it remains a stupid policy," said Marshall, the son of the late Supreme Court justice and civil rights icon. Dukakis also later defended Gore, saying he raised the issue in a legitimate way.

THERE WAS VERY LITTLE LEGITIMATE about Gore's final week in New York. It turned into a one-ring circus, starring Ed Koch. Here Gore had spent a year struggling for visibility, and now he finally had it, and it made him cringe. There was the mayor, standing at a subway stop. *Hi, everybody. It's us! Al Gore and me!* Wherever they went, the irascible Koch stole the show. And at every stop, he could not resist taking another dig at Jackson. He accused Jackson of lying about being the last person to cradle Martin Luther King Jr. after he was shot (a legitimate question raised by many of the civil rights activists who were in Memphis that day). He said that Jews would be "crazy" to vote for Jackson. And there was Gore standing ashen at his side, blanching at the fury he had unloosed. "The mayor is speaking for himself," was all he could muster by way of disavowal. It was, for the staff, alternately painful and comical and fattening (Koch was also Gore's culinary guide: canolis, kosher pickles, fried bananas—"every place we went, the essential attraction was food," recalled Gore aide Jerold Mande).

On the Sunday morning before the vote, Gore sat in a studio in midtown Manhattan, waiting to appear as a guest on ABC's *This Week* with David Brinkley. Richard Holbrooke, one of his foreign policy advisers, sat at Gore's side, briefing him on the nuances of questions they anticipated. Some financial backers, Sarah and Victor Kovner, were also on hand to lend moral support. Their jaws dropped as they watched the segment before Gore's, which featured Ed Koch and Jesse Jackson in full fervor, scrapping at one another and throwing insults back and forth as though they were at a local council meeting. Holbrooke considered it the single most memorable moment he had witnessed in politics. "I remember at the ad break, we were just sitting there in total silence, like all the preparations are just out the window. What do you say? What do you do? Gore struggled through it with great tenacity. We staggered out into the street, and Gore started walking in the [Salute to Israel] parade, and Koch was walking about two blocks ahead of him, and at every street corner, Koch stopped and gave another attack on Jesse. Someone was saying, you could actually *see* votes being lost. It was the worst day of his political life, I'm sure." Compounding the weirdness, Gore walked in the parade wearing a flak jacket and short raincoat, having received a death threat.

Coinciding with the struggle with Jackson was a struggle within Gore between his ambition and his guilty conscience. By day, after every Koch eruption, Gore stood by his benefactor, signaling his tacit acquiescence in the mayor's increasingly strident attacks. But at night, he would call Jackson to apologize, full of remorse and self-disapproval. *Why doesn't he just stop appearing with the guy?* asked Jackson's campaign manager, Gerald J. Austin. *Doesn't he understand that he looks bad?*

You don't understand, Jackson replied. *He's really calling me more as a minister because he feels badly about this and wants absolution.*

Gore campaigned vigorously on election day, even after his staff had given up hope. One aide remembered going into Fred Martin's hotel room and finding the campaign manager sprawled on his bed, lamenting the lost campaign. *It's remarkable,* Martin said, *how you can take a guy with so much potential and see his campaign get blown to smithereens!* Late that night, after the results showed Gore finishing third behind Dukakis and Jackson, with barely 10 percent of the vote, Martin placed a call to Jesse Jackson's room and asked if Gore could come see him. Jackson was finishing a late soul food meal. As difficult as the last few weeks had been, he felt at ease with Gore now, as he always did when he could find a moral high ground from which to operate, manipulating a conversation on several levels. Gore came and apologized again and told Jackson that he was going to close up his campaign. Jackson accepted Gore graciously and asked for his endorsement. Gore was sorry, but not *that* sorry. He said it was too soon to think about things like that.

Two days later, Gore withdrew from the race, leaving with a speech laced not with bitterness but with humor. "I was doing great until I turned forty," he said. He had turned forty on March 31, in the mess of New York. And he spoke of lessons he had learned from his rivals: from Gephardt that passion in the service of policy is powerful; from Dukakis that competence is charisma. And from "my friend Jesse Jackson," he said, he learned that "we are a better party and a better nation when we break down barriers and fight for justice." Then, as if to atone for his earlier remark, he added: "As Theodore Roosevelt first noted when he talked about the bully pulpit, a successful president must be both a chief executive *and* a preacher." Karenna was there wearing her favorite antiestablishment vest, black with safety pins, but her mourning now was far different from what she felt that long ago day when her father had entered the race. She had grown to enjoy politics, and to identify with some of her father's economic populist rhetoric, saying that he "sounded similar to the D.C. hard-core bands that I used to listen to."

He left the race with a $1.6 million debt, which he vowed to erase before the convention. He set up another fund-raising group, known as 40-40, forty people committed to raising $40,000 each, and this time he did it. His friends said they had never seen Gore work the phones harder than when he was paying off that debt. There was no mystery why it meant so much to him. This was just his first race, and he wanted a clean start for the next one.

THE CONVENTION IN ATLANTA was not easy for Gore. His staff had to haggle with the Dukakis people even to get stage time for their guy, and the best they could do was a brief appearance Tuesday afternoon. While he maintained a buoyant appearance, Gore's friend Guthrie Castle sensed at first that Gore felt "snubbed . . . some feeling of not having been accorded enough due respect for what he had accomplished, being such a young man at the time." Gore worked the convention hotels as though it still meant something, talking to one delegation after another, urging support for the party and Dukakis.

Late Wednesday night, after being locked out of the convention hall when the fire marshals closed the doors, Gore suddenly loosened up. Nothing more to lose. He threw an open party on the top floor of the Atlanta Hilton and Towers, and invited the Gore Corps folks along with newfound friends from down the hall, delegates from California and Rob Lowe and members of the Hollywood Brat Pack. The drinks were flowing, and sometime past midnight John F. Kennedy Jr. walked through the door. Gore grinned broadly and pulled the handsome young political heir aside.

You know, John, he said. *You and I, we should talk sometime.* They had so much in common, he said. Both part of American royalty. The kid was twenty-eight (the same age Gore had been when he ran for Congress) and was showing his first signs of political interest, having delivered a well-received speech in Atlanta introducing his Uncle Ted. *There are a fair number of things I can show you about how I've been able to navigate that world and come out of it doing pretty well,* Gore said. *The next time you're down in Washington, call me. We'll talk.*

There would be no great twenty-eight-year cycle, but still there was this connection. Family tragedies. Prep schools. Harvard. Controversial fathers. Aggressive foreign/domestic policies. Expectations. In four more years AGJ would still be only forty-four. He went back to his friends and partied into the night.

CHAPTER EIGHTEEN

THE NEW
WORLD WAR

*H*MMM, THOUGHT EDITOR JOHN STERLING. *This might be inter-esting. But then again, it might not.* He was reading a eight-page pro-posal that had been submitted to him at Houghton Mifflin by literary agent Mort Janklow on behalf of a prospective first-time author, Sena-tor Al Gore of Tennessee. The book would deal with the global envi-ronment and how it should be protected. That much was apparent, if little else. It was hard to discern whether this was meant to be a guided tour of the earth's far-flung ecological hot spots, a compendium of ob-scure congressional hearings, or a philosophical treatise on the inter-connectedness of the physical and spiritual worlds. There was no clear story line and the ideas went all over the place. Finally there was a problem with the tentative title. Gore wanted to call his tome *The New World War*.

When he finished reading the proposal, Sterling told Janklow that he might consider the book depending upon the answers to two ques-tions. Would there be a ghostwriter? The environment was a tough subject to sell anyway, and Sterling wanted nothing to do with a manu-script from a senator seeking to advance a political platform and using a ghostwriter. Second, were they in this for the money and looking for a big advance? If so, no dice. Janklow passed the questions along to Gore and called back with the answers. No, they were not looking for a huge sum of money. Gore was serious, the agent said. He would not need a ghostwriter and he was not intending to use it as a campaign platform. The proof was there in a sentence in which Gore had boldly declared: "I have decided to risk my entire political career with a series of extremely controversial proposals."

That was enough to lure Sterling out of Manhattan to visit Gore at his Senate office on July 27, 1990. On the way down, he wondered who would be in the room with the senator, assuming it would be crowded with press handlers and policy aides. He also assumed that Gore would behave like a typical politician with too many meetings scheduled and too little time, and give him perhaps thirty minutes, at most an hour. Instead, he was surprised to find Gore utterly alone and ready and eager to talk for hours, from 2:00 to 4:50 in the end. Here was Gore the irrepressibly spirited pedagogue, all substance, synapses firing away, going laterally across a vast swath of material at a hundred miles an hour and then deep into a single subject. *He's doing a data download to some extent,* Sterling thought, and though it was obvious that Gore was showing off it was still quite a sight to behold. It became immediately obvious to the editor that Gore had no idea how to structure the book. But it was also clear that he "absolutely was going to write the book or had to write the book because it was all inside him. He was genuinely passionate about the subject."

At some point in the conversation Sterling told Gore that he would have to find a new title. But, Gore argued, the degradation of the environment has to be considered on the level of a world war. People need to mobilize to address the problem in the same way they would to fight a world war. Sterling understood the metaphor, but made it clear that "The New World War" would not work.

Gore accepted the advice without further resistance, and the makings of an agreement were at hand. On August 2, the deal was done for an untitled work, with the understanding that Sterling would be willing to come down to Washington regularly to help Gore "find a shape to the book." Their first session was unforgettable. They met at the Capitol Hill apartment in the Methodist Building kept by the old man and Pauline, a prime location on the Hill that was home to senators and congressmen and former members, along with a row of progressive religious organizations that gave the place its nickname—the God Box. When Sterling entered the Gore residence, he saw papers everywhere, piles of material categorized by topic on every chair, couch, and table in the place. What followed, as the editor put it later, was "a tour through the apartment and thus through the book and to some extent through the mind of Al Gore."

• • •

AT LEAST AS FAR BACK AS 1984, Gore had talked about writing a book. He and aide Steve Owens were driving out of the Memphis airport one day when Gore said he had a book idea and even a title for it: *Salt III*. Oh, said Owens, a book about arms control. *No*, said Gore, *a book about the different ways sodium affects our lives.* Owens burst out laughing. *Doesn't grab you, huh?* Gore said. But he was serious. He had held congressional hearings about contact lenses and saline solutions and about the high sodium content in food and he thought he could put it all together into a book about salt. *Forget about the best-seller lists for that one*, Owens said. He never heard his boss mention the idea again.

The notion of undertaking a larger project on the environment had been on Gore's mind since the summer of 1988, after he had withdrawn from the presidential nomination race and faced a variation of little Albert's question one more time: *Now what?* How do you shake off the stale stench of bureaucratic sameness that permeates the senses as you walk down the familiar congressional corridors after a year out running for president? Even when you are sputtering and faltering out there, you are still up on that high fat road to the White House, and in comparison the basement subway ride from Russell Senate Office Building to the Capitol seems piddling indeed. There were some matters that Gore had to attend to when it was over, like paying off his debt and repopulating a Senate staff depleted by burnout, but beyond those obligations came the question of what he truly wanted to do next.

Part of the answer came to him in a series of tell-me-what-I-did-wrong dinners he held in Washington in 1988, at which friends and advisers gave him their critiques of his first presidential run. From those he concluded that he had failed himself in several respects. He had been unable to convey any sense of who he was and why he believed what he did. And he had further failed in the way he had dealt with his favorite issue, which was not defense but the environment, because he had not successfully persuaded voters of its importance. As usual, he looked at this largely as a matter of knowledge that could be resolved factually. The issue was right, but the public needed to be educated properly to embrace it. The other part of the answer came as a means of averting the stultifying sensation of being trapped again in the Senate cloakroom with a club of men who did not much like him. He would find ways to escape, traveling the world from the Amazon rain forest to the Trans-Antarctic range to the Aral Sea desert, an earnest politico-scientist studying the global ecology.

Marla Romash, a tough former Connecticut statehouse reporter who was hired as press secretary in January 1989, noticed as soon as she arrived that Gore was now fixated on the environment, eager to reclaim it as his issue, perhaps fearful that he had lost standing as the singular environmental senator while he was out on the campaign trail. Before teaching the public, he would educate Romash and other staff assistants who were unfamiliar with the nuances of global warming, and bring in other staffers such as Carol Browner and Katie McGinty to further his environmental agenda. He also took on the role of tutor for journalists. His old *Tennessean* friend Frank Sutherland remembered Gore's first visit to the paper after Sutherland became editor. Gore spent ninety minutes explaining global warming to the editorial board. "And the scary part was, it made sense," Sutherland said. "I thought I understood it, anyway." At a Washington dinner party, Gore arrived with an easel and tri-level flip chart tracking carbon dioxide emissions and global temperatures. The last chart projected where temperatures were going, and David Brinkley and other media guests watched slack-jawed as the senator bounded up on a chair to flip the final chart toward the ceiling. "Cokie Roberts called the next day hysterical about it," Romash remembered. "Of course we knew what he did because we had seen it twenty times already."

The concept of global warming through what was called the greenhouse effect was at the center of Gore's thinking about the environment. It was an idea that had intrigued and disturbed him since his college days, when he had taken a course from Harvard professor Roger Revelle, the first scientist to systematically monitor carbon dioxide in the atmosphere, using data collected at the Mauna Loa volcano in Hawaii. It was during Gore's years at Harvard in the mid-1960s that Revelle began sharing the results of his study. He told his students that over eight years of measurements, the concentration of carbon dioxide levels had increased markedly each year, and that this would cause the earth to grow warmer. It was from Revelle, Gore said later, that he realized that "nature is not immune to our presence, and that we could actually change the makeup of the earth's entire atmosphere in a fundamental way."

Now, a quarter-century later, Gore wanted to spread Revelle's message to the world, and he was thinking big. The idea struck him that he should create his own documentary television series with a companion book, something on the order of Jacob Bronowski's *The Ascent of Man* or Carl Sagan's *Cosmos*. Through his longtime friend in Los Angeles, Gary Allison, he got in touch with Geoff Haines-Stiles, who had been one of the producers of *Cosmos* and was known for his ability to translate complicated scientific concepts into compelling television. Was Haines-Stiles interested in doing a documentary series on the environment? That was the question being considered in the spring of 1989, just before Gore and Tipper and six-year-old Albert joined a group of friends from their Arlington, Virginia, neighborhood in attending the April 3 home opener of the Baltimore Orioles—an outing that might have brought all of this to an end, but instead did just the opposite.

There was a buoyant feeling among Orioles fans walking back to their cars in the early evening of that radiant first day of baseball. They had watched the home team defeat the Red Sox ace, Roger Clemens, and now streamed out of Memorial Stadium in what amounted to a string of postgame victory parades leading in every direction through the working-class neighborhoods of northeast Baltimore. The Arlington entourage had parked more than a half-mile away over near Lake Montebello and was moving with the flow of fans heading in that direction. Al and Albert and two neighborhood kids slightly trailed the rest of the pack. Tipper was talking to a friend nearby, assuming that her husband had control of their son. Suddenly Albert broke free from his father and darted into the middle of the street, where he was struck by a 1977 Chevrolet. Gore's neighborhood pal and jogging partner, James Kohlmoos, who had organized the outing, "heard the screech and turned around and there was Albert flying through the air . . . a terrible image." It seemed to Gore that Albert was in the air thirty feet and scraped along the pavement several more feet before coming to rest at the edge of a gutter. When he reached his son's side, Gore wrote later, the boy was "motionless, limp and still, without breath or pulse. His eyes were open with the nothingness state of death, and we prayed, the two of us, there in the gutter, with only my voice."

Whether Albert had in fact stopped breathing and lost a pulse is unclear. Soon after the accident, two nurses from the Johns Hopkins intensive care unit came upon the scene on their way to work from an opening day party. When they saw an anxious crowd gathered at the curb, they slammed on the brakes and bolted out of their cars. Vicky

Costin-Siegel opened her trunk, took out a visiting nurse's bag, and made her way through the crowd with nursing colleague Esther Ocampo at her side. They assumed at first that they would be dealing with a heart attack victim, Costin-Siegel remembered, but "we looked at each other and said, 'Oh, my God, it's a kid!' " They knew how to treat children, they had been taught the CPR pneumonic for pediatrics, five compressions on the chest to one breath, pushing down a half-inch or inch. But it was obvious to them that CPR was not necessary. The boy was breathing and crying, "screaming his head off," according to Costin-Siegel. She turned to Gore and instructed, "Please, put his head down and leave him straight."

The two nurses covered a cut on Albert's forehead and created a makeshift splint out of tongue depressors for his injured left leg. Costin-Siegel checked his breathing with her stethoscope and measured his blood pressure, and in a cursory eye examination detected that his pupils were unequal. When she reported this to Ocampo, Tipper overheard it. There was a gasp. "Please tell me he's going to live," she said, then began praying aloud. A man in the crowd came forward and led a prayer as well. It "seemed like forever until the ambulance came," Ocampo remembered. When it did, Gore climbed in the ambulance and rode with Albert and the paramedics to the Children's Center at Johns Hopkins Hospital, with Tipper following in a police car.

Marla Romash was on the telephone with her new boyfriend, Jim O'Hara of the *Tennessean*, doing what they often did in their long-distance romance, chatting while watching the same sports event on television sets hundreds of miles apart. Their conversation was interrupted by an operator who came on Romash's line and said there was an emergency. Romash hung up and Gore got through to her. "Albert's been hit by a car," he said. "We're at the hospital. He's being operated on. I don't know what's going to happen." He did not say it explicitly, but Romash feared from her boss's tone that he thought his son would die.

Albert came out of the operating room in serious but stable condition. His injuries were all over his body: concussion, broken rib, broken left thigh, ruptured spleen, bruised lung, nerve damage in his right shoulder. The initial fears that he might not survive were gone, but it remained uncertain for some time whether any of the damage might be permanent. Sixty percent of his spleen was removed in a second operation. He was placed in a full body cast. His lungs were suctioned hourly. The only way he could communicate was by squeezing his father's hand to form words from alphabet cards. Romash issued a public statement for the Gores in which they said their son would survive through "God's healing grace." Notes and letters of well-wishing flowed into the hospital by the hundreds and then thousands. For three weeks, Gore scrapped his Senate calendar and spent most of his time in Baltimore. He and Tipper took a room in a hotel across the street and alternated spending the night at Albert's side in the hospital. In the next bed lay little Brett Philpott from suburban Atlanta who had undergone surgery on his brain. The Philpotts and Gores, according to Brett's father, Mitch Philpott, "did a lot of talking, a lot of praying, a lot of crying." On April 20 the doctors said that Albert had passed the period of major risk, and on April 26 he went home, where he slept on a hospital bed in the dining room, attended to by his parents and three older sisters.

It was during that difficult April, back while Albert was still recovering in the hospital, that Gore held his first meeting with Geoff Haines-Stiles to discuss the series and book on the environment. They had talked at Albert's bedside. "I want to do something like *Cosmos*," Gore had said.

To look back on that period from the distance of more than ten years makes one consider a central question of human nature: Do people really change, or when confronted with familiar circumstances do they tend to revert again and again to ingrained patterns of personality and character? The Al Gore who emerged from the trauma of April 1989 believed that he had "changed in a fundamental way." Losing the presidential race, turning forty, and then nearly losing his only son, he said, gave him "a new sense of urgency" about things he valued most, made him "increasingly impatient with the status quo, with conventional wisdom, with the lazy assumption that we can just muddle through," and equally impatient with what he described as his own "tendency to put a finger to the political winds and proceed cautiously." Whether Al Gore in his run for president reflected those changes is debatable. He seemed as cautious as ever, beholden to polls and conventional wisdom, relying on consultants to calibrate his image and message. But if, over time, he could not fully transform himself, he showed back then that he knew the person he wished he could be.

He wanted to break away from his past tendencies. He had never been the warmest boss, but now he brought in a corporate consultant, Jane Hopkins, to help him create a more collegial atmosphere in his Senate office after the 1988 campaign. He promised himself that he would spend more time with his wife and children, worry less about trivial political matters, and devote himself to something that connected his brain with his soul and showed that he could be profound and daring. And that calling, he said, was the environment. There were inevitable contradictions in his plan to change himself, the most obvious being that just as he intended to spend more time with his family he took on another obsession, the series and book idea, to add to his political duties. He dealt with the trauma of Albert's accident, and the stress he was feeling at midlife, by throwing himself into something that consumed him intellectually and spiritually—at the same time that Tipper was falling into a long and difficult depression triggered by those same circumstances.

Gore said that from those weeks he had spent at his son's side, when he largely ignored the daily burdens of politics, he had learned that nothing could be more important than his family. It was a revelation to him, he said, that events on his schedule that once had seemed so heavy in fact "were as light as a feather, and the substance was nothing." Yet he eventually replaced them with other events that he thought had more weight. He traveled to the Amazon again and began a series of roundtable congressional hearings with oceanographers and climatologists, while also holding regular tutorials in his Senate office, organized by his old St. Albans friend Reed Hundt, in which scientists and economists were brought in to discuss the latest ideas on chaos theory and the network effects of the information economy. Throughout this period, while carving out hours to attend the school and sports activities of his children, he also continued his routine of traveling back to Tennessee on weekends for town meetings, which he now infused with more spiritual and environmental references, seeing if he could explain complex ideas in ways the average person could understand.

Haines-Stiles accompanied Gore to Tennessee to watch him in action, and came away impressed by the way he could lead the audience "one step beyond what they were thinking." He saw that when and if they produced the television series, Gore would be an effective narrator, more educator than politician. They retreated to the farm in Carthage and began putting together a list of stories and storytelling devices, what Haines-Stiles thought might be the outline for a documentary series, but what instead became the first rough draft of the proposal for *The New World War.*

A TOUR OF AL GORE'S MIND. That is what John Sterling experienced in the Methodist Building apartment the first time he came down to Washington to work on the book with his senator-author. Gore's staff had caught glimpses of it many times, if not the full tour. They knew that his brain tended to work visually. Most of them at some point had walked into his office and found him sitting behind his desk, a pair of scissors in hand, carefully cutting an oblong sliver of a thought, a few words, a paragraph, from a memo or paper, and putting it into a pile of similar oblong slivers. He might gather a pile and hand it over and say "Think about this" or "Get back to me on this"—leaving it to them to interpret his meaning by figuring out the connections in the jumble of words and phrases.

They could be certain that the connections would cross several disciplines, and that he would be looking for commonality in disparate pieces of information. They would less likely find a pile of oblong slivers on gun control legislation than on various concepts of violence drawn from theology, science, history, and anthropology. Gore thought in terms of metaphor. When physicist Per Bak came to his tutorial and taught him the theory of self-organized criticality—how every grain of sand poured onto a sandpile subtly changes the dynamics until a single additional grain can reconfigure the entire pile or cause an avalanche—he immediately applied this theory to the world environment and to his own midlife crisis.

When he met with Sterling in his parents' apartment, Gore displayed not a few piles of oblong slivers but a roomful of larger piles—notes and charts that he had already sorted out according to broader themes. Gore dashed from one pile to another, from chair to sofa to bed, making connections all along the way. He might start out with a description of the brain, the neocortex for abstract thought and the limbic system for emotional thought, and move from there to the separation of mind and body and the difference between physical pain and psychic pain, and from there to the increasing distance between man and nature, and the resulting spiritual loss and the hunger for authenticity, which if not addressed could cause feelings of powerlessness that would be deadened by the mechanism of denial that leads to the addiction of consumption, which endangers the earth.

Or he would come to the separation of mind and body from a different direction, using material from a pile on the couch about food: moving from the switch from hunting-gathering to agriculture, and on to Thomas Malthus's nineteenth-century theory that population would outpace food production, and how Malthus was right about population growth but wrong about food production because of improved food production technology, but that these scientific advances created a Faustian bargain of soil erosion and fertilizer contamination and pesticide damage, and that the genetic engineering of crops through biotechnology has led to a loss of genetic diversity and led to humankind's hubris that technology could conquer all, further separating the mind from the body and man from nature.

Five hours of this, Gore racing back and forth, his passion for the subject never flagging. Sterling took it all in with amazement. *This is unusual,* he thought. *But I'm up for it.* In their second session, Gore produced ninety-three index cards on which he had summarized an idea or theme—greenhouse effect, Global Marshall Plan, biofeedback loops, ecology of the spirit—and he and Sterling spread the cards on the dining room table and began to reorganize them in smaller groupings that ultimately led to a rough outline of the chapters of the book.

While Gore had dropped the idea of doing a television series simultaneously (putting off the documentary until later), he still tended to think of the book in visual more than literary terms. He imagined that he would be "a very strong first-person presence all the way through," taking the reader along on his tour. Sterling gradually steered him away from that idea, suggesting instead that Gore choose a few points where writing in the first person seemed appropriate, particularly at the beginning and end, but then get out of the way of the story. Sterling was also struck by the interplay of science and spirituality in Gore's thinking. Gore was in essence a fact-based thinker, but his spiritual search had become so strong since Albert's accident that he wanted to infuse a number of chapters with religion and philosophy and his own search for the lessons of life. They talked this over while reshuffling the index cards, until it became clear that a separate chapter on ecology and spirituality would be more effective.

GORE BEGAN WRITING THE BOOK in the late fall of 1990 and early winter of 1991. This was not an otherwise uneventful period of his life. He had a wife who was still struggling with her post-accident depression. She had stopped exercising and gained twenty-five pounds and was feeling increasingly withdrawn. At the same time, Gore had a Senate reelection campaign to run, though with minimal opposition. And in January 1991 he faced a major foreign policy issue in the Senate, the handling of the Gulf War.

In what he later called an "excruciating" decision, Gore ended up voting to authorize use of military force in Operation Desert Storm, one of ten Democrats to support President Bush in the close 52–47 vote. Republican Senate leaders Bob Dole and Alan Simpson later ridiculed Gore for trying to shop his vote to whichever side would give him more television time, but that charge evaporates under scrutiny. It is true that before the vote he asked both sides whether they could provide television time for him, but that is because he had not yet made up his mind which way he would vote. He had asked Leon Fuerth, who had joined his staff as a foreign policy aide, to prepare him detailed memos on the pros and cons, but not a conclusion. He went to the Senate floor with a speech that had a hole in it where he would announce his decision. Under those circumstances, he thought it would be unfair to ask only the antiwar side for time if he ended up speaking in support of the war.

Even during that period, Gore's staff carved out large chunks of time for him in the early morning and evening so that he could slip over to the Methodist Building and write. He became known for pulling all-nighters there while consuming gallons of Diet Coke. He was often cranky and slow to thank those assisting him, which they generally attributed to a lack of sleep, and which they tolerated only because he seemed hardest on himself. The most popular account of his writing effort concerns the night he apparently fell asleep at the computer and awoke hours later to discover that his elbow had inadvertently hit the keyboard and written thousands of r's . . . or k's or m's, depending on who told the story.

The writing could be clunky in any case. Gore told Sterling that he just wanted to get it all down, and worry about style later. Though he engaged a researcher in the early stages of the work, and drew upon staff members at various points to help gather information and to read drafts, the work product was decidedly his and not that of a hired hand. Gore had vowed to be bold, both in his proposals and in his personal statements, and in that latter area the early drafts of the manuscript were even stronger than the eventual book. At one point he showed staff members a version in which he said that his commitment to pushing a strong environmental agenda was more important to him than holding public office and that he might not run again. One staff member, upon reading that section, bluntly told him, "Gore, you are so full of shit it's ridiculous. You are making a promise you can't keep. Make the point about how real these issues are to you. Make the point about too often holding your finger to the wind and not being driven to do the right things. Make those points, but don't take yourself out of the game. It doesn't make sense!" That section was deleted.

The first real test of Gore's commitment came in the summer of 1991, when he turned in the first draft. It was more than seven hundred pages long and needed substantial reworking. But there were also rumblings that Gore was going to run for president again. Sterling knew that it would be impossible for Gore to run for president and revise the book at the same time. Which would it be? The final decision would not be made until Gore left Washington for a family vacation on a houseboat on a lake in middle Tennessee. His careerism, his attention to politics over family, his need to meet the expectations of others—all the failings that had led to Gore's self-flagellation were played out one more time. His family did not want him to run, he wanted to, but he had said and written too much already that would make him seem the ultimate hypocrite if he ran. The dilemma only made him angry at himself. He could not run. Back to the book, which he told Sterling he wanted to come out in January 1992.

That's going to be a trick, Sterling thought. But he could see Gore's reasoning. Any later than that, and the book would come up against the presidential primary season and perhaps get lost among the campaign issues of the day. Who would care then about the ideas of some senator who was not running for president? It would look funny for him to be out on the road in March or April trying to round up book buyers while his political compatriots were out there looking for votes. The tour would work for Gore in January, but not in April, he said. Sterling agreed, and decided to begin editing the beginning of the book while Gore was rewriting the middle sections and finishing the final chapters. If Gore was not the surest writer, he was always eager for an expert editor's help, appreciative of changes that smoothed out or rewrote his sentences and sharpened his points.

While scientists helped Gore revise factual misconceptions in his drafts, and Sterling helped him rearrange chapters and rewrite sections, the rhetoric in the manuscript remained passionate and urgent from beginning to end. In one of his more strident metaphors, Gore related the global environmental situation to Hitler's rise in Germany, saying that an ecological Kristallnacht was at hand and an environmental Holocaust was imminent. Protecting the earth, he said, had to become the central organizing principle of humankind. He called for a Global Marshall Plan that would stabilize the world population, educate the world's citizens on the environmental emergency, develop cleaner technologies (leading to the elimination of the internal combustion engine in twenty-five years), and establish ways to measure and assign economic consequences to every corporate and governmental act that affected the environment.

The Marshall Plan concept went back to Gore's original idea that the environmental dilemma had to be confronted with the vigor of a world war. But if Sterling vetoed the title *The New World War*, what should it be? They did not settle on the answer until the final hour of the deadline for putting out the catalogue listing Houghton Mifflin's winter backlist. In a long list of possible titles, the word "earth" had been in several of them as well as the word "balance." What if they put them together? Sterling uttered the phrase "earth in the balance" to agent Janklow, who liked it. Gore was not certain, but finally said, "Yeah. Yeah, that sounds like it could really work when you think about it."

The last words Gore wrote for the book were for the dedication. He considered "a lot of different possibilities" before the obvious came to him. He was Bo again, and he typed NANCY LaFON GORE HUNGER — "and it just unleashed a huge . . . I didn't stop crying, you know, for a long time. Just typing that much. And then I knew obviously that was who the book would be dedicated to." The publication date for *Earth in the Balance* was the third week in January 1992. It came out to favorable reviews, and moved onto the best-seller list just as the nation was getting its first look at the provocative young governor of Arkansas, Bill Clinton. After his book tour that spring, Gore was once again the American politician most strongly identified with the environment, and he wanted to further enhance that reputation by getting back to the television series.

The plans were grander now. The book became a blueprint for

what the documentary might do, but some of it would be difficult to translate into television, so they concocted more imaginative ways to present the material. They talked about getting a group of satirists, comedians from *Saturday Night Live* and *Monty Python*, perhaps, to represent the dysfunctional family, the dysfunctional cabinet, the dysfunctional ecology. They thought about getting George C. Scott to play General Patton attacking trees that were polluting the world, since Ronald Reagan had said trees were the enemy. John Cleese and Dan Aykroyd and Dana Carvey and Mike Myers might take roles. The idea was broached with executives at *Saturday Night Live*, who were interested enough to schedule another meeting after Gore got back from the Earth Summit in Rio de Janeiro. Haines-Stiles and a production crew accompanied Gore to Brazil, along with his friend Reed Hundt, who had helped put together the seed money for the production. They traveled north in Brazil to the Atlantic rain forest with a Senate colleague, Paul Wellstone of Minnesota.

At one point in the adventure, Hundt accompanied Wellstone on a boat ride through a rain forest estuary while Gore headed off with the production crew to find a more remote place for shooting. As Hundt then remembered the scene, "It begins to rain. Pour exceedingly. We get drenched. Senator Wellstone is just standing there in the bow of the boat. It's like a lake in Minnesota. He did not look senatorial soaking wet. He prided himself in not looking senatorial. That was the whole idea. Then above us we hear chum-chum-chum-chum. And it's Al coming overhead in a chopper and he looks down—and Wellstone looks up." And one need know no more to understand why Gore was not the most popular man in the Senate. But here he seemed in his element. He ad-libbed his lines and presented them far better than he delivered campaign commercials or political speeches. He seemed closer to realizing his dream of being Carl Sagan than to his old man's dream of him being president.

Then again, he had also made sure to call Bill Clinton from Rio, providing the likely Democratic presidential nominee with a private briefing on the Earth Summit. Gore had a sense, he told his traveling companions, that he and Clinton would resume their conversation when he returned to the States.

THE FAMILY SEEMED to be making another turn. More than two years had passed since Albert's accident, and doctors were now confident that he had fully recovered. Tipper was emerging from a long period where she had withdrawn from the world and become sluggish, wanting only to be with her family, or utterly alone. She began exercising and jogging again and undertook a search for a spiritual balance of her own.

CHAPTER NINETEEN

TIPPER'S
EVERYDAY LIFE

AL GORE'S POLITICAL RISE would not have been possible without Tipper, even though it took her places that she did not necessarily want to be. Ambition, insecurity, expectations—the tensions of his life were all eased by her presence. She had been with him since she was sixteen, influencing him more year by year, in ways that the old man and Pauline never could, with her expansiveness of spirit. If his sister, Nancy, in a sense represented the genetic missing side of Gore, Tipper's central place in his life showed that he knew what was missing and tried to fill it, choosing for a mate someone with spontaneity and emotional honesty, someone who could, in the words of one friend, "light up his eyes" every time she walked into the room and force him to see "outside the fog" of his self-absorption. He wanted to figure out how everything in the world worked and then use that knowledge to do something big for humankind. She was more interested in exploring the mysteries of an individual human being's mind and soul.

The public life that she confronted as part of her husband's career, as a congressman's wife, a senator's wife, and finally a vice president's wife, forced her to play an artificial role in an artificial world. The more prominent the Gores became in that world, the more Tipper felt the need to find a release from it. During the congressional years, when her husband was gone to Tennessee virtually every weekend, she built a darkroom in the basement of their Arlington home and shot and developed pictures when she could, hoping to document life in all its pain and beauty. By the time she became the second lady of the United States, when her daily life was shaped by royal power, inhuman power, the power of getting what you ask for, she was drawn more than ever to seek out the other, the everyday world of the powerless.

HERE IS WHERE Tipper Gore would rather be. She has escaped the White House and her daily rituals in the Old Executive Office Building and is walking through a nearby park in downtown Washington on a sunny day in February. A homeless man taps her on the shoulder and points to a woman talking loudly to herself—someone new to help. Her name is Marye and she has come from California hauling her life's belongings in green plastic bags.

Come with us, Tipper tells her, hoping to persuade her to go for a shower and a meal at a homeless shelter.

No, I've got to wait for my husband, Marye says.

Where is he?

He lives over there, Marye says, pointing to the White House across the street. He works there as president. Tipper nods. Marye says she wants to see him. She says she is eight months' pregnant though her stomach is flat. She says she keeps it flat by smoking fat-free rocks given to her by a California doctor. Tipper listens and nods again. She wants to get this woman some housing and mental health treatment. Marye will not budge until she sees her husband.

Tipper escorts her across the street to a gate in front of the White House. The guard recognizes her and stands at attention. *Mrs. Gore,* he begins . . . She motions him to stop, and asks him to check the schedule to see whether Marye will have time for a shower before President Clinton returns from an event. The security guard, perplexed at first, catches on and obliges. There is plenty of time, he says. Tipper asks him to write a note informing the president of where Marye is going and when she will return. Then Tipper, Marye, and Pat Letke-Alexander, a physician's assistant, lug Marye's green plastic bags over to a van marked "Health Care for the Homeless" and get in for the drive to a clinic on Columbia Road in Adams Morgan. They eat lunch there. *I want my reality back,* the schizophrenic woman says, and the wife of the vice president of the United States understands.

IT BEGAN ONE AFTERNOON in 1985, when Tipper was a senator's wife driving the kids home from the Capitol after having lunch with their dad. They saw a woman standing at the curb, talking to herself and gesturing. *Mom, what's wrong with her,* one of the kids asked. Tipper said the woman was probably mentally ill and that she might be hearing voices. The girls wanted to take the woman home with them. Tipper said they could not do that, but she promised that they would do something. She disliked herself for turning away, she said later, in an interview for *Parade* magazine. "Denial can have a corrosive effect. It takes a toll. It's true when you deny problems in your family, and it takes a toll on all of us when we deny problems in society."

Nine years after that incident with her kids, on her birthday in August 1994, she celebrated by heading out on the streets for the first time, driving along with Letke-Alexander in search of people like Marye who were living in the deepest shadows of powerful Washington, on the streets, in the parks, under the bridges. "The lower you are by the world's definition, the higher you are on her priority list," is the way one of Tipper's friends put it. Volunteering for Health Care for the Homeless was a way for her to deal with the guilt that had nagged at her, but it also provided her with a means to express herself without being defined by her connection to the White House. On the street, she was only that blond lady with the van, not the vice president's wife. The work was "her passion," Letke-Alexander said of her mental health partner. "She's able to be a normal, everyday person in a role that she gets everyday life from."

Her work with the homeless and mentally ill is one reflection of an empathetic personality that seems different from her husband's. In some ways it is more like that of Al's late sister, Nancy Gore Hunger. Like Nancy, Tipper is more spontaneous and natural, and like Nancy, there were times in her life when she felt lost, though she never had Nancy's sophisticated sense of the political world. There is also, as more than one friend has noticed, a touch of Bill Clinton in Tipper. She deals more from intuition than analysis, and has an easy warmth to her, reaching out to people, literally, the way Clinton does, touching a stranger's face or holding a stranger's hand, though Tipper's reaching out seems to come from a more selfless impulse. And she has rhythm, her love of music bringing out her extroverted side. As Clinton played the sax on *Arsenio,* Tipper gigged on the drums with the Grateful Dead. She is in every sense the other side of Al Gore.

• • •

BEFORE GOING OUT in the van, Letke-Alexander and Tipper struck a deal. One Secret Service agent would ride with them, but he would have to dress as they did. There would be no cameras, no reporters, no motorcades. In the park that first afternoon, they met a man Letke-Alexander did not know. He was disheveled and disoriented, lying on the ground. Tipper sat on the grass with him and listened as he began to pull from his wallet, one by one, rumpled business cards, snapshots, an old library card. Every scrap of paper, every photo, had a story with it—a man who had done something for him, a woman he had once known. Tipper sat there engrossed, then leaned out of his view and mouthed the words, *Let's take him with us.*

No, Pat mouthed back. *Secret Service.* They had promised the agents that they would not carry anyone that Letke-Alexander did not recognize from her work on the streets.

Tipper ignored the comment and asked the man whether he would like to come along in the van, which he did.

She stayed with the van all afternoon, and undertook one final gesture before returning to the White House for a joint celebration with the president, who shared her birthday. She had met another man, a substance abuser, who wanted to get home to see his family. Tipper and Letke-Alexander called the bus station to find out what times buses ran to his hometown in South Carolina and whether they could get a ticket. She provided the money for the ticket. Letke-Alexander took the man to the bus station, bought his ticket, and made sure he had something to eat, then left. A few hours later, Tipper drove to the bus station, found the man and shared a cup of coffee with him, not leaving until he boarded the bus.

For years, Tipper went out with Letke-Alexander every Friday morning at nine o'clock, their route taking them to parks that were gathering places for people with schizophrenia, bipolar disorder, depression. Over time, Tipper became familiar with the regulars. In Farragut Park there was Captain Kersh, a former Army captain who had done two tours in Vietnam and had been a dentist. For months the van people had tried to get him in for treatment, without success. Tipper would sit next to him on the park bench and hold his hand. She told the captain that her husband had been in the Army, the 20th Engineers in Vietnam. He eventually responded to her interest in him until one day she was able to coax him to Christ House, which had a temporary shelter of thirty-four beds. Eight months later he was doing well enough to be moved to a group home for the mentally ill, but he balked at the last minute, only to be persuaded when Tipper brought him a letter from her husband saying that he was proud of the captain's progress and signed, "Your fellow Vietnam veteran, Al Gore."

There was another regular named Jack, a homeless man Tipper had seen for years as she jogged through Rock Creek Park. She lured him into Christ House, and shortly thereafter he was admitted to St. Elizabeths Hospital for treatment. Tipper visited him there, unannounced, and she and Letke-Alexander talked to the resident doctor, who did not recognize Tipper and treated her like she had no understanding of mental illness. Nearby, another patient was ranting loudly about the Clintons and the Gores. It was a scene that Letke-Alexander would never forget, with the "crazy lady behind us, the resident in front of us, nobody having a clue who Tipper is, and she's just acting like it's totally normal."

Sometimes Tipper Gore told people who she was, but usually not. After the homeless became comfortable with her, she might bring along her camera and shoot a picture, then print it, sign it, and give it to them. Some of the photos are contained in her 1996 book, *Picture This*, what she called a "visual diary" of her family's life. But for the most part, she considered her work with Washington's street people private. She became furious when a Canadian journalist gave a homeless man a dollar and a pack of cigarettes to tell him when and where she would show up. Then she sat down with the homeless man and calmly explained that she wanted to keep this low-key and would not be able to do it if there were reporters who knew about it.

HER INTEREST in mental health goes back to her childhood, when her mother, Margaret Carlson Aitcheson, suffered from serious bouts of depression that sometimes required hospitalization. The illness was bad enough, Tipper recalled in her book, but the stigma made it worse. "Once, when my mother was in the hospital for something else, I wanted to tell the doctors about the medication she was taking," Tipper wrote. "But she was so terribly fearful of anyone finding out—even a doctor—that she wouldn't let me tell them. It broke my heart." The pain she felt watching her mother suffer and feeling unable, as a child, to help, explains much about Tipper, her friends say. "It's part of where her empathy came from," said Sally Aman, her former press secretary. It is also the source of her fierce protectiveness—of homeless people, her parents, her husband, her children.

"She is like this mother person," observed one longtime friend, Carmala Walgren. "She really does feel like she wants to make sure everybody's okay." Her own mother's life certainly was not easy. She lost her first husband in World War II, then married John Kenneth Aitcheson in 1947, had Tipper a year later, and filed for divorce a year after that. The divorce records describe a marriage that was troubled from the start, in some ways apparently echoing the trauma of alcoholism and claims of physical abuse that darkened Bill Clinton's childhood home. Margaret Aitcheson asserted that John Aitcheson caused her "great physical pain and anguish" and that he was "exceedingly abusive to her," when she asked him to account for where he had been, and that on several occasions he told her that "he did not love her" and "ordered her out of the house." John Aitcheson denied ever hitting her, and said his language was no more abusive than hers. Unlike Bill Clinton, who testified on his mother's behalf during divorce proceedings when he was fifteen, Tipper was a baby when her parents' painful divorce took place. And unlike Virginia Clinton, Margaret Aitcheson did not take her husband back, though they had long since returned to good terms by the time Tipper made it to the vice president's mansion.

John Aitcheson's testimony appeared to reflect a young man's inability to cope with his wife's depression. He asserted in his affidavit that she was "lazy and indolent, would lie abed late in the mornings and sleep through, and refuse to prepare breakfast for her husband or their child . . . and from the onset of their marriage was erratic, volatile and flighty." The divorce was granted in 1952, when Tipper was four. "The marriage was a mistake, except for Tipper," Margaret Aitcheson would later say. Tipper and her mother went to live with Tipper's grandparents in Arlington, in a red-brick Tudor house built in 1938 by her grandfather E. J. Carlson, the son of Swedish immigrants who had risen to become head of the Prudential Building and Loan Association in Washington. Though Tipper was doted on by adults, divorce was less common in those days and she felt the sting of being teased by classmates for "having no father." She saw him only on Sunday, after church.

The grandfather died in 1958 at home on South 26th Street, leaving a household of women. "Mother, grandmother, and Tipper. Just the three of them. A matriarchal society," remembered Mead Miller, one of the St. Albans boys who dated Tipper during her freewheeling high school days. "Anything that happened on a date, Tipper'd go talk to them. . . . I loved the atmosphere. The warmth of the house. They had a warm, natural, non-Washington household." With her mother struggling with depression and alcoholism, Tipper relied greatly on her grandmother Verda Louise Carlson, who offered a "safe place" where the granddaughter could find unconditional love. She was protective but also wanted Tipper to enjoy life. She bought Tipper her first drum set, took her to practice with her rock band, the Wildcats, and drove her—when she was still in high school—all the way to Cambridge so she could spend a weekend with Al Gore at Harvard. Her death in 1987 was devastating for Tipper, and coming as it did less than two years before her son, Albert's, near-fatal accident, left her without an important source of strength when depression later flooded over her.

Long before she went public with the depression in her family, Tipper shared it privately with friends. Carmala Walgren, who met Tipper in 1977 when her husband, Doug, and Al entered Congress together, bonded with Tipper over the similarities in their lives, including the depressed and alcoholic mother and nourishing grandmother. When Walgren herself suffered from bouts of depression, she turned to Tipper. Once, Walgren was so incapacitated she called Tipper, who took herself away from an event and spent an hour on the phone with her. *Don't get mad at yourself about this,* Tipper told her. *Pick one thing you can do, even if it's just to get up and get dressed. Just give yourself a break.* It was a disease, she kept telling people, and herself, not something for which her mother or herself or anyone should be blamed. When Doug Walgren was on a House Energy and Commerce subcommittee looking into insurance companies, Tipper told Carmala: "Tell Doug to have them look at these insurance companies because they don't understand that heads are part of our bodies, that depression is an illness. It's just crazy that they don't understand this."

It is that sentiment that would become her singular policy obsession from the moment her husband was chosen as Clinton's running mate. On the long bus trips where the Clintons and Gores would spend so much time together, Tipper would take every opportunity to talk about mental illness. When they reached the White House and Hillary became health care czar, Tipper was named the president's adviser on mental health. Her first victory was in federal hiring, so that job seekers no longer had to disclose whether they had family or marriage counseling, and the question "Have you ever seen a psychiatrist?" is no longer placed next to "Have you ever committed a felony?" Making that simple change required meetings with the CIA, FBI, and Defense Department. When the health care package led by Hillary eventually disintegrated, Tipper's "ragged little band" of mental health advocates, as aide Skila Harris referred to it, focused on smaller pieces of legislation. They had one key bipartisan success: requiring companies to provide the same coverage for mental illness as for other illnesses.

It was not until May 1999, with her husband's campaign for the presidency getting underway, that Tipper took another step toward removing the stigma attached to mental illness by talking about her own struggles with depression. She had touched lightly around the subject for years, talking about how traumatic little Albert's accident was, how she had gained twenty-five pounds after that and gone to see a counselor. But now she used the word "depression" for the first time. "When you get to this point of being seriously depressed, or what we call clinically depressed, you just can't will your way out of that or pray your way out of that or pull yourself up by the boot straps out of that. You really have to go and get help, and I did," she said in an interview with *USA Today*.

The interview drew much praise, but there was also a measure of skepticism regarding it. There was an understandable political element to her going public when she did—to remove the potential distraction from her husband's campaign, and to control when and how she would disclose her condition rather than let the media do it for her. The interview was also notable for what it did not disclose. She spoke in flat, clinical language, imbuing it with no revealing personal detail that might allow others to identify with her struggle. She backed away from discussing any relationship between her mother's illness, which seemed chronic, and her own, which might have been situational. Many of her friends and associates said they had not known that she had been treated for depression, though in retrospect they were not surprised. That was part of everyday life.

Every so often, Tipper would invite her mentally ill friends over for lunch at the Naval Observatory. She would lead a toast, her guests hoisting glasses filled with sparkling cider. Her staff, dressed in Navy whites, would bring out a first course and a second course, and then

Captain Kersh would get up and announce that he was going outside for a smoke, and soon others would join him, drawing on their cigarette butts recycled from the street.

Nice house, old Jack said one day to Pat Letke-Alexander, as she drove him back from lunch. *Her husband must have a good job.*

Well, he does, she responded. *He's the vice president.*

Oh, said Jack, and they drove on as though it were nothing.

CHAPTER TWENTY

TWO GUYS

T HE STORY OF HOW Al Gore became vice president begins and ends with two guys. They were about the same age, from neighboring states in the middle south, both moderate, tall, articulate, and competitive. Their political careers had been rumbling down parallel tracks year after year, moving toward the same destination without colliding. For all they had in common, they hardly knew each other, had rarely met since they had entered public life simultaneously in the elections of 1976. Go back now to May 1991. They were both in Cleveland for the annual convention of the Democratic Leadership Council. The opening speech would be delivered by Bill Clinton, governor of Arkansas and chairman of the DLC, who had spent the previous several months traveling the country with the group's president, Al From, testing a new message on opportunity and responsibility. The closing address would come from Al Gore, senator from Tennessee, who years earlier had helped From draft the original press release announcing the formation of this organization of new Democrats.

They had been sizing each other up from a distance, these two postwar baby boomers who believed they should be president. One had run already in 1988, and the other almost ran, but backed out at the last minute. As the next election season began its preliminary phase, From was not alone in thinking, when he studied the lineup card listing his starter and his closer in Cleveland, that "one of these two guys is going to be our nominee."

The night before Clinton's appearance, one of From's aides

stayed up nearly until dawn retyping the latest revision of the speech, which the governor and From had worked on for days. The next morning at breakfast, Clinton took out a sheet of paper and wrote a few words on it. When he walked into the convention hall and studied the crowd, he scrapped the text and spoke extemporaneously using cues from his morning scribbles. "You gotta start slow and let 'em off with a crescendo," he had told From beforehand, and that is what he did, delivering a speech that had those who heard it buzzing all day and then telling their friends about it when they got back to their hometowns. If it was not "the speech of his life," as From described it, the performance was the sort where one could see conventional wisdom taking shape. The early word spread across the Democratic political network: Watch Clinton, he has a message about moving beyond the orthodoxies of left and right that could take us back to the White House.

At dinner on the eve of Gore's speech, the senator turned to From and asked, "Anything I should do to prepare for tomorrow?"

"Yeah," came the reply. "Take whatever speech you have and cut it in half."

Gore went back to his hotel room and labored over his text for hours, adding here and cutting there. At three o'clock in the morning, Marla Romash, his press secretary, urged him, "Al! Quit writing. You've got to practice!" But Gore kept writing until he had what he considered a perfect draft. The next day he walked into the convention hall and began his speech with a story about the first time he came to Cleveland on a political trip and went out for a morning jog and got lost and spent an hour running around in a desperate search for his hotel. Then he pulled out his prepared text and read it word for word, obliterating his well-crafted phrases about what he called "the Republican Syndrome" of pessimism with a deadly dull rote delivery that left members of the audience wishing they were lost on a morning jog instead of trapped in the hall listening to him. The most emotion he elicited was from his press secretary, who took to the privacy of her room and cried at the thought of her boss's uninspired performance.

From that moment on it seemed that the Clinton and Gore tracks were no longer running parallel. There were still a few campaign sputterings from Gore and his inner circle—an encouraging poll and a gathering of consultants at Le Brasserie one night, going over the field and the money and the logistics, all enough to send Gore out on a houseboat with his family for a summer vacation during which he was to make up his mind. For two weeks, Al and Tipper and their four kids and two dogs, Coconut and Shiloh, floated from one end of the lake to the other. They water-skied, fished, took long swims, dove off their special ledge, which later became known as "Al Gore's Jump," tied up the boat at night between two trees in a little cove, and talked about the political future. The close quarters became too much for at least one of them, Shiloh, who kept trying to bail out, diving into the water and then thinking better of it and demanding to be pulled up to safety. There was a cell phone on board, but Gore had issued a strict ban against its use, a ban that only he was allowed to break to call Washington to see what was going on.

The family's presidential discussions were careful weighings of the pros and cons. One of the pros, according to Karenna, was that "my dad felt that he could win, and that he would be able to make a difference in people's lives by changing some of the national policies that he thought needed to be changed." And one of the cons, she remembered, was "the race—and potentially the job itself—would mean that he would be very, very busy with work and wouldn't have a lot of time to be with the family. Another con was that we couldn't have much privacy." Her father, Karenna said, "listened to all our thoughts carefully and talked it through with us individually." When he made up his mind, there was no complaint from his mates on the houseboat.

And that was that: Al Gore went back to writing his book on the environment, while Bill Clinton used Cleveland as the departure station for his improbable ride to the White House.

A year later they were like traveling salesmen, these two guys, hustling from city to city, from media market to media market, trying to close the deal in the winter and spring of 1992. Gore was promoting *Earth in the Balance.* Clinton was selling himself as a candidate for the Democratic presidential nomination. And they were winning in unexpected ways. Gore was surprising the publishing establishment with a book whose mix of crisis rhetoric, incisive analysis, and New Age spiritualism struck a chord with readers. Clinton was surprising the political establishment by surviving (with what would become his familiar arsenal of will, skill, and uncommon luck) a series of near-fatal controversies involving the big three of the baby boom generation: sex, drugs, and the draft.

Gore watched Clinton's melodramatic rise with equal parts jealousy, awe, admiration, and disdain. When one story broke about Clinton evading the draft, Gore was in a bar in Denver unwinding after a long day on the book circuit. At his side was a friend from Tennessee, another military veteran. The subject soon came around to presidential politics, and Gore's decision not to run, and the tribulations of Bill Clinton. *What kind of guy was Clinton? Was he a draft dodger?* Gore said he didn't know him that well and wasn't really sure. Then he shook his head and growled in a mock macho drawl, "He's the kind of guy we would have beat the shit out of."

Be that as it may, Clinton was also the kind of guy who read *Earth in the Balance* when a mutual acquaintance gave it to him, and who, once he clinched the nomination and started the process of selecting a running mate, did not scratch Gore from the original list of forty possibilities that his advisory committee prepared for him. Nor did Gore's feelings about Clinton stop him from saying yes when he got the call from an intermediary asking him whether he might be interested.

UNDER THE DIRECTION OF Warren Christopher, the picking of a running mate for Bill Clinton was organized as though it were a top secret physics experiment. While his public partners in the enterprise were well-known Democratic figures, Vernon Jordan and Madeleine Kunin, the detail work was done by a cadre of five young lawyers who worked in private in unmarked rooms at the Jones Day law firm's Washington office. Each of the lawyers was assigned a batch of eight names from the original list of forty. The candidates had been subdivided into three groups: the C list included names of people who were there only for defensive reasons, so they would not feel slighted and cause trouble. The B list included long shots, some from outside government, in case Clinton decided to do something unusual. And the A list included the better known politicians and most likely choices. A vetting memo for the C list was to be only one page, for the B list three to five pages, and for the A list, ten pages, single spaced.

The Christopher trio—and Clinton—leaned toward some favorites as the process began, Colin Powell and Bill Bradley in particular, but the general and the senator rejected all entreaties and were scratched from the list. The first round of memos, based mostly on public information gleaned from computer searches plus a few discreet interviews, went to Christopher and then on to Clinton by Memorial Day. At the time, the process might have seemed like an academic exercise. Even as he clinched the Democratic nomination,

Clinton was running third in the national polls in early June, behind President Bush and Reform Party candidate Ross Perot. Clinton was frustrated and moody, looking for a way to break through the Perot clamor. Picking the right running mate was for him both a welcome distraction and a possible way out.

When he read the ten-page memo put together on Senator Albert Gore Jr., he got a decidedly evenhanded view. On the plus side, the report said that putting Gore on the ticket would help Clinton in two areas, foreign policy and the environment, where he was considered weak; that his previous experience running for president would mean "less of a risk of surprise when reporters probe Gore's background"; that his views on most major issues were compatible with Clinton's; and that his Senate record would "invite favorable comparisons" with the record of his Republican counterpart, Dan Quayle. On the negative side, aside from the "obvious drawback" of not offering regional balance, it was said that Gore "could be difficult at times," noting the number of staffers who quit after the 1988 campaign; that he "can at times display a wooden personality"; that it was "unclear whether Gore has the personality to be a deferential partner"; and that he still seemed "vulnerable to criticism" of his 1988 campaign, especially charges of "political opportunism."

There was nothing in the memo that eliminated Gore when the list of forty was winnowed. The vetting of each of the remaining contenders was overseen by a different "wise man," in Gore's case Harry McPherson, a former LBJ aide. The stately and refined McPherson seemed to know everyone in town, though his dealings with Gore had been minimal. His perceptions of the Gore family were shaded somewhat by his memory that President Johnson thought that Gore Senior, who had turned against him on the Vietnam war, was self-righteous. Assisting McPherson as a junior partner in the Gore vetting was Gary Ginsburg, a lawyer who had worked on the original vetting memo of Gore and had been an aide to Gore during his unsuccessful run in 1988.

While Ginsburg and another associate, Michael Vandenbergh, went down to Carthage to root around in the Gore family's public records, McPherson began a round of calls checking him out with friends, associates, and congressional colleagues. The conversations were off the record; no one would be identified in the memos to Clinton. McPherson tracked down John Seigenthaler in Prague, where

Gore's old editor was advising a newspaper. "Harry, let's not fool each other," Seigenthaler said as the conversation came to a close. "You and I both know they are both southern Baptists from small southern states and we just wasted forty-five minutes of this campaign's money talking about Gore." To which McPherson replied, "Well, John, all I'm doing is what I'm asked. I might agree with you about that, but I'm not going to say it to anybody else and I hope you don't."

Seigenthaler immediately placed a call to Gore and spilled the beans about the vetting, saying, "I'm telling you about this not because I think you're going to be a vice presidential candidate, but because I don't." Gore expressed surprise and laughed.

In his interviews with Gore's colleagues in the House and Senate, McPherson was struck by the flatness of most responses. Here was a free shot for anyone who hated Gore and wanted to sink him—but there was none of that. And here was an opportunity for people to say what a great guy Gore was—and there was virtually none of that, either. The common themes were that Gore was intelligent, well informed, and very ambitious. The one word McPherson took away from his interview with Gore's Tennessee colleague in the Senate, Jim Sasser, who had been close to the entire Gore family, whose wife had been one of Nancy Gore's dearest friends, was *okay—the middling term okay*. It was not meant as a negative, but nor did it sing. Where was the emotion? Where were the deep friendships? There was maybe one in the House, with Tom Downey of Long Island, but when McPherson talked to other congressmen who were said to be close to Gore, it seemed that they did not know him very well.

A luncheon appointment was set for McPherson and his gumshoes to meet with Gore at his parents' Methodist Building apartment. When Gore answered the door and ushered them in, he seemed like a prince who was annoyed at having to endure the vetting process. The apartment was cluttered with antiques, with a decorating style that McPherson judged to be flounce, heavy curtains and tables covered with petticoat layers. Gore showed his guests the computer where he had written *Earth in the Balance*, then led them to a dining room table where they were served tuna fish sandwiches. At one point the discussion turned to policy. With surprising sharpness, Gore dismissed Clinton's proposal for a middle-class tax cut, saying it would never happen. He and Tom Downey had tried a variation on that theme a year before, co-sponsoring the Working Family Tax Relief Act, which was funded by a surtax on the rich, but the proposal had gone nowhere. After lunch, sitting in the living room, McPherson gently broached the subject of Gore and friends. It was an awkward moment, as Gore stumbled and paused trying to answer the question. "It confirmed my suspicions," McPherson told his compatriots later, exaggerating slightly to make his point. "Damn, the guy has no friends!"

If that impression was bewildering, it was by no means disqualifying. In most respects, when held up against the other finalists — Senators Bob Graham of Florida, Bob Kerrey of Nebraska, Harris Wofford of Pennsylvania, and Congressman Lee Hamilton of Indiana — Gore seemed impressive, for his intellect, appearance, and fit with Clinton. The fact that he, like Clinton, came from a small southern state was counterbalanced by the ways that he bolstered Clinton's weak spots. He was a Vietnam veteran who had a strong image on defense issues and had voted in support of the Gulf War, which could give the draft-avoiding Clinton political cover. Furthermore, his personal life seemed solid, another valuable counterpoint to Clinton's saturnalian appetites.

To be doubly certain of that last point, McPherson made a series of discreet calls to friends in the Washington media elite to see if there were any new rumors about Gore. *Know anything? Anything in the '88 campaign?* The answer he got back from all quarters: *Almost certainly not.* He also went back to the Methodist Building for a second meeting with Gore, this time alone so that he could deal with the most sensitive topic. "Al," he began, "I don't want to ask you this question, and I'm embarrassed to ask you, but you'll understand more than anybody that with Clinton undergoing the scrutiny that he is that he really would be in a bad way if he has a running mate with the same problems of the same kind . . ."

Gore got the drift, and decided to answer the question before McPherson had to utter the difficult words. It was a hot early summer day and there was no air-conditioning in the apartment and the windows were open, letting in the whirrs and moans of Capitol Hill tour buses. Gore turned slightly sideways in his chair and looked directly at McPherson with perfect sincerity, and as he started to talk a diesel bus rumbled noisily up the street, drowning out the answer. McPherson thought he had read Gore's lips forming the words, "There won't be any problems," but he was not sure, and he was too embarrassed to ask Gore to say it again.

• • •

THERE WAS AN ELEMENT of the grade B spy movie to the enterprise, Mark Gearan thought in retrospect, but at the time it all seemed so important and necessary. The one thing the Clinton campaign did not want was a process that resembled the embarrassment of 1984, when Walter Mondale paraded his collection of veep prospects around like they were poodles and terriers and German shepherds vying for top prize at the Westminster dog show. Gearan, a trusted political operative, was given the assignment of making sure that did not happen. So here it was, a clandestine operation in the late evening darkness of June 30: A red Bronco with tinted windows pulls up to the Senate office, Gore slips into the back seat for the ride across town to the Washington Hilton, then down the ramp to the service entrance and up a service elevator to the suite reserved under Herlihy, Gearan's wife's maiden name, and Bill Clinton and Al Gore are together at last.

Clinton moved like a predaceous shark through the ocean darkness of American politics, never stopping, rarely sleeping, so for him an eleven-at-night meeting was habitual, but not for Gore. Even though he was known for pulling an occasional all-nighter when he was obsessed with a project, he was not naturally a night person, and tended to grow increasingly cranky and dull as his energy level diminished. His staff understood that to have him operating effectively, Gore needed his rest. Even more than that, he demanded preparation. He had to know everything he could about a subject before he walked into a meeting—so much so that Gearan, after working at Gore's side the rest of the campaign, looked back on that initial fateful interview and imagined that "he must have known what color the drapes were in every suite."

Perhaps he also took a pre-interview nap. In any case, there were no signs of Gore fatigue on this night. He and Clinton met like college pals who had not seen each other since the 1960s and were picking up where they had left off, able to communicate effortlessly in the shorthand of their shared generational experiences. Now they could show each other how smart they were and how much they knew without provoking the normal feelings of jealousy or tension. They were not competing directly, they were sensing what it would be like if they combined to take on the rest of the world. The interviews with other finalists took no more than an hour. Clinton and Gore talked on and on. The meeting became less an interview and more a strategy session on how the two would operate as a team, the first discussion of the spheres of interest such as the environment and technology where Gore would take the lead role in the campaign and in the White House.

Gearan and Gary Ginsburg and Clinton aide Bruce Lindsey watched television while they waited on the other side of a closed door. At one point they knocked. *What in the hell's going on in there?* The door opened to the sight of two guys lounging in the living room with their jackets off and shirttails hanging out, like buddies having a good-natured chat at the end of a rewarding day of deal-making. "No, no, no," said Clinton to the curious aides. "We're doing fine. Don't worry about us." And the door closed again.

"We realized that history was being made," Ginsburg said later. The two guys emerged from the conversation at 1:40, nearly three hours after they had started. Gore and his escorts retraced their route down the service elevator and out the back garage and into the Washington night. He might have been an easy mark as a poker player at Harvard, but Gore was giving nothing away now. Gearan and Ginsburg both remembered an eerie sensation on the drive back to the Hill. *Wow, that went well,* one of them said, trying to get something from Gore. He offered not a word. "He didn't talk. It was silence, awkward silence," Gearan said. "I didn't know what to make of it then." Later he decided that Gore was simply "exhausted, wiped out" from having to perform at the highest level during what was for him the worst time of day. Ginsburg, who had more experience with Gore, going back to 1988, had a different take on the silent ride. "He's playing this thing very typically Gore-ish," Ginsburg said to himself, meaning close to the vest.

This was not, in any other sense, a quiet time for the silent man in the back of the Bronco. He was on the biggest roll of his career. His book had been published to excellent reviews, and now it looked as though he would be on the Democratic ticket. The two lives of Al Gore, the writer he wanted to be and the politician he was expected to be, had somehow reached this felicitous and unanticipated intersection.

There were mild rumblings down in Little Rock over the next few days. The gang from the War Room, James Carville and Paul Begala and George Stephanopoulos, were not keen on Gore and made final pushes for their preferences, Wofford and Mario Cuomo. But everything pointed to Gore. Clinton was taken by his intellect and his aura of discipline and loyalty. In many respects Gore reminded him of his one invaluable political ally through the years, his wife, Hillary. With Hillary, he had an implicit trust that whatever he asked her to do would be done right, and he sensed the same would be true of Gore. Harry McPherson got the word to place another round of calls to ensure that there were no last-minute surprises. He reached Bill McSweeney, the old man's friend and associate from Occidental, and asked him whether there was anything in the relationship between the Gores and Armand Hammer that might prove embarrassing.

"Harry," McSweeney said to his fellow LBJ White House alumnus, "let me put it to you this way. Pauline Gore and I spent twenty years making sure that Armand Hammer was never alone in the same room with Al Gore so I could answer this phone call." McPherson and Warren Christopher, listening in on the speakerphone, both broke into laughter. The focus turned from what the vetters might not know to what they knew. Gearan asked Ginsburg to prepare a memo for Clinton on what sorts of tough questions he and his running mate might have to deal with when and if Gore got the nod.

Gore took his family and inner circle down to Carthage after the Fourth of July and waited for the phone to ring. They knew the call from Little Rock had to come soon, whether it brought life-changing news or not. Roy Neel and Peter Knight, aides who had been with Gore since his first days in Congress, holed up in Al's old room at the big house across the river with Miz Pauline and Senator Senior, making contingency plans, putting together their own list of the calls they would have to make if the news was positive. Bob Squier, the consultant, began plotting the role Gore could play at the convention in New York the following week and then the fall campaign. Marla Romash, the press secretary, stayed with longtime Gore staffer Alberta Winkler at her farmhouse a few miles down the road, preparing updated biographies of her boss and wondering how to handle the growing village of press trucks congregating at the edge of the farm. At night the group would gather at the big house and eat housekeeper Mattie Lucy Payne's fried chicken and listen to the old man tell stories and enjoy his guided tour of the lifetime gallery of political pictures hanging on the kitchen walls.

Clinton was still working the phones, widening the net of people who could tell him more about Gore. On the Sunday night of July 5 he called Marty Peretz, publisher of *The New Republic*, who would have preferred Gore on the top of the ticket, but offered Clinton one crucial assessment of his former student at Harvard: *Al Gore will not knife you in the back.* Then Clinton called Thomas Archimedes (Ark) Monroe III, a relative of Gore's who lived in Little Rock and had been active in Arkansas politics. Monroe told Clinton that he had just returned from a visit with his ninety-five-year-old grandmother, who grew up in Carthage and was Albert Gore's first cousin. "She was standing there with her hands on her hips and she said, 'Well, Ark, is your governor going to pick Al as vice president?,' " Monroe recalled. He said he was unsure what Clinton would do. "And she made this statement: 'Can you think of anything better than those two young men leading this country into the twenty-first century?' "

Great line, Clinton said. Then he asked: *But what does Gore bring?*

He's run a campaign, Monroe said. *He knows what it takes. He brings your campaign money. He has an ability to raise money quickly. And you would get along.*

Early on the evening of July 8, Ginsburg finished his tough-questions memo and was about to send it to Little Rock, but decided first to run it by Greg Simon, the senator's legislative director. The memo addressed the sensitive issues of pot smoking, Vietnam, legislative flip-flops on abortion and gun control—matters that were by no means disqualifying but that might require considered responses. Ginsburg had never felt close to Gore, but admired his intellect and work ethic and thought he was by far the best choice for the vice-presidential slot. He had become such an advocate that he urged Bruce Reed, Gore's well-respected former speechwriter, to have lunch with McPherson to make the case. In writing the memo, he felt he was doing his job, undertaking the sort of hard but necessary opposition research that smart campaigns should do on themselves.

But when the fax came to Simon, it seemed only like a laundry list of every bad thing that could be said about his boss, and he faxed it down to Carthage, where it was greeted as a last-minute attempt at subversion. Ginsburg was in the hideaway office at Jones Day, having just returned from dinner, when Roy Neel called at about eight o'clock. Ginsburg sensed from a clicking sound that Gore was listening silently on a second line, but Neel did the talking, or screaming. *What an incredibly stupid thing to put this memo out on a fax machine*, Neel said. *Who knows who might get hold of it? This is all a bunch of crap, full of factual inaccuracies. We need a chance to correct this thing.* They were

venting at the vetter, and Ginsburg took it, keeping to himself one crucial fact that Neel and Gore did not yet have. What he wanted to say
but felt obliged not to was, *Relax, it's over. Clinton has decided on Gore
and will be calling in a few hours.*

The phone rings at 11:30 that night. Gore takes the call in his
back bedroom, and then Tipper gets on the line, and the deal is done,
and there is a dizzying rush of adrenaline. Neel slips across the Caney
Fork to start making his calls, and the news leaks to the Associated Press
in Little Rock, and the press village down at the end of the farm starts
rumbling, and the group has to think about packing and getting over to
Arkansas for the announcement at the governor's mansion, but no one
can sleep. The next morning when Mark Gearan waits at the airport to
accompany the family to Little Rock, he sees Al driving up in his own
van — driving for the last time in years — and the number two guy looks
focused, no bouncing around like a hyperactive adolescent, no Dan
Quayle on that boat in New Orleans (he has that four-year-old memory
deeply etched in his mind, they all do), and following behind in another van comes the staff, rolling down Interstate 40 at eighty miles an
hour, catching up, everything a blur, as Alberta Winkler shouts with
glee, "If you wanna run with the big dogs, you've gotta get off the
porch!"

NEW YORK CITY, less than a week later. Here was a moment
the old man had once yearned for himself. Thirty-six years had now
passed since he made his futile bid at the 1956 Democratic convention
in Chicago, his face distorted with ambition as he worked himself into
a frenzy trying to get on Adlai Stevenson's ticket. Now his son was right
there in his place, a Gore on the podium at Madison Square Garden,
looking out on the swelling, buzzing, placard-bobbing crowd of delegates, preparing to deliver a speech accepting his party's vice presidential nomination. Gore Senior had heard parts of the speech the day
before, when Junior had rehearsed it on a mock stage at the Intercontinental Hotel. The old man had entered the room halfway through the
oration, listened to the end, shook his head, and offered a critique. He
had never heard a worse speech, he said. Be extemporaneous. This was
too dull and wooden. Al bit his lip and said nothing. He had put his
heart into the text, and his advisers liked it; there was no way he was
going to wing it for the most important speech of his life. This was
never easy, the transference of a political dream from one generation

to the next, but the son understood from years of experience that, in the end, no matter what was said or left unsaid between them, it was all an expression of love.

Special places were reserved for Senator and Pauline Gore on the podium. Al was already up there, concentrating on his speech, when his parents appeared backstage and stepped onto the handicapped lift, an open air elevator that would bring them up to their seats. The lift rose no more than a yard off the ground, then jerked to a stop and would move neither up nor down. Senior and Pauline were stuck there as the clock ticked on toward their son's shining hour. The commotion drew Gore backstage, where he looked down to see his elderly father grabbing the top of the lift and trying to find footing so that he could hoist himself out. The old man, a frisky cattle rancher who had scaled many a fence in his eighty-four years, was in no mood to get stuck in a handicapped lift. But this time his escape was cut short by Pauline's cry for dignity, "Oh, Albert!" From the front came a warning to the speaker. *Sir, you have two minutes,* and in the chaos of that tableau, until the electricians arrived just in time, one saw the whole Gore family saga played out as a comedy of life, with the torn and achieving son, the poised mother, and the irrepressible father clambering out of the backstage lift as though he might get left behind in Possum Hollow.

CHAPTER TWENTY-ONE

BEING THERE

M ARK GEARAN DID NOT EXPECT to be on the road during the 1992 campaign, but there he was, bouncing along on the No. 2 bus as it rolled out of New York toward the American heartland. How did this happen? When he was selected by the Clinton team to manage the vice-presidential candidate, Gearan assumed that he would spend the summer and fall in Little Rock, setting strategy with the rest of the inner circle, and that Al Gore would take his chief of staff, Roy Neel, on his traveling squad. That was the usual method, the way Lloyd Bentsen had done it four years earlier. But Gore had a different plan. *Gearan comes with me,* he said. And he sent Neel down to headquarters where the loyal aide could look after his interests. That was the first move Gore made as Clinton's running mate, an early marker that defined the relationship over the ensuing eight years.

If this was the job that the old man so coveted, the son would make the most of it. He was determined not to be forgotten or ignored. He expected this to be a partnership of the two principals and a merger of their staffs below, not an uneasy and imbalanced alliance, and from the start he worked relentlessly to make that the case. No sooner had the caravan left New York than Gore faced what he considered a direct threat to his status. Susan Thomases, the campaign scheduler and close friend of Hillary Clinton's, tried to boot Al and Tipper off the bus long before it reached the Gateway Arch in St. Louis. In a conference call with Little Rock on the first day of the trip, Gore "just lost it," one participant recalled, and insisted that he and his wife would stay put to the end. Thomases backed down after a heated exchange, and the bus trip became the signature event of the campaign, sticking in the public imagination as a romantic evocation of two handsome couples touring the backroads on a double date.

It was all a matter of proximity—being there. Gore not only stayed the course on that first bus trip, he spent as much time as possible scrambling off his coach and onto Clinton's, where he could ride shotgun right next to his new partner and talk policy and tell stories and develop a bond that would imbue him with an aura of trustworthiness and indispensability. If Gore wanted to ride with him, "Clinton was fine with it," as one aide said, since it allowed him to study his running mate for hours on end in an unstructured setting, a chance that might never come again. There were only a few minor irritations that arose, perhaps reflecting larger differences in style between the disciplined Gore and freewheeling Clinton. When Gore was on the Clinton bus, the M&Ms disappeared, replaced by fruit and carrot sticks. Al and Tipper were getting into fighting shape. In desperation, Clinton occasionally whispered to an aide to sneak in some chocolate, but Gearan noticed that "the typical Clinton largesse in terms of snack foods was gone."

Dealing with Gore was a new experience for the Clinton team. He had a regimen that seemed to them more rooted in the bureaucracy or military than in the give-and-take of campaign politics. He demanded eight hours of sleep each night, and if he could not get it one night the scheduling staff had to find ways to make it up for him later. Everything had to be neatly organized, even on the bus trips. Clinton treated them like a rolling extemporaneous acting class; Gore wanted briefing meetings every night and index cards listing the dignitaries at the next stop and themes for the day. The information man could not function without up-to-date information. This was still the era before ready access to the Internet, so Gore devised his own hard-copy version. After every stop, he hopped back on the bus, or later the plane, and shouted "Wires!"—and staffers knew they had to round up faxes of the latest wires from the AP, UPI, Reuters, the Hotline, the Greenwire, anything that had campaign news or gossip. This task soon fell to an aide named Michael Gill, who began compiling what the others called the Gill Book. Gore loved nothing more than to devour the Gill Book. "He was meticulous about reading it. Absolutely meticulous," Gearan recounted. "He would study how an event was covered, the issues, how he was portrayed. The Net didn't really exist then so this was it—the Gill Book."

As the campaign wore on, Gore's insistence on being part of everything, his constant calling back to Little Rock to make sure his ideas and interests were being served, at once irritated and impressed Clinton's top tacticians in the War Room, James Carville and George Stephanopoulos. One afternoon, after finishing a telephone conversation with Gore, Carville went into one of his eye-squinting, drawling rants. "That Gore! He has an opinion on everything we're doing! And he thinks we oughta do *this* different. And he thinks we oughta do *that* different! He's driving me crazy!" Carville began. Then, without changing his facial expression or tone of voice or even pausing, he went on to say, "But I'll tell you something. I'll still take him over anybody else! Because he is the most disciplined, on-message person I have ever worked with. And I'll put up with all the rest, because this guy knows how to be a disciplined campaigner."

The concern raised in the first vetting memo about Gore before his selection, that he might not have the personality to be a "deferential partner," proved groundless. He would never stop scrapping for power, for a place at the table, but he would do it without seeming disrespectful or publicly embarrassing himself or Clinton. He certainly did not covet the vice presidency in the manner that his father once had. He wanted to be *president*, he kept telling his aides during the brief period when he was deciding whether to accept Clinton's offer if it came. And there could be something imperious in his nature when he dealt with subordinates, stingy with compliments. But he had been trained in the ways of being number two. He was the second Albert Gore, the second Congressman Gore, the second Senator Gore, always the son of a famous father. In his early days he acceded not just to the old man, but to a brilliant mother and provocative older sister. At St. Albans he was one step behind Dan Woodruff, the football hero and top prefect. At Harvard he was often considered a moon in the orbit of another star, Tommy Lee Jones. Deferential might be the wrong word to describe him, there was an edge in those relationships, but he knew from a lifetime of experience how to adapt to the role, the prince quietly exerting power while waiting for his time alone at the top.

THERE ARE, IN THE END, only a few important moments for a running mate during a presidential campaign. Gore had already passed the critical moment of first impression — or moments, since the first impressions came in waves as the public paid more attention: the announcement in Little Rock, the speech at the New York convention, the first bus trip to the Midwest. He had more than held his own in all three settings, bringing a handsome family and a two-smart-young-guys vibrancy to the ticket, seemingly enough to knock independent candidate Ross Perot temporarily out of the race and to lift Clinton's poll ratings by nine percentage points. The second important moment came in the fall, when he would stand alone in front of a national audience for the first time, debating the incumbent vice president, Dan Quayle. The Democratic team was on its way to victory by then, in retrospect many political analysts would say the race was already over, but Gore took to it with utmost seriousness and betrayed no signs of overconfidence.

In preparation for the October 13 debate, Gore's handlers took him off the road and constructed a makeshift television studio in a barn near Carthage, hoping that the familiar rural setting would relax him. He prided himself on being a ferocious and effective debater, and had certainly had enough practice in his life, going back to the Government Club at St. Albans and including more recently the dozens of debates in the 1988 primaries. But the consequences were far greater now, and this would be a single performance with only one real opponent, rather than the traveling tag-team wrestling-match debates of four years earlier. (Actually, there would be a third man on the stage, the second pale coming of Perot bringing forth Admiral James Stockdale for that one existential moment of "Who am I? Why am I here?" discombobulation.) Gore had served in the Senate with Quayle and considered him smarter than the lampoon version of him that had developed during the vice presidency. The higher the stakes, the more perfect Gore wanted to be, and his conception of being perfect was to know everything there was to know, which did not necessarily translate into effective television.

This tendency was familiar to his friend and former House colleague, Dennis Eckart, who came down to play Quayle in the debate preps. "He was very serious and in some ways was the quintessential Gore as folks think they know him, which is to put seventeen facts back on the table to totally rebut what you've said, to show his depth of knowledge and his overwhelming competence," Eckart recounted. "It was, 'You know, you're kind of putting too much out there.' " Gore's recall was indeed impressive, but there was a sense among his advisers that he might be using it as a crutch, returning to facts when he was in trouble as a means of changing the subject. The message discipline that Carville so admired could come undone if Gore started dropping down to those levels C, D, E, and F of fact finding that made him such a favorite of policy aides. "One fact! One message! One theme! Say it three times!" Carville instructed. "We don't need three facts, three themes that you say one time!" Under the direction of Bob Squier, Gore's most trusted consultant, they even tried severely editing his debate books for the same purpose. "Take those seven pages of facts out," Squier said one day. "He doesn't need them."

The mock rounds in the Tennessee barn revealed more about Gore than did the real debate when it was televised from Georgia Tech. Eckart had mastered the Quayle persona. He had performed the same role in 1988 for Lloyd Bentsen, developing a thick file on Quayle and watching hours of videotape of him in action. It was Eckart, the last time around, who had first noticed from the tapes that Quayle kept jabbing his hand into his coat pocket JFK-style. He anticipated correctly that Quayle would try to compare himself to the youthful Kennedy, a concept that bewildered Bentsen during a mock debate but readied him for his winning "I knew JFK" line when the scene really happened. But Eckart's knowledge of Quayle this time was not as important as what he was learning about Gore.

Not long after it was reported that Eckart was helping Gore with the debates, he received an unsigned envelope in the mail one day with a Tennessee postmark. Inside was a copy of a letter from U.S. Representative Al Gore Jr. to a constituent from the fourth congressional district in which Gore was explaining that he, like the person to whom he was writing, was a strong opponent of abortion. The franked envelope in which Gore had sent the letter was also included, along with another page citing the times and votes when Gore was on the side of the anti-abortion movement. During the 1992 campaign Gore had been presenting himself as someone who was and always had been strongly pro-choice.

Eckart was always looking for ways to throw Gore off stride during the debate rehearsals. He purposely "misquoted the hell out of" Gore speeches and twisted around phrases from *Earth in the Balance*. He made up a letter that Gore supposedly sent to an autoworker in Cleveland about his desire to eliminate the internal combustion engine and put the man out of work. "And in a letter you wrote to UAW Local 17, you write, 'I'm sorry we disagree on this, but I promise that I will do everything in my power to see that you are retrained,' " Eckart began. He could see Gore's computer mind punching in the category—congressional letters, internal combustion engine, retraining—looking for the seventeen facts. Nothing came spitting out. "And then he went into, 'Well, what I meant . . . ,' " Eckart recalled. "He wasn't sure whether he had written that letter or not."

The abortion letter was even more disconcerting for Gore. He *knew* that he had written letters of that sort, he just did not know that any of them were still floating around. As Eckart began his attack, he could "see out of the corner of my eye" that Gore's staff was getting nervous, wondering what was going on. The subject was particularly uncomfortable for Marla Romash, Gore's press secretary, who was strongly pro-choice and had grilled him extensively on his abortion position before she went to work for him in 1989. Gore gave a stuttering, mixed response now. When the mock debate was over, Roy Neel shook his head and muttered, "Well, if Eckart got this letter, the Republicans *have to* have this letter."

If they did, it never came up in the debate with Quayle, and would not resurface until Gore was running for president in 2000. Quayle and his advisers chose instead to pound away at Clinton, challenging Gore indirectly by disparaging Clinton's credibility. This tactic seemed to confound Gore and diminished the effectiveness of his aggressive style. And it nibbled away a little at Gore's standing with at least one member of the Clinton inner circle, Hillary Clinton, who was disturbed by his tendency to change the subject and recite a few facts instead of coming directly and strongly to Clinton's defense.

There was then and always a quiet but unavoidable strain in the relationship between Al and Hillary. Bill Clinton had said at the start that one of the reasons he chose Gore as his running mate was that he seemed much like Hillary: stable, reliable, loyal, smart, interested in policy as much as politics. And the shared personality traits of the two couples did not go unnoticed by the press. It was said that from the two couples Al and Hillary were the dispassionate technocrats. Those are stereotypes, but there is some measure of truth to them, and what became increasingly obvious was that precisely because Al Gore and Hillary Clinton were so alike, and since they both intended to be Bill Clinton's political partner once they reached the White House, there was a sharper rivalry between them than would ever develop between the two guys.

The election was over before it was over, long before Al Gore's campaign plane landed in Nashville in the first predawn hours of election day. The old man and Pauline were there waiting for him, joining the caravan that would carry the Gore family down the Interstate in the darkness of middle Tennessee, across the barrens of rock and cedar and flat cactus, passing near Possum Hollow and turning up toward the Caney Fork and Carthage, where ten busloads of people would sign up for the inaugural trip to Washington.

EPILOGUE: THE STRUGGLE WITHIN

AL Gore's relationship with Bill Clinton was defined in an agreement they worked out in Little Rock after the 1992 election and before the inauguration. The document furthered a concept the two men had discussed as early as their first meeting at the Washington Hilton back during the selection process. Gore would be a managing partner. He would have an office in the West Wing. Members of his staff would be integrated into the president's staff. The president and vice president would meet for lunch once each week and the meeting would be inviolate, held no matter what else was preoccupying them. And Gore would have what he called *spheres of interest* in which Clinton would defer to him and let him take the lead for the administration.

Though it was not stated in those terms, within the White House it became understood that Gore was essentially president of the subjects within his spheres of interest. The list grew over time, as Clinton gave him new assignments at their weekly lunches, eventually including all environmental issues, science, high tech, the Internet, communications, space, reinventing government, voluntary ratings for network television, family and medical leave, the tobacco industry, nuclear disarmament of former Soviet states, air traffic safety, and defense contracting. Clinton was willing to cede these spheres of interest to Gore because there were other policy matters that he was more interested in, and because he implicitly trusted Gore to handle them with skill and discretion. He took pride in saying that he had the most powerful vice president in American history.

There was nonetheless serious concern among Gore's aides and advisers that he did not take full advantage of the power Clinton gave him because he tried too hard to impress the president. They sensed in him an overpowering need to prove to Clinton that he had made the right choice, that he could offer invaluable help, compelling him to attend every meeting, master every issue, keep abreast of every personnel decision, and prove that he was at least the second smartest person in the room. His aides would wonder why they were gathering data on those C, D, E, and F policy levels for every minor meeting at which the president might be present. *Stop staffing this guy*, they would plead. *You don't have to be there at every meeting. You don't have to be there for every decision. You don't have to be at his side all the time. You don't have to be the wooden Indian standing behind him in every picture.*

So which was it? Gore the partner or Gore the staffer? The bold Gore or the subservient Gore? Those questions go to the struggle within Al Gore that has long been evident—a duality that he brought with him into the vice president's job, that became more pronounced once he was there, and that remained unresolved as he sought to move up to the Oval Office. He was at once competent and self-confident about anything that he could translate into a question of scientific fact, yet often insecure and riddled with self-doubt when it came to perceptions and emotions and aspects of life that could not be established with mathematical certainty.

That is why he could deliver an hour-long extemporaneous lecture on global warming and yet need index cards as a crutch when saying a simple thank you and goodbye to an aide who was resigning. It is why he could be described simultaneously, by the same people, as "the only adult in the White House" and "the most insecure person I've ever met in my life." It is why he could have a far subtler sense of humor and more even disposition than Bill Clinton, yet be perceived as a stiff while Clinton was thought of as an easygoing guy. Those first words of self-doubt that Gore uttered during his 1976 congressional campaign—*How'm I doin'? How'm I doin'?*—became the private mantra of his political career. Literally and figuratively, he had to see the Gill Book to get a reading on himself.

Variations on the theme were recounted by people who worked for him and admired him yet could recall scenes like the one offered by Lorraine Voles, who served as his director of communications from 1993 to 1997: "There was a situation where he was asking me how he did, how he did, how he did, and I guess I was getting annoyed, and he said, 'Lorraine, don't you know how insecure I am?' " She could tell that he meant it, she said later, and that he was not being flippant. One former adviser reached the conclusion that insecurity was "the seminal force that motivates Gore," a trait, this adviser said, that tended to obscure his better side—"an insightful, intelligent, subtle, and well-intentioned person." And it was insecurity, many of his former aides concluded, that brought out his tendency to be bureaucratic, defensive about his turf, wooden in public presentation, prone to exaggerate his own accomplishments, impressed by résumés and the conventions of the establishment, and more timid than he wanted to be.

Gore is self-aware enough to understand this about himself. He has now and then tried to overcome it, as he demonstrated in *Earth in the Balance,* with its introductory self-criticism followed by chapters that were bold and for the most part nonbureaucratic. In the White House, ironically, it was when he assumed the status of Clinton's senior staffer that he could be firm and confident, pressing the president to act decisively in the Balkans and Haiti, and not to relent in the face of the Republican revolution's budget-cutting agenda. He had a comfort level from that distance, the strong supporting role he had played all his life. But his presidential ambitions tended to increase his insecurity and bring out its problematic side effects. In the controversies that hounded him in recent years, ranging from the White House fundraising investigation to the Clinton impeachment to the tumult of his presidential campaign, the louder he insisted that he had no regret, the more likely it was that he had pushed too hard and was battling self-doubt, which would then seep out in the form of a hedge or a contradiction or a sudden change of direction.

THE NATURE OF GORE'S INSECURITY, and the various ways it manifested itself, became evident to former White House consultant Dick Morris when he was laying plans for the 1996 Democratic convention. It was a classic encounter between the self-styled modern Machiavelli and the prince of Tennessee. Morris began with the goal of keeping the prime-time spotlight away from any of the party's iconic liberals like Jesse Jackson, Ted Kennedy, or Mario Cuomo. Monday night would go to Christopher Reeve and Sarah and Jim Brady. Tuesday would be Hillary remodeled as the midwestern high school girl home again in Chicagoland. But there was a hole Wednesday night, and Morris wanted Gore to fill it. The vice presidential nominee traditionally spoke on Thursday night, after the delegate vote and before the presidential candidate.

When Morris asked him if he would anchor the Wednesday night program, Gore's response was "immediately negative." He said there were no ratings on Wednesday and that he did not want to be shuffled to a night when nobody was watching. Morris came back with a ratings history that showed that the Wednesday night averages were only slightly below those of Thursday. "You can be the highlighted figure on Wednesday night, the star," Morris argued. "Even if the ratings are higher on Thursday, all the attention goes to the presidential nominee. If you give a speech on Wednesday night, it will give you a leg up for 2000." Gore, skeptical of Morris's numbers, as others have been over the years, demanded to see raw data. Morris gave it to him.

The next time the two men met, Gore was still resistant, and making another argument. "Look, Dick," he said. "You don't understand what this is all about. This is not simply a speech. This is a formal address in which I accept the nomination of my party after a vote of the delegates. I can't give the acceptance speech the night *before* I'm nominated."

Morris temporarily dropped the idea, saying perhaps they would revisit it after the Republican convention in July. He got nervous when the GOP ticket of Bob Dole and Jack Kemp emerged from San Diego with a glimmer of hope, cutting the Democrats' lead in half. He took his case to Clinton. *We've got to have Gore speak Wednesday night,* he said. *We don't have another big-name centrist Democrat who can do it.* Clinton agreed and said Morris could tell Gore that the president wanted him to do it.

Morris visited Gore at his office in the West Wing. "The president would really like you to speak on Wednesday night," he said.

Gore gave a "heavy sigh," as Morris recalled the scene. Morris started talking about what he might say in the speech. Gore was not listening. He got up from his normal seat and walked across the room and sat in a chair near the American flag. He murmured something . . . *What if I . . .*

Morris could not hear it all.

Excuse me, sir?

Gore raised his voice only slightly.

"What if I fuck up?" he muttered.

Morris was stunned. He thought it was like hearing a home-run hitter saying that he did not want to go to bat. When he analyzed it later, he saw that all of the manifestations of Gore's insecurity came into play. First the concern about protecting his turf. Then the bureaucratic response, seeking the cover of facts and figures. Then the establishment response, citing tradition. Finally the acknowledgment of timidity and self-doubt. But like many friends and aides who have worked closely with Gore over the years, Morris emerged from the experience believing that the vice president was the sort of person who could overcome his weaknesses and learn from his mistakes.

In the introduction to *Earth in the Balance*, Gore chided himself for one of the consequences of his insecurity, his propensity toward caution. "The voice of caution whispers persuasively in the ear of every politician, often with good reason," he wrote. "But when caution breeds timidity, a good politician listens to other voices." Throughout his years as vice president, Gore was often persuaded by the voice of caution, even on the environment, the issue that meant the most to him and for which he promised to take the most political risks. There were, as he had written, good reasons for this. He was being realistic, hoping to achieve the possible, always mindful that he had a presidential race ahead. But those good reasons bred timidity, until he broke free for a few days in December 1997.

World talks aimed at reaching a protocol on global warming seemed on the verge of collapse one week after they began in Kyoto, Japan. European countries wanted the United States to agree to steeper cuts in pollution emissions. The American delegates and other wealthy nations wanted developing countries to make a stronger commitment to pollution controls. Gore was caught in the middle of it all. He knew that without his intervention, the Kyoto talks were likely to fail. But there was enormous pressure on him not to go. He was told that the agreement might do major damage to the economy, endangering everything that had been gained, socially and politically, over the Clinton boom years. Furthermore, whatever he did would not be enough to please the environmentalists, and the business community was strongly opposed to the talks and hoped they would collapse. His trusted consultant, Bob Squier, armed with polling data, came to him and said he was absolutely convinced that it was political suicide. *You can't go*, he told Gore. *If you go, I can't help you. No one can help you. This is going to kill you.*

If Squier was caution whispering persuasively in his ear, Gore was not listening this time. Before he left, he met with a dozen senior administration staffers in his West Wing office. Only one person in the room thought he should go. That was Al Gore. During the meeting, he went around the room, asking aides one by one for their opinion. Some said that the decision was very difficult and that they would not offer a position. Others were adamant that he should not go. *Thank you very much*, Gore said. *I'm going to think about this.* There was no way he was not going to Japan. He worked on his speech on the flight over, then conferred by telephone with President Clinton from his hotel room, working out the final wording, before heading over to the conference room—cavernous, windowless, and beige—where hundreds of delegates were waiting. The room fell silent as he walked in. He said that the Americans were willing to show "an increased negotiating flexibility"—words that refueled the talks. After meeting privately with officials from South America, Japan, China, India, Brazil, and Europe to broker a consensus, the treaty was kept alive. As he left, he flashed a thumbs-up sign to his aide, Katie McGinty. Go get 'em, he said. Call me if you need me. On the plane back, Gore walked through the cabin, pumped by adrenaline, as his staff slept in utter exhaustion.

It could be said that the victory was hollow. The treaty drew loud opposition from Republicans in the Senate, and knowing that it would fail, the White House did not even attempt to send it to the Hill. Again there was disappointment from some environmentalists who felt that Gore should have exerted even stronger leadership. But for those around him who had seen the struggle between his idealism and ambition, and who knew how his insecurity could hold him back, this was a victory of a deeper sort. He had found his gut.

EARLY IN THE SPRING OF 1997, John Seigenthaler, Gore's longtime mentor and former editor at the *Tennessean*, delivered a lecture at Colby College in which he said that political fund-raising was the big story the press missed in the 1996 presidential campaign. He sent a copy of his speech to the vice president, but never heard back from him. Gore was by then dealing with tough questions about his own role in fund-raising, the beginning of a lingering controversy that aides say rattled him more than any other event during his vice presidency, including the Clinton impeachment. How could someone who once made his living as a tough investigative reporter end up dialing for dollars from his White House office, hitting up corporate executives for large contributions, and not sense that this might raise serious questions of propriety if not legality? The answer again can be found in Gore's internal struggle between self-righteousness and self-doubt.

His tendency is to think of life as a series of missions. In 1996 his mission was to defeat the Republicans and their budget-cutting agenda. He had already resolved the budget fight as a mathematical equation, concluding that the Republicans were wrong, that it was as simple as two plus two equals four, with no possibility of another answer. Of that he had no doubt, no reason to question himself. Raising money was part of the mission, and here his insecurity started to come into play. It was another way to impress the boss, to demonstrate his competence, to prove that he was invaluable. If he was given a call sheet, he would make every call. Clinton would fake it, slough it off, avoid the task, but the loyal Gore would come through.

When Gore felt insecure in politics, he tended to close down his intuitive side and look at life as a bureaucrat. There was a procedure for everything he was doing. Lawyers and aides were vetting every list, telling him what calls he could make, what phones he could use. He wanted only facts, or so he told FBI agents later. He said that he ignored any memos concerning fund-raising that were written by Harold Ickes, the president's deputy chief of staff, because he knew that Ickes hated Dick Morris, the mastermind of the television campaign for which the money was being raised. The Ickes memos would be rhetoric, not fact, he believed, intended only to undercut Morris. So he set them aside, unread, letting them pile up day after day until an aide took them away. That, he explained, is why he did not see the memos from Ickes that talked about the mix of hard money and soft money that was to be raised. If he read a memo, he put a right-handed check mark in the upper left hand corner. The Ickes memos went unchecked.

The story that raised questions about Gore's fund-raising inside the White House was written by Bob Woodward and appeared in the *Washington Post* on March 2, 1997. It was based on more than one hundred interviews and quoted donors as saying that they were made to feel uncomfortable by the direct appeals from the vice president. It also quoted several former vice presidents as saying they did not make direct solicitations from the White House. Gore's fund-raising prowess, the article said, made him known by insiders as the administration's "solicitor-in-chief." With equal parts self-righteousness and insecurity, Gore created his own version of reality to explain the story: Woodward was trying to settle a score. In explaining his thinking later to FBI agents, Gore said that before the article appeared, Woodward had asked him "about writing a book about the campaign." He told the agents that he turned down the request, and that rejection explained why Woodward would "come after me." He said this to the FBI even though several of Gore's own aides knew that he talked to Woodward twice for *The Choice*, his book about the 1996 presidential race.

Gore also told the FBI agents that he was relieved after reading Woodward's article because there was nothing in it that would hurt him. Yet the article obviously worried him greatly. The day after it appeared, he was struggling with both self-righteousness and self-doubt. What embarrassed him most, according to friends, was that his judgment and character were being called into question by the Washington elite. "Clinton is more concerned about what the mother shopping at Wal-Mart thinks about him," one former Gore aide explained. "Gore could give a shit about that. It is his parents, his classmates at St. Albans, all the usual suspects" in the establishment that he worried about. The embarrassment compelled him to go out and defend himself, so the day after the article appeared he told his staff that he wanted to hold a press conference right away. There was time for one discussion with his aides and lawyers before he appeared at the White House briefing room. During the discussion, his counsel, Charles Burson, used the phrase "no controlling legal authority" to explain that case law regarding the legality of Gore's actions seemed fuzzy at best. "Everything I did I understood to be lawful," Gore told the press. Then, in the bureaucratic persona brought on by insecurity, he used the phrase "no controlling legal authority" seven times before the press conference was over.

As they left the briefing room, his staff told him that he had done a great job. They talked about how Wolf Blitzer on CNN had compared it to his masterful dismantling of Ross Perot in their debate over free trade. When they turned the corner and walked past the Oval Office, Clinton emerged and stuck a big paw around Gore's shoulder and ushered him inside. They were both smiling. Later, when Gore came back to his own office, his insecurity resurfaced. *How'd I do? How'd I do?* The reports got tougher as the night wore on, and Gore became more and more critical of himself. This was a tendency that helped to soften him in the eyes of his staff. As hard as he could be on them, he was always hardest on himself.

In the days after the press conference, the consensus was that Gore had blown an opportunity and made himself look worse. On most days, he talked to an inner circle of five or six advisers. Now he called in a larger group of advisers and consultants and asked for a no-holds-barred critique. *What did I do wrong? What should I do now?* Someone suggested that he should volunteer to testify before Congress. Another said he should go on *60 Minutes*. The advice, said Carter Eskew, one of the consultants, was "brutally frank." Many agreed that he had to make a grand gesture of some fashion and that he was finished if he didn't act. They said it had damaged him terribly. "Mr. Vice President," said one friend, "with all due respect, the bill is coming due for Bill Clinton, and you are going to pay for it."

Gore listened calmly, no icy stares, thanking each person in turn. "I'm listening," he said. Then he concluded by saying that he disagreed with the consensus. "I don't believe it was wrong, legally, ethically, or morally. In fact, I believe it was right," he said. "We had a job to do, an agenda to fulfill, that was right." The doubt was gone again as Gore looked at the issue as a mathematical equation with only one right answer. The message one friend took with him from the meeting: *Thanks, but no thanks.* But even as he disagreed with Gore's assessment, this friend left the White House that day feeling oddly more positive about Gore. "I thought what it said about him was that he could be president of the United States," the friend said. "It was moral relativism. If you don't have it, you can't have the job. He has missions. His mission is to get through it. He has figured that out."

GORE WAS NEAR THE DOORWAY of the Oval Office when Clinton told him that he did not have sex with Monica Lewinsky. As soon as Clinton turned around, a look of disbelief crossed the vice president's face. He tried not to talk about the scandal around his staff, except to complain about its secondary effects, how it was getting in the way of policy, how it was making it impossible for him, without seeming disloyal, to start breaking away and forming his own identity apart from the president. There were times when they could sense that he was thinking he might be president sooner than he expected. And there were times when they sensed he thought that this might prevent him from ever being president. Publicly, he said that the president was his friend and that he believed him. Once, late in the day, he closed the door to his office and asked an aide in a quiet voice, *Do you believe him?* No, came the response, and Gore said nothing to indicate he thought otherwise.

During that whole long year of 1998 as the Clinton drama played itself out, the old man was dying down at the big house above the Caney Fork. Pauline decided that he would go in style. Before, when she was recovering from a stroke, he would take her out on the balcony of the house and walk her back and forth, back and forth, for hours at a time. Now she was dressing him and cleaning him up and getting him in the car and taking him around to the neighbors, just enough "so people could see him, but not have him exposed to any embarrassment," said friend Bill McSweeney. He told the same stories all the time. The one about how Cordell Hull had arranged for him to meet President Roosevelt in his office because of some legislation coming up and how he bought a new suit and briefcase for the occasion, never had a briefcase before, so he could look official when he called on the president. And he went in and they had a nice long talk and he got so excited when it was over that he ran out the door to drive home to tell Pauline about it and then realized that he had to go back to the president's appointments secretary and say, "I forgot my briefcase!" He loved to tell that story when his son came home. People'll be leaving briefcases in Al's office.

The son's mission was to get through it in the months after he buried his father that December in Grave 3, Lot 18, Section C of the Smith County graveyard. His oldest friends, Steve Armistead and Goat Thompson, two members of the Snow Creek Gang, watched him struggle whenever he came back to the Caney Fork.

STEVE: "Al's having a tough time, I can tell, and if you're around him you can tell, too, since his dad died."

GOAT: "I used to tell him, when he was a senator, 'Why you fool around with this stuff?' "

STEVE: "I can see it in his face. And his anguish."

GOAT: "I noticed Al, he's aged a lot, too, in the last couple three years."

STEVE: "On the phone, I could just tell by the tone and the condition he was in. He was at the house and Miz Pauline was hollerin' at him to come and eat. You could tell by the sound of his voice that he hadn't had time."

NOTE ON SOURCES

THIS BOOK is based on interviews or correspondence with five hundred people, mostly conducted during a fourteen-month period between March 1999 and June 2000, as well as boxes of memos, letters, and other documents. Many key sources were interviewed several times. This is in no way an authorized biography, although Vice President Gore agreed to six interviews, none of more than an hour. Parts of this book have been published in the *Washington Post*, beginning with an article on Gore's years as a journalist published in January 1998. Other articles were published in October and December 1999 and August 2000.

People interviewed for this book included: Richard Abalos, John Adams, John Aitcheson, William Allen, Gary Allison, Graham Allison, Beth Alpert, Dennis Alpert, Ian Alsop, Richard Alston, Sally Aman, Barry Ancona, Calvin Anderson, Victoria Anderson, Donna Armistead, Linda Armistead, Steve Armistead, Lloyd Armour, Mark Armour, Victor Ashe, Rob Atkinson, John Atkisson, Eli Attie, Les AuCoin, Gerald J. Austin, Tony Badger, Donald Baer, Walter Bailey, David Baker, John Bandeian Jr., Charles Bartlett, David Bartlett, James Bass, Albert Bates, William Batoff, Chris Bayley, Gordon Beall, Larry Belinsky, Roberts Bennett, Jerome Berlin, Richard Betts, Edd Blair, Jeff Blattner, James Blumstein, Dennis Bolte, Charles Bone, Robert Boorstin, David Bositis, Donna Brazile, Stephen B. Bright, Paul Brock, William Brock, Lew Brodsky, Kathy Brooks, Richard Brooks, Ted Brown, Carol Browner, Tom Burke, Charles Burson, Robert A. Butterworth, Gayle Byrne, Deb Callahan, Terry Calvani, Mary Campos, Lee Caplin, Lisa Caputo, William Carrick, Tom Carroll III, Chris Carter, Hodding Carter III, Jackie Carver, F. Guthrie Castle, Rick Chappell.

Also: Henry Cisneros, Phillip E. Clapp, Alzeda Clark, Bayard (Stocky) Clark, Eileen Claussen, Faith Clay, Stephen Claywell, Emily Clyburn, James E. Clyburn, Steve Cobb, David J. Cocke, Doug Coe, Anne Cohn-Donnelly, Joseph Colla, Nelson P. Conover, John Conyers, Ken Cook, James Cooney, Kenneth B. Cooper, Dolly Cowan, Richard Ben Cramer, Charles Crawford, Leo (Mac) Cropsey, Valerie Crotty, Stanley Crouch, Sherry Cummings Sloan, James Cutting, Leslie Dach, William Dalton, Preston Daniels, Kert Davies, John Claiborne Davis, Bart Day, Richard Deerin, Bob Delabar, Mike Delgiudice, Norm Dicks, Wayne Dirksen, Tom Downey, Greg Duckett, Blake Early, Betty Eastman, Maria Echaveste, Dennis Eckart, Steve Eckart, the Reverend Craig Eder, Robert Edgar, Christopher Edley Jr., Everett Ehrlich, Charles Elrod, George Elsey, Paul Elston, Frank Empson, Carter Eskew, David A. Everett, Edward Farley, Richard Fife, Evelyn Fisher, Georgia Fisher, James Fleming, Nancy Fleming, James Florio, Charles Fontenay, Harold Ford Sr., Chris Foreman, David Forman, H. Jackson Forstman, John Hope Franklin, James C. Free, David Friedman, Al From, Sandy Frusher, Lawrence Fuchs, Leon Fuerth, Jerry Futrell, Abe Gainer, William Galston, James Gardner, Stephen Gaskin, Robert Gass.

Also: Frankie Gaye, Mark Gearan, James Gibbs, Kenyon Gibbs, Kumiki Gibson, Don Gilligan, James Gilliland, Gary Ginsburg, Peter Goldberg, Tim Golding, Warren Gooch, Gary Goodman, Jamie Gore, Jill Gore, Jimmy Gore, Louise Gore, Mark Gore, Pauline LaFon Gore, Tipper Gore, Karenna Gore-Schiff, Celeste Gore-Schreck, Schuyler Gott-Andrews, Fred Graham, Hugh Davis Graham, Otis Graham, Dewey Grantham, James Gray Jr., Tom Grumbly, Charles Guggenheim, Lani Guinier, Donald Lee Hackett, William S. Haddad, Geoff Haines-Stiles, Walter Harrelson, J. Lawrence Harrington, Mark Harris, Skila Harris, Alexander Haslam, Alexander Boyd Hawes Jr., Johnny Hayes, Wade Henderson, Maurice Hendrick, John Hennigan, Frederick Hessick, Shirley Hiett, George (Buddy) Hillow, Richard Holbrooke, Jane Holmes Dixon, Pat Holt, John Hook, Benjamin Hooks, Dennis Horger, Barbara Howar, Jeff Howard, Lewis Frank Huck, James Thomas Hudson Jr., Phillip Huffines, Reed Hundt, Frank Hunger, John Hurd, Wallace Hyde, Richard Hyland, John D. Isaacs, Jesse Jackson, Tamar Jacoby, James Jensen, Bruce Jentleson, Brooks Johnson, Robert Johnson, Kenneth Jost, Joel Kachinsky, David Kaiser.

Also: Mickey Kantor, Michael Kapetan, Spurgeon M. Keeny Jr., Diane Kefauver, Peter Keiser, Peter G. Kelly, George Kendall, John Kifner, Jamie Kilbreth, William Kirk, Ron Klain, Marty Knanishu, Peter Knight, James Kohlmoos, Mike Kopp, Emmanuel Krasner, James Kreuttner, Geoffrey Kuhn, the Reverend Samuel Billy Kyles, Wade Ladue,

Dawn LaFon, Tommy LaFon, Whit LaFon, Hershel Lake, Nate Landow, Bruce La Pierre, Weldon Latham, Greg Lawler, John L. Laycock, Irving Lazar, Michael Lemov, H. Alan Leo, Pat Letke-Alexander, Eric Lewis, John Lewis, Joseph Lieberman, John Lillard, Tom Lindley, Robert Loftus, Esther Ocampo Lombardo, Kyle Longley, Eddie Long, Glenn C. Loury, Thomas Lovejoy, Joseph E. Lowery, Janice Lucas, Alfred MacFarland, John Maddux, Thomas E. Magee, Mary Blue Magruder, Andrew Maguire, Jerold Mande, Ed Markey, Ivin N. Marks, Thurgood Marshall Jr., Will Marshall, Fred Martin, Jack Martin, Larry Martinez, Bill Mason, Roy P. Mays, Michael B. McElroy, Katie McGinty, Joseph McGrath, Richard McKinney.

Also: Patrick McLain, Terrence McNally, Bob McNeely, Harry McPherson, William S. McSweeney, Ned McWherter, Don Meir, Mark Mellman, Gilbert S. Merritt, Kyle Michel, Mead Miller, Tom Miller, Edward Mitchell, Thomas Archimedes Monroe III, Curtis Moore, Irving Moore, Dick Morris, Agnes Mouton, Bill Moyers (by fax), Tom Murray, Bruce Nairn, Bob Nash, James Neal (archivist), James F. Neal (attorney), Roberta Neal, Ralph Neas, Roy Neel, Jean Nelson, Richard Neustadt, David Nichols, Betty Sue Nixon, Eleanor Holmes Norton, Jim O'Hara, Mike O'Hara, Don Oberdorfer, Dave Ogilvy, Mildred Beasley Oldham, Ivan Ourusoff, Steve Owens, Neil Oxman, John Passacantando, Mattie Lucy Payne, Anne D. Percy, Charles Percy, William Percy, Anne Peretz, Martin Peretz, David Perry, Charles Peters, David G. Petty, Gordon Petty, Mitch Philpott, Charles Pieper, James P. Pinkerton.

Also: Rafe Pomerance, Carl Pope, Terry Pope, Jerome Powell, John Powers, Hugh Price, Jerry Pritchard, Wes Proffett, Kyle Pruett, Jack Quinn, Franklin Raines, Bruce Rathbun, William T. Ray Jr., Eddie Reasoner, Coates Redmon, Bruce Reed, Kenneth Rietz, Paul Risley, Donald Ritchie, Jonathan Ritvo, Jack Robinson Sr., Tamara Trexler Robinson, Michael J. Roche, Lawrence Rockefeller, Stanley Rogers, William Rollings, Marla Romash, Phil Rosenbaum, Roger Rosenblatt, Barth Royer, Anthony J. Rubino, Randy Rubino, Andrew Rudnik, Martin Russo, Clayton Ryce, Charles Saltzman, David Sandalow, James Sasser, Mary Sasser, Harriet Hawes Savage, Tim Schaeffer, Arlie Schardt, William Denny Scharf, Gail Kefauver Scharf, Andrew Schlesinger, Robert Scott, Walter Searcy, John Seigenthaler, David Seivers, Jerry Sheehan, Mark Sherry, Robert Shetterly Jr., Mark Shields, Thomas J. Shields, George Shipley, Andy Shookhoff, Blake Silkwood, Matthew Simchak, Greg Simon, John Sims, John Siscoe, Phil Sloan, Lawrence Smith, Maxine Smith, William D. Smith, Frank Snowden, Caren Solomon, Bob Somerby, Lewis Sorley.

Also: Gary South, Gene Sperling, Ben Spratling, Bob Squier, Mildred T. Stahlman, Ron Stakem, Guenter Stanisic, John Stanton, Warren Steel, Shelby Steele, Jay Stein, Rick Steinberg, Ronnie Steine, George Stephanopoulos, John Sterling, Frank Thatcher Steuart, Bryan Stevenson, Andrew Stevovich, Dess Stokes, Ray Strother, Robert L. Suettinger, Russell Sugarmon, Frank Sutherland, Thomas (Doc) Sweitzer, Alan Symonds, Ronald Takaki, Willford Brent Taylor, Ginny Terzano, Eugene TeSelle, Jo Thackston, Abigail Thernstrom, Alfred Pembroke Thom, Gordon (Goat) Thompson, Margo Thorning, Tom Tisch, William M. Tomlinson, Adrian Traas, Jimmy Trainham, Jorge Tristani, Cadwell Tyler III, Humphrey Tyler, John Tyson, Carl Vigeland, Lorraine Voles, Peter van Wagenen, Carmala Walgren, Nolan Walters, William Walton Jr., Charles Brandon Waring, John Warnecke, Wes Watkins, Mark Weiner, Dan Weiss, Arnold Welles, Eddie West, General William Westmoreland, Chris White, Jim White, Rosie White, Victoria White-Berger, Wayne Whitt, Glenn Wild, Peggy Wilhyde, Roger Wilkins, Sam Williams, Eleanor Willis, Stanley Willis, David K. Wilson, Shelby Wilson, William Julius Wilson, Elizabeth Winthrop, Tim Wirth, Dwaine Witte, Dan Woodruff, James S. Wright, Robert Wright, Robert S. Wright, David Wylie, William Yates, Mark Zern, Eve Zibart, Michael Zibart, Paul Zofnass.

ACKNOWLEDGMENTS

THIS BOOK GREW from a series in the *Washington Post*, and would not have been possible without the great generosity and encouragement of our colleagues there, starting with publisher Don Graham and associate publisher Bo Jones. That they both attended St. Albans and then Harvard, perhaps setting the path for young Al Gore to follow, should not be held against them or him. Our editors at the *Post*, Leonard Downie Jr., Steve Coll, Jackson Diehl, Bill Hamilton, Maralee Schwartz, Liz Spayd, Mike Abramowitz, Ruth Marcus, Glenn Frankel, Bob Barnes, and JoAnn Armao gave us tremendous freedom to pursue the Gore story in our own way. We would also like to thank the many first-class journalists at the *Post* who gave us guidance, including David Broder, Dan Balz, Bob Woodward, Tom (the owner-coach) Edsall, John Harris, Ceci Connolly, David Finkel, David von Drehle, Al Kamen, Mike Allen, Peter Baker, Susan Glasser, Mary McGrory, Terry Neal, Ben White, Chuck Babington, Hanna Rosin, John Mintz, David Ignatius, Joel Achenbach, Kevin Merida, and Tom Jackman. Without the expert and indefatigable work of news researcher Madonna Lebling, this work would not have been possible. Thanks also to researchers Lynn Davis, Bobbye Pratt, Donna Mackie, Nancy Shiner, Mary Lou White, Karl Evanzz, Heming Nelson, Roland Matifas, Bob Lyford, and Margot Williams, and to dictationists Olwen Price, Carol Van Horn, and Kathy Allesi.

Alice Mayhew, our editor, pushed this project to the end with her inimitable energy and wisdom, as did her unflappable deputy, Roger Labrie. The Simon & Schuster family was unfailingly helpful: thanks to Carolyn Reidy, David Rosenthal, Victoria Meyer, Fred Chase, Jennifer Thornton, Leslie Jones, Michael Accordino, and the incomparable Kerri Kennedy. Rafe Sagalyn, our agent and friend, was always encouraging, as were his assistants, Dan Kois and Megan Devine, and reader Jim Warren.

Though six time zones away, Janet and Shigemitsu Nakashima were of great encouragement to us, as were Karen Kimura, Michael Nakashima, and Gerry Nakashima. And a special thank you to Alan Sipress, for his faith, support, and sharp eye. Once again the family of Marani warmed the way: thanks to Elliot and Mary Maraniss (the perpetual editors), Jim Maraniss and Gigi Kaeser, Jean and Michael Alexander, Brian Keeling—and most of all to Andrew, Sarah, Heather, and Linda, who kept everything in balance.

INDEX